JPEG2000 Standard
for Image Compression

JPEG2000 Standard for Image Compression

Concepts, Algorithms and VLSI Architectures

Tinku Acharya

Avisere, Inc.
Tucson, Arizona
&
Department of Electrical Engineering
Arizona State University
Tempe, Arizona

Ping-Sing Tsai

Department of Computer Science
The University of Texas—Pan American
Edinburg, Texas

A JOHN WILEY & SONS, INC., PUBLICATION

Library of Congress Cataloging-in-Publication Data:

Acharya, Tinku.
    JPEG2000 standard for image compression : concepts, algorithms and VLSI
architectures / Tinku Acharya, Ping-Sing Tsai.
       p. cm.
    "A Wiley-Interscience publication."
    Includes bibliographical references and index.
    ISBN 0-471-48422-9 (cloth)
    1. JPEG (Image coding standard)   2. Image compression.   I. Tsai, Ping-Sing, 1962–   II.
Title.

TK6680.5.A25 2004
006.6—dc22
                                                    2004042256

Printed in the United States of America

10 9 8 7 6 5 4 3 2

To my mother *Mrs. Mrittika Acharya*,
my wife *Lisa*, my daughter *Arita*,
and my son *Arani*

— Tinku Acharya

To my family *Meiling, Amy,* and *Tiffany*

— Ping-Sing Tsai

Contents

Preface   xiii

1 Introduction to Data Compression   1
   1.1   Introduction   1
   1.2   Why Compression?   2
         1.2.1   Advantages of Data Compression   3
         1.2.2   Disadvantages of Data Compression   4
   1.3   Information Theory Concepts   5
         1.3.1   Discrete Memoryless Model and Entropy   5
         1.3.2   Noiseless Source Coding Theorem   6
         1.3.3   Unique Decipherability   8
   1.4   Classification of Compression algorithms   9
   1.5   A Data Compression Model   11
   1.6   Compression Performance   12
         1.6.1   Compression Ratio and Bits per Sample   13
         1.6.2   Quality Metrics   13
         1.6.3   Coding Delay   15
         1.6.4   Coding Complexity   15
   1.7   Overview of Image Compression   15
   1.8   Multimedia Data Compression Standards   17

	1.8.1	Still Image Coding Standard	17
	1.8.2	Video Coding Standards	18
	1.8.3	Audio Coding Standard	18
	1.8.4	Text Compression	19
1.9		Summary	20
		References	20
2	**Source Coding Algorithms**		**23**
2.1		Run-length Coding	23
2.2		Huffman Coding	24
	2.2.1	Limitations of Huffman Coding	27
	2.2.2	Modified Huffman Coding	28
2.3		Arithmetic Coding	30
	2.3.1	Encoding Algorithm	31
	2.3.2	Decoding Algorithm	33
2.4		Binary Arithmetic Coding	34
	2.4.1	Implementation with Integer Mathematics	38
	2.4.2	The QM-Coder	39
2.5		Ziv-Lempel Coding	44
	2.5.1	The LZ77 Algorithm	44
	2.5.2	The LZ78 Algorithm	46
	2.5.3	The LZW Algorithm	49
2.6		Summary	52
		References	53
3	**JPEG: Still Image Compression Standard**		**55**
3.1		Introduction	55
3.2		The JPEG Lossless Coding Algorithm	56
3.3		Baseline JPEG Compression	60
	3.3.1	Color Space Conversion	60
	3.3.2	Source Image Data Arrangement	61
	3.3.3	The Baseline Compression Algorithm	62
	3.3.4	Discrete Cosine Transform	63
	3.3.5	Coding the DCT Coefficients	66
	3.3.6	Decompression Process in Baseline JPEG	72
3.4		Progressive DCT-based Mode	75
3.5		Hierarchical Mode	76
3.6		Summary	77

References   78

4   Introduction to Discrete Wavelet Transform   79
    4.1   Introduction   79
    4.2   Wavelet Transforms   80
          4.2.1   Discrete Wavelet Transforms   82
          4.2.2   Concept of Multiresolution Analysis   83
          4.2.3   Implementation by Filters and the Pyramid Algorithm 85
    4.3   Extension to Two-Dimensional Signals   87
    4.4   Lifting Implementation of the Discrete Wavelet Transform   91
          4.4.1   Finite Impulse Response Filter and Z-transform   92
          4.4.2   Euclidean Algorithm for Laurent Polynomials   93
          4.4.3   Perfect Reconstruction and Polyphase Representation
                  of Filters   94
          4.4.4   Lifting   96
          4.4.5   Data Dependency Diagram for Lifting Computation   102
    4.5   Why Do We Care About Lifting?   103
    4.6   Summary   103
          References   104

5   VLSI Architectures for Discrete Wavelet Transforms   107
    5.1   Introduction   107
    5.2   A VLSI Architecture for the Convolution Approach   109
          5.2.1   Mapping the DWT in a Semi-Systolic Architecture   110
          5.2.2   Mapping the Inverse DWT in a Semi-Systolic
                  Architecture   112
          5.2.3   Unified Architecture for DWT and Inverse DWT   116
    5.3   VLSI Architectures for Lifting-based DWT   118
          5.3.1   Mapping the Data Dependency Diagram in Pipeline
                  Architectures   119
          5.3.2   Enhanced Pipeline Architecture by Folding   120
          5.3.3   Flipping Architecture   121
          5.3.4   A Register Allocation Scheme for Lifting   121
          5.3.5   A Recursive Architecture for Lifting   124
          5.3.6   A DSP-Type Architecture for Lifting   125
          5.3.7   A Generalized and Highly Programmable Architecture
                  for Lifting   126
          5.3.8   A Generalized Two-Dimensional Architecture   127
    5.4   Summary   133

References   133

6 JPEG2000 Standard   137
   6.1   Introduction   137
   6.2   Why JPEG2000?   139
   6.3   Parts of the JPEG2000 Standard   142
   6.4   Overview of the JPEG2000 Part 1 Encoding System   145
   6.5   Image Preprocessing   145
         6.5.1   Tiling   145
         6.5.2   DC Level Shifting   146
         6.5.3   Multicomponent Transformations   146
   6.6   Compression   147
         6.6.1   Discrete Wavelet Transformation   149
         6.6.2   Quantization   152
         6.6.3   Region of Interest Coding   153
         6.6.4   Rate Control   156
         6.6.5   Entropy Encoding   157
   6.7   Tier-2 Coding and Bitstream Formation   158
   6.8   Summary   158
         References   159

7 Coding Algorithms in JPEG2000   163
   7.1   Introduction   163
   7.2   Partitioning Data for Coding   164
   7.3   Tier-1 Coding in JPEG2000   164
         7.3.1   Fractional Bit-Plane Coding   165
         7.3.2   Examples of BPC Encoder   177
         7.3.3   Binary Arithmetic Coding—MQ-Coder   185
   7.4   Tier-2 Coding in JPEG2000   195
         7.4.1   Basic Tag Tree Coding   196
         7.4.2   Bitstream Formation   197
         7.4.3   Packet Header Information Coding   201
   7.5   Summary   211
         References   211

8 Code-Stream Organization and File Format   213
   8.1   Introduction   213
   8.2   Syntax and Code-Stream Rules   213

	8.2.1	Basic Rules	215
	8.2.2	Markers and Marker Segments Definitions	216
	8.2.3	Headers Definition	216
8.3	File Format for JPEG2000 Part 1: JP2 format		218
	8.3.1	File Format Organization	220
	8.3.2	JP2 Required Boxes	220
8.4	Example		223
8.5	Summary		225
	References		225

9 VLSI Architectures for JPEG2000   **227**

9.1	Introduction		227
9.2	A JPEG2000 Architecture for VLSI Implementation		228
9.3	VLSI Architectures for EBCOT		231
	9.3.1	Combinational Logic Blocks	233
	9.3.2	Functionality of the Registers	235
	9.3.3	Control Mechanism for the EBCOT Architecture	237
9.4	VLSI Architecture for Binary Arithmetic Coding: MQ-Coder		242
9.5	Decoder Architecture for JPEG2000		245
9.6	Summary of Other Architectures for JPEG2000		246
	9.6.1	Pass-Parallel Architecture for EBCOT	246
	9.6.2	Memory-Saving Architecture for EBCOT	247
	9.6.3	Computationally Efficient EBCOT Architecture by Skipping	248
9.7	Summary		249
	References		249

10 Beyond Part 1 of JPEG2000 Standard   **253**

10.1	Introduction		253
10.2	Part 2: Extensions		253
	10.2.1	Variable DC Offset	254
	10.2.2	Variable Scalar Quantization Offsets	254
	10.2.3	Trellis-Coded Quantization	254
	10.2.4	Visual Masking	255
	10.2.5	Arbitrary Wavelet Decomposition	256
	10.2.6	Arbitrary Wavelet Transformation	257
	10.2.7	Single Sample Overlap Discrete Wavelet Transformation	257
	10.2.8	Multiple Component Transforms	258

	10.2.9 Nonlinear Transformations	259
	10.2.10 Region of Interest Extension	261
	10.2.11 File Format Extension and Metadata Definitions	261
10.3	Part 3: Motion JPEG2000	261
10.4	Part 4: Conformance Testing	264
10.5	Part 5: Reference Software	265
10.6	Part 6: Compound Image File Format	265
10.7	Other Parts (7–12)	265
10.8	Summary	266
	References	267
Index		269
About the Authors		273

Preface

The growing demand for interactive multimedia technologies, in various application domains in this era of wireless and Internet communication, necessitated a number of desirable properties to be included in image and video compression algorithms. Accordingly, current and future generation image compression algorithms should not only demonstrate state-of-the-art performance, it should also provide desirable functionalities such as progressive transmission in terms of image fidelity as well as resolution, scalability, region-of-interest coding, random access, error resilience, handling large-size images of different types, etc. Many of these desired functionalities are not easily achievable by the current JPEG standard. The algorithms to implement different modes of the current JPEG standard are independent from each other. The lossless compression algorithm in current JPEG standard is completely different from the lossy compression mode and also the progressive and hierarchical modes. JPEG2000 is the new still image compression standard that has been developed under the auspices of the International Organization for Standardization (ISO). The systems architecture of this new standard has been defined in such a unified manner that it offers a single unified algorithmic framework and a single syntax definition of the code-stream organization so that different modes of operations can be handled by the same algorithm and the same syntax definition offers the aforementioned desirable functionalities. Moreover, the JPEG standard was defined in 1980s before the emergence of the Internet age. Many developments since then have changed the nature of research and development in multimedia applications and communication arena. The JPEG2000 standard takes these new developments into consideration.

The JPEG2000 algorithm has been developed based on the *discrete wavelet transform* (DWT) technique as opposed to the *discrete cosine transform* (DCT) based current JPEG. The nature of DWT helps to integrate both the lossless and lossy operations into the same algorithmic platform as well as it allows one to perform different kinds of progressive coding and decoding in the same algorithmic platform. Also the bit-plane coding of the transformed coefficients and the underlying structure of the bitstream syntax is very suitable to achieving different progressive operations during both encoding and decoding.

In this book, we present the basic background in multimedia compression techniques and prepare the reader for detailed understanding of the JPEG2000 standard. We present both the underlying theory and principles behind the algorithms of the JPEG2000 standard for scalable image compression. We have presented some of the open issues that are not explicitly defined in the standard. We have shown how the results achieved in different areas in information technology can be applied to enhance the performance of the JPEG2000 standard for image compression. We also introduced the VLSI architectures and algorithms for implementation of the JPEG2000 standard in hardware. The VLSI implementation of JPEG2000 will be an important factor in the near future for a number of image processing applications and devices such as digital camera, color fax, printer, scanner, etc. We also compile the latest publications and results in this book. Throughout the book we have provided sufficient examples for easy understanding by the readers.

This book consists of 10 chapters. The first two chapters provide an overview of the principles and theory of data and image compression with numerous examples. In Chapter 3, we review the current JPEG still standard for image compression, discuss the advantages and disadvantages of current JPEG, and the need for the new JPEG2000 standard for still image compression. We discuss the principles of discrete wavelet transformation and its implementation using both the convolution approach and the lifting approach in Chapter 4. In this chapter, we discuss the theory of multiresolution analysis and also the principles of lifting factorization for efficient implementation of discrete wavelet transform. In Chapter 5, we discuss VLSI algorithms and architectures for implementation of discrete wavelet transform and review different architectures for lifting-based implementation. In Chapters 6 to 8, we concentrate on descriptions of the JPEG2000 building blocks, details of the coding algorithms with examples, code-stream organization using JPEG2000 syntax, and formation of the compressed file of the JPEG2000 standard. Chapter 9 is devoted to the VLSI architectures of the standard in great detail, which cannot be found in current books in the marketplace. In Chapter 9, we also summarize the latest results and developments in this area. Chapter 10 provides a discussion on the JPEG2000 extensions and other parts of the standards as of writing this book. Every chapter includes sufficient references relevant to the discussion.

The book may be used either in a graduate-level course as a part of the subject of data compression, image compression, and multimedia processing, or as a reference book for professionals and researchers. This book is particularly useful for the engineers and professionals in industry for easy understanding of the subject matter and as an aid in both software and hardware developments of their products.

We would like to express our sincere thanks to many friends and colleagues who directly or indirectly helped us in different ways. We sincerely thank Dr. Val Moliere of John Wiley & Sons, Inc., for her assistance all through this project. We extend our gratitude to Professor Chaitali Chakraborti of Arizona State University for her guidance and assistance in compiling some of the chapters in this book. We also thank Dr. Kishore Andra for supplying some useful materials to enrich this book. We thank Dr. Andrew J. Griffis for reviewing and making suggestions to better explain some of the materials. Mr. Roger Undhagen and many other friends deserve special thanks for their continuous encouragement and support toward the compilation of this treatise. We would also like to thank the anonymous reviewers of our book proposal for their very constructive review and suggestions.

Finally, we are indebted to each member of our families for their active support and understanding throughout this project. Especially, Mrs. Baishali Acharya and Mrs. Meiling Dang stood strongly behind us with their love and supports which helped us to attempt this journey, and were cooperative with our erratic schedules during compilation of this book. We would also like to express our sincere appreciation to our children, who were always excited about this work and made us proud.

Tinku Acharya
Ping-Sing Tsai

1

Introduction to Data Compression

1.1 INTRODUCTION

We have seen the revolution in computer and communication technologies in the twentieth century. The telecommunications industry has gone through sea-changes from analog to digital networking that enabled today's very powerful Internet technology. Transition from the analog to the digital world offered many opportunities in every walk of life. Telecommunications, the Internet, digital entertainment, and computing in general are becoming part of our daily lives. Today we are talking about digital networks, digital representation of images, movies, video, TV, voice, digital library—all because digital representation of the signal is more robust than the analog counterpart for processing, manipulation, storage, recovery, and transmission over long distances, even across the globe through communication networks. In recent years, there have been significant advancements in processing of still image, video, graphics, speech, and audio signals through digital computers in order to accomplish different application challenges. As a result, multimedia information comprising image, video, audio, speech, text, and other data types has the potential to become just another data type. Telecommunication is no longer a platform for peer-to-peer voice communication between two people. Demand for communication of multimedia data through the telecommunications network and accessing the multimedia data through Internet is growing explosively. In order to handle this pervasive multimedia data usage, it is essential that the data representation and encoding of multimedia data be standard across different platforms and applications. Still image and video data comprise a significant portion of the multimedia data and they occupy the lion's share of the communication bandwidth for multimedia communication. As a result, development of efficient image compression techniques continues to be an important challenge to us, both in academia and in industry.

1.2   WHY COMPRESSION?

Despite the many advantages of digital representation of signals compared to the analog counterpart, they need a very large number of bits for storage and transmission. For example, a high-quality audio signal requires approximately 1.5 megabits per second for digital representation and storage. A television-quality low-resolution color video of 30 frames per second with each frame containing 640 × 480 pixels (24 bits per color pixel) needs more than 210 megabits per second of storage. As a result, a digitized one-hour color movie would require approximately 95 gigabytes of storage. The storage requirement for upcoming high-definition television (HDTV) of resolution 1280 × 720 at 60 frames per second is far greater. A digitized one-hour color movie of HDTV-quality video will require approximately 560 gigabytes of storage. A digitized 14 × 17 square inch radiograph scanned at 70 μm occupies nearly 45 megabytes of storage. Transmission of these digital signals through limited bandwidth communication channels is even a greater challenge and sometimes impossible in its raw form. Although the cost of storage has decreased drastically over the past decade due to significant advancement in microelectronics and storage technology, the requirement of data storage and data processing applications is growing explosively to outpace this achievement.

Interestingly enough, most of the sensory signals such as still image, video, and voice generally contain significant amounts of superfluous and redundant information in their canonical representation as far as the human perceptual system is concerned. By human perceptual system, we mean our eyes and ears. For example, the neighboring pixels in the smooth region of a natural image are very similar and small variation in the values of the neighboring pixels are not noticeable to the human eye. The consecutive frames in a stationary or slowly changing scene in a video are very similar and redundant. Some audio data beyond the human audible frequency range are useless for all practical purposes. This fact tells us that there are data in audio-visual signals that cannot be perceived by the human perceptual system. We call this *perceptual redundancy*. In English text files, common words (e.g., "the") or similar patterns of character strings (e.g., "ze", "th") are usually used repeatedly. It is also observed that the characters in a text file occur in a well-documented distribution, with letter *e* and "space" being the most popular. In numeric data files, we often observe runs of similar numbers or predictable interdependency among the numbers. We have mentioned only a few examples here. There are many such examples of redundancy in digital representation in all sorts of data.

Data compression is the technique to reduce the redundancies in data representation in order to decrease data storage requirements and hence communication costs. Reducing the storage requirement is equivalent to increasing the capacity of the storage medium and hence communication bandwidth. Thus the development of efficient compression techniques will continue to be a design challenge for future communication systems and advanced multimedia applications.

1.2.1 Advantages of Data Compression

The main advantage of compression is that it reduces the data storage requirements. It also offers an attractive approach to reduce the communication cost in transmitting high volumes of data over long-haul links via higher effective utilization of the available bandwidth in the data links. This significantly aids in reducing the cost of communication due to the data rate reduction. Because of the data rate reduction, data compression also increases the quality of multimedia presentation through limited-bandwidth communication channels. Hence the audience can experience rich-quality signals for audio-visual data representation. For example, because of the sophisticated compression technologies we can receive toll-quality audio at the other side of the globe through the good old telecommunications channels at a much better price compared to a decade ago. Because of the significant progress in image compression techniques, a single 6 MHz broadcast television channel can carry HDTV signals to provide better quality audio and video at much higher rates and enhanced resolution without additional bandwidth requirements. Because of the reduced data rate offered by the compression techniques, computer network and Internet usage is becoming more and more image and graphic friendly, rather than being just data- and text-centric phenomena. In short, high-performance compression has created new opportunities of creative applications such as digital library, digital archiving, videoteleconferencing, telemedicine, and digital entertainment, to name a few.

There are many other secondary advantages in data compression. For example, it has great implications in database access. Data compression may enhance the database performance because more compressed records can be packed in a given buffer space in a traditional computer implementation. This potentially increases the probability that a record being searched will be found in the main memory. Data security can also be greatly enhanced by encrypting the decoding parameters and transmitting them separately from the compressed database files to restrict access of proprietary information. An extra level of security can be achieved by making the compression and decompression processes totally transparent to unauthorized users.

The rate of input-output operations in a computing device can be greatly increased due to shorter representation of data. In systems with levels of storage hierarchy, data compression in principle makes it possible to store data at a higher and faster storage level (usually with smaller capacity), thereby reducing the load on the input-output channels. Data compression obviously reduces the cost of backup and recovery of data in computer systems by storing the backup of large database files in compressed form.

The advantages of data compression will enable more multimedia applications with reduced cost and hence aid its usage by a larger population with newer applications in the near future.

1.2.2   Disadvantages of Data Compression

Although data compression offers numerous advantages and it is the most sought-after technology in most of the data application areas, it has some disadvantages too, depending on the application area and sensitivity of the data. For example, the extra overhead incurred by encoding and decoding processes is one of the most serious drawbacks of data compression, which discourages its usage in some areas (e.g., in many large database applications). This extra overhead is usually required in order to uniquely identify or interpret the compressed data. For example, the encoding/decoding tree in a Huffman coding [7] type compression scheme is stored in the output file in addition to the encoded bitstream. These overheads run opposite to the essence of data compression, that of reducing storage requirements. In large statistical or scientific databases where changes in the database are not very frequent, the decoding process has greater impact on the performance of the system than the encoding process. Even if we want to access and manipulate a single record in a large database, it may be necessary to decompress the whole database before we can access the desired record. After access and probably modification of the data, the database is again compressed to store. The delay incurred due to these compression and decompression processes could be prohibitive for many real-time interactive database access requirements unless extra care and complexity are added in the data arrangement in the database.

Data compression generally reduces the reliability of the data records. For example, a single bit error in compressed code will cause the decoder to misinterpret all subsequent bits, producing incorrect data. Transmission of very sensitive compressed data (e.g., medical information) through a noisy communication channel (such as wireless media) is risky because the burst errors introduced by the noisy channel can destroy the transmitted data. Another problem of data compression is the disruption of data properties, since the compressed data is different from the original data. For example, sorting and searching schemes into the compressed data may be inapplicable as the lexical ordering of the original data is no longer preserved in the compressed data.

In many hardware and systems implementations, the extra complexity added by data compression can increase the system's cost and reduce the system's efficiency, especially in the areas of applications that require very low-power VLSI implementation.

1.3   INFORMATION THEORY CONCEPTS

The *Mathematical Theory of Communication*, which we also call *Information Theory* here, pioneered by Claude E. Shannon in 1948 [1, 2, 3, 4] is considered to be the theoretical foundation of data compression research. Since then many data compression techniques have been proposed and applied in practice.

Representation of data is a combination of *information* and *redundancy* [1]. Information is the portion of data that must be preserved permanently in its original form in order to correctly interpret the meaning or purpose of the data. However, redundancy is that portion of data that can be removed when it is not needed or can be reinserted to interpret the data when needed. Most often, the redundancy is reinserted in order to regenerate the original data in its original form. Data *compression* is essentially a redundancy reduction technique. The redundancy in data representation is reduced such a way that it can be subsequently reinserted to recover the original data, which is called *decompression* of the data. In the literature, sometimes data compression is referred to as *coding* and similarly decompression is referred to as *decoding*.

Usually development of a data compression scheme can be broadly divided into two phases—*modeling* and *coding*. In the modeling phase, information about redundancy that exists in the data is extracted and described in a model. Once we have the description of the model, we can determine how the actual data differs from the model and encode the difference in the *coding* phase. Obviously, a data compression algorithm becomes more effective if the model is closer to the characteristics of the data generating process, which we often call the *source*. The model can be obtained by empirical observation of the statistics of the data generated by the process or the source. In an empirical sense, any information-generating process can be described as a source that emits a sequence of symbols chosen from a finite alphabet. Alphabet is the set of all possible symbols generated by the source. For example, we can think of this text as being generated by a source with an alphabet containing all the ASCII characters.

1.3.1   Discrete Memoryless Model and Entropy

If the symbols produced by the information source are statistically independent to each other, the source is called a *discrete memoryless source*. A discrete memoryless source is described by its source alphabet $A = \{a_1, a_2, \cdots, a_N\}$ and the associated probabilities of occurrence $P = \{p(a_1), p(a_2), \cdots, p(a_N)\}$ of the symbols $a_1, a_2, \cdots, a_N$ in the alphabet A.

The definition of the *discrete memoryless source* model provides us a very powerful concept of quantification of *average information content per symbol* of the source, or *entropy* of the data. The concept of "entropy" was first used by physicists as a thermodynamic parameter to measure the degree of "disorder" or "chaos" in a thermodynamic or molecular system. In a statistical sense, we can view this as a measure of degree of "surprise" or "uncertainty." In an intuitive sense, it is reasonable to assume that the appearance of a less probable event (symbol) gives us more surprise, and hence we expect that it might carry more information. On the contrary, the more probable event (symbol) will carry less information because it was more expected.

With the above intuitive explanation, we can comprehend Shannon's definition of the relation between the source symbol probabilities and corresponding codes. The amount of *information* content, $I(a_i)$, for a source symbol a_i, in terms of its associated probability of occurrence $p(a_i)$ is

$$I(a_i) = \log_2 \frac{1}{p(a_i)} = -\log_2 p(a_i). \tag{1.1}$$

The base 2 in the logarithm indicates that the information is expressed in binary form, or bits. In terms of binary representation of the codes, a symbol a_i that is expected to occur with probability $p(a_i)$ is best represented in approximately $-\log_2 p(a_i)$ bits. As a result, a symbol with higher probability of occurrence in a message is coded using a fewer number of bits.

If we average the amount of information content over all the possible symbols of the discrete memoryless source, we find the average amount of information content per source symbol from the discrete memoryless source. This is expressed as

$$E = \sum_{i=1}^{N} p(a_i)I(a_i) = -\sum_{i=1}^{N} p(a_i)\log_2 p(a_i). \tag{1.2}$$

This is popularly known as *entropy* in information theory. Hence entropy is the expected length of a binary code over all possible symbols in a discrete memoryless source.

The concept of entropy is very powerful. In "stationary" systems, where the probabilities of occurrence of the source symbols are fixed, it provides a bound for the compression that can be achieved. This is a very convenient measure of the performance of a coding system. Without any knowledge of the physical source of data, it is not possible to know the entropy, and the entropy is estimated based on the outcome of the source by observing the structure of the data as source output. Hence estimation of the entropy depends on observation and assumptions about the structure of the source data sequence. These assumptions are called the *model* of the sequence.

1.3.2 Noiseless Source Coding Theorem

The *Noiseless Source Coding Theorem* by Shannon [1] establishes the minimum average code word length per source symbol that can be achieved, which in turn provides the upper bound on the achievable compression losslessly. The *Noiseless Source Coding Theorem* is also known as *Shannon's first theorem*. This is one of the major source coding results in information theory [1, 2, 3].

If the data generated from a discrete memoryless source A are considered as grouped together in blocks on n symbols, to form an *n-extended source*, then the new source A^n has N^n possible symbols $\{a_i\}$, with probability $P(a_i) = P(a_{i_1})P(a_{i_2})\cdots P(a_{i_n}), i = 1, 2, \cdots, N^n$. By deriving the entropy of the new n-extended source, it can be proven that $E(A^n) = nE(A)$, where $E(A)$ is the entropy of the original source A. Let us now consider encoding blocks of n source symbols at a time into binary codewords. For any $\epsilon > 0$, it is possible to construct a codeword for the block in such a way that the average number of bits per original source symbol, $\bar{L}$, satisfies

$$E(A) \leq \bar{L} < E(A) + \epsilon$$

The left-hand inequality must be satisfied for any uniquely decodable code for the block of n source symbols.

The *Noiseless Source Coding Theorem* states that any source can be losslessly encoded with a code whose average number of bits per source symbol is arbitrarily close to, but not less than, the source entropy E in bits by coding infinitely long extensions of the source. Hence, the noiseless source coding theorem provides us the intuitive (statistical) yardstick to measure the information emerging from a source.

1.3.2.1 **Example:** We consider a *discrete memoryless source* with alphabet $A_1 = \{\alpha, \beta, \gamma, \delta\}$ and the associated probabilities are $p(\alpha) = 0.65$, $p(\beta) = 0.20$, $p(\gamma) = 0.10$, $p(\delta) = 0.05$ respectively. The entropy of this source is $E = -(0.65 \log_2 0.65 + 0.20 \log_2 0.20 + 0.10 \log_2 0.10 + 0.05 \log_2 0.05)$, which is approximately 1.42 bits/symbol. As a result, a data sequence of length 2000 symbols can be represented using approximately 2820 bits.

Knowing something about the structure of the data sequence often helps to reduce the entropy estimation of the source. Let us consider that the numeric data sequence generated by a source of alphabet $A_2 = \{0, 1, 2, 3\}$ is $D = 0\ 1\ 1\ 2\ 3\ 3\ 3\ 3\ 3\ 3\ 3\ 3\ 3\ 2\ 2\ 2\ 3\ 3\ 3\ 3$, as an example. The probability of appearance of the symbols in alphabet A_2 are $p(0) = 0.05$, $p(1) = 0.10$, $p(2) = 0.20$, and $p(3) = 0.65$ respectively. Hence the estimated entropy of the sequence D is $E = 1.42$ bits per symbol. If we assume that correlation exists between two consecutive samples in this data sequence, we can reduce this correlation by simply subtracting a sample by its previous sample to generate the residual values $r_i = s_i - s_{i-1}$ for each sample s_i. Based on this assumption of the model, the sequence of residuals of the original data sequence is $\bar{D} = 0\ 1\ 0\ 1\ 1\ 0\ 0\ 0\ 0\ 0\ 0\ 0\ 0\ -1\ 0\ 0\ 1\ 0\ 0\ 0$, consisting of three symbols in a modified alphabet $\bar{A}_2 = \{-1, 1, 0\}$. The probability of occurrence of the symbols in the new alphabet $\bar{A}$ are $P(-1) = 0.05$, $p(1) = 0.2$, and $p(0) = 0.75$ respectively as computed by the number of occurrence in the residual sequence. The estimated entropy of the transformed sequence is $\bar{E} = -(0.05 \log_2 0.05 + 0.2 \log_2 0.2 + 0.75 \log_2 0.75) = 0.992$ (i.e., 0.992 bits/symbol).

The above is a simple example to demonstrate that the data sequence can be represented with fewer numbers of bits if encoded with a suitable entropy encoding technique and hence resulting in data compression.

1.3.3   Unique Decipherability

Digital representation of data in binary code form allows us to store it in computer memories and to transmit it through communication networks. In terms of length of the binary codes, they can be *fixed-length* as shown in column A of Table 1.1 with alphabet $\{\alpha, \beta, \gamma, \delta\}$, as an example, where all the symbols have been coded using the same number of bits. The binary codes could also be *variable-length* codes as shown in columns B or C of Table 1.1 in which the symbols have different code lengths.

Table 1.1   Examples of Variable-Length Codes

Symbol	A	B	C
α	00	0	0
β	01	10	1
γ	10	110	00
δ	11	111	01

Consider the string $S = \alpha\alpha\gamma\alpha\beta\alpha\delta$. The binary construction of the string S using variable-length codes A, B, and C is as follows:

$$C_A(S) = 00001000010011$$

$$C_B(S) = 001100100111$$

$$C_C(S) = 000001001.$$

Given the binary code $C_A(S) = 00001000010011$, it is easy to recognize or uniquely decode the string $S = \alpha\alpha\gamma\alpha\beta\alpha\delta$ because we can divide the binary string into nonoverlapping blocks of 2 bits each and we know that two consecutive bits form a symbol as shown in column A. Hence the first two bits "00" form the binary code for the symbol α, the next two bits "00" is similarly mapped to the symbol α, the following two bits "10" can be mapped to symbol γ, and so on. We can also uniquely decipher or decode the binary code $C_B(S) = 001100100111$ because the first bit (0) represents the symbol α; similarly the next bit (0) also represents the symbol α according to the code in column B. The following three consecutive bits "110" uniquely represent the symbol γ. Following this procedure, we can uniquely reconstruct the string $S = \alpha\alpha\gamma\alpha\beta\alpha\delta$ without any ambiguity.

But deciphering the binary code $C_C(S) = 000001001$ is ambiguous because it has many possibilities—$\alpha\gamma\gamma\beta\gamma\beta$, $\alpha\gamma\alpha\delta\gamma\beta$, or $\alpha\alpha\alpha\alpha\beta\gamma\beta$ to name a few. Hence the code $C_C(S) = 000001001$ is not uniquely decipherable using the code in column C in Table 1.1.

It is obvious that the *fixed-length* codes are always uniquely decipherable. But not all the *variable-length* codes are uniquely decipherable. The uniquely decipherable codes maintain a particular property called the *prefix property*. According to the prefix property, no codeword in the code-set forms the *prefix* of another distinct codeword [5]. A codeword $C = c_0 c_1 c_2 \cdots c_{k-1}$ of length k is said to be the prefix of another codeword $D = d_0 d_1 \cdots d_{m-1}$ of length m if $c_i = d_i$ for all $i = 0, 1, \cdots, k-1$ and $k \leq m$.

Note that none of the codes in column A or in column B is a prefix of any other code in the corresponding column. The codes formed using either column A or column B are uniquely decipherable. On the other hand, binary code of α in column C is a prefix of both the binary codes of γ and δ.

Some of the popular variable-length coding techniques are Shannon-Fano Coding [6], Huffman Coding [7], Elias Coding [8], Arithmetic Coding [9], etc. It should be noted that the *fixed-length* codes can be treated as a special case of uniquely decipherable *variable-length* code.

1.4 CLASSIFICATION OF COMPRESSION ALGORITHMS

In an abstract sense, we can describe *data compression* as a method that takes an input data D and generates a shorter representation of the data $c(D)$ with a fewer number of bits compared to that of D. The reverse process is called *decompression*, which takes the compressed data $c(D)$ and generates or reconstructs the data D' as shown in Figure 1.1. Sometimes the *compression* (coding) and *decompression* (decoding) systems together are called a "CODEC," as shown in the broken box in Figure 1.1.

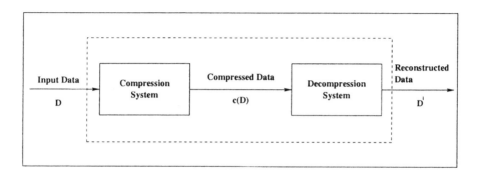

Fig. 1.1 CODEC.

The reconstructed data D' could be identical to the original data D or it could be an approximation of the original data D, depending on the reconstruction requirements. If the reconstructed data D' is an exact replica of the original data D, we call the algorithm applied to compress D and decompress $c(D)$ to be *lossless*. On the other hand, we say the algorithms are *lossy* when D' is not an exact replica of D. Hence as far as the reversibility of the original data is concerned, the data compression algorithms can be broadly classified in two categories — *lossless* and *lossy* . Usually we need to apply lossless data compression techniques on text data or scientific data. For example, we cannot afford to compress the electronic copy of this text book using a lossy compression technique. It is expected that we shall reconstruct the same text after the decompression process. A small error in the reconstructed text can have a completely different meaning. We do not expect the sentence "You should *not* delete this file" in a text to change to "You should *now* delete this file" as a result of an error introduced by a lossy compression or decompression algorithm. Similarly, if we compress a huge ASCII file containing a program written in C language, for example, we expect to get back the same C code after decompression because of obvious reasons. The lossy compression techniques are usually applicable to data where high fidelity of reconstructed data is not required for perception by the human perceptual system. Examples of such types of data are image, video, graphics, speech, audio, etc. Some image compression applications may require the compression scheme to be lossless (i.e., each pixel of the decompressed image should be exactly identical to the original one). Medical imaging is an example of such an application where compressing digital radiographs with a lossy scheme could be a disaster if it has to make any compromises with the diagnostic accuracy. Similar observations are true for astronomical images for galaxies and stars.

Sometimes we talk about *perceptual lossless* compression schemes when we can compromise with introducing some amount of loss into the reconstructed image as long as there is no perceptual difference between the reconstructed data and the original data, if the human perceptual system is the ultimate judge of the fidelity of the reconstructed data. For example, it is hardly noticeable by human eyes if there is any small relative change among the neighboring pixel values in a smooth non-edge region in a natural image.

In this context, we need to mention that sometimes *data compression* is referred as *coding* in the literature. The terms *noiseless* and *noisy coding*, in the literature, usually refer to *lossless* and *lossy compression* techniques respectively. The term "noise" here is the "error of reconstruction" in the lossy compression techniques because the reconstructed data item is not identical to the original one. Throughout this book we shall use *lossless* and *lossy compression* in place of *noiseless* and *noisy coding* respectively.

Data compression schemes could be *static* or *dynamic*. In *static* methods, the mapping from a set of messages (data or signal) to the corresponding set of compressed codes is always fixed. In *dynamic* methods, the mapping from the set of messages to the set of compressed codes changes over time. A dynamic method is called *adaptive* if the codes adapt to changes in ensemble characteristics over time. For example, if the probabilities of occurrences of the symbols from the source are not fixed over time, we can adaptively formulate the binary codewords of the symbols, so that the compressed file size can adaptively change for better compression efficiency.

1.5 A DATA COMPRESSION MODEL

A model of a typical data compression system can be described using the block diagram shown in Figure 1.2. A data compression system mainly consists of three major steps—*removal or reduction in data redundancy, reduction in entropy,* and *entropy encoding.*

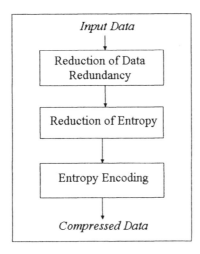

Fig. 1.2 A data compression model.

The redundancy in data may appear in different forms. For example, the neighboring pixels in a typical image are very much spatially correlated to each other. By correlation we mean that the pixel values are very similar in the non-edge smooth regions [10] in the image. In the case of moving pictures, the consecutive frames could be almost similar with or without minor displacement if the motion is slow. The composition of the words or sentences in a natural text follows some context model based on the grammar being used. Similarly, the records in a typical numeric database may have some sort of relationship among the atomic entities that comprise each record in the database. There are rhythms and pauses in regular intervals in any natural audio or speech data. These redundancies in data representation can be reduced in order to achieve potential compression.

Removal or reduction in data redundancy is typically achieved by transforming the original data from one form or representation to another. The popular techniques used in the redundancy reduction step are prediction of the data samples using some model, transformation of the original data from spatial domain to frequency domain such as Discrete Cosine Transform (DCT), decomposition of the original data set into different subbands such as Discrete Wavelet Transformation (DWT), etc. In principle, this step potentially yields more compact representation of the information in the original data set in terms of fewer coefficients or equivalent. In case of lossless data compression, this step is completely reversible. Transformation of data usually reduces entropy of the original data by removing the redundancies that appear in the known structure of the data sequence.

The next major step in a lossy data compression system is to further reduce the entropy of the transformed data significantly in order to allocate fewer bits for transmission or storage. The reduction in entropy is achieved by dropping nonsignificant information in the transformed data based on the application criteria. This is a nonreversible process because it is not possible to exactly recover the lost data or information using the inverse process. This step is applied in lossy data compression schemes and this is usually accomplished by some version of *quantization* technique. The nature and amount of quantization dictate the quality of the reconstructed data. The quantized coefficients are then losslessly encoded using some entropy encoding scheme to compactly represent the quantized data for storage or transmission. Since the entropy of the quantized data is less compared to the original one, it can be represented by fewer bits compared to the original data set, and hence we achieve compression.

The decompression system is just an inverse process. The compressed code is first decoded to generate the quantized coefficients. The inverse quantization step is applied on these quantized coefficients to generate the approximation of the transformed coefficients. The quantized transformed coefficients are then inverse transformed in order to create the approximate version of the original data. If the quantization and inverse quantization steps are absent in the codec and the transformation step for redundancy removal is reversible, the decompression system produces the exact replica of the original data and hence the compression system can be called a lossless compression system.

1.6 COMPRESSION PERFORMANCE

Like any other system, metrics of performance of a data compression algorithm are important criteria for selection of the algorithm. The performance measures of data compression algorithms can be looked at from different perspectives depending on the application requirements: amount of compression achieved, objective and subjective quality of the reconstructed data, relative complexity of the algorithm, speed of execution, etc. We explain some of them below.

1.6.1 Compression Ratio and Bits per Sample

The most popular metric of performance measure of a data compression algorithm is the *compression ratio*. It is defined as the ratio of the number of bits to represent the original data to the number of bits to represent the compressed data. Consider an image of size 256 × 256 requiring 65536 bytes of storage if each pixel is represented by a single byte. If the compressed version of the image can be stored in 4096 bytes, the compression ratio achieved by the compression algorithm will be 16:1.

A variation of the *compression ratio* is *bits per sample*. This metric indicates the average number of bits to represent a single sample of the data (e.g., *bits per pixel* for image coding). If 65536 pixels of an image are compressed to 4096 bytes, we can say that the compression algorithm achieved 0.5 bits per pixel on the average. Hence the *bits per sample* can be measured by the ratio of the *number of bits* of a single uncompressed sample to the *compression ratio*.

It should be remembered that the achievable compression ratio using a lossless compression scheme is totally input data dependent. If the same algorithm is applied in a number of distinct data files, the algorithm will yield a different compression ratio in different files. The maximum compression ratio and hence the bits per sample that can be achieved losslessly is restricted by the entropy of the data file according to the *noiseless source coding theorem* by Shannon. Sources with less redundancy have more entropy and hence are more difficult to achieve compression. For example, it is very difficult to achieve any compression in a file consisting of mainly random data.

1.6.2 Quality Metrics

This metric is not relevant for lossless compression algorithms. The quality or fidelity metric is particularly important for lossy compression algorithms for video, image, voice, etc., because the reconstructed data differ from the original ones and the human perceptual system is the ultimate judge of the reconstructed quality. For example, if there is no perceivable difference between the reconstructed data and the original ones, the compression algorithm can be claimed to achieve very high quality or high fidelity. The difference of the reconstructed data from the original ones is called the *distortion*. One expects to have higher quality of the reconstructed data, if the distortion is lower. Quality measures could be very subjective based on human perception or can be objectively defined using mathematical or statistical evaluation. Although there is no single universally accepted measure of the quality metrics, there are different objective and subjective quality metrics in practice to evaluate the quality of the compression algorithms.

1.6.2.1 Subjective Quality Metric   Often the subjective quality metric is defined as the *mean observers score* (MOS). Sometimes, it is also called *mean opinion score*. There are different statistical ways to compute MOS. In one of the simplest ways, a statistically significant number of observers are randomly chosen to evaluate visual quality of the reconstructed images. All the images are compressed and decompressed by the same algorithm. Each observer assigns a numeric score to each reconstructed image based on his or her perception of quality of the image, say within a range 1–5 to describe the quality of the image—5 being the highest quality and 1 being the worst quality. The average of the scores assigned by all the observers to the reconstructed images is called the *mean observer score* (MOS) and it can be considered as a viable subjective metric if all the observers evaluate the images under the same viewing condition. There are different variations of this approach to calculate MOS—absolute comparison, paired comparison, blind evaluation, etc.

The techniques of measurement of the MOS could well be different for different perceptual data. The methodology to evaluate the subjective quality of a still image could be entirely different for video or voice data. But MOS is computed based on the perceived quality of the reconstructed data by a statistically significant number of human observers.

1.6.2.2 Objective Quality Metric   There is no universally accepted measure for objective quality of the data compression algorithms. For objective measure, the most widely used objective quality metrics are root-mean-squared error ($RMSE$), signal-to-noise ratio (SNR), and peak signal-to-noise ratio ($PSNR$). If I is an $M \times N$ image and $\bar{I}$ is the corresponding reconstructed image after compression and decompression, $RMSE$ is calculated by

$$RMSE = \sqrt{\frac{1}{MN} \sum_{i=1}^{M} \sum_{j=1}^{N} [I(i,j) - \bar{I}(i,j)]^2}, \qquad (1.3)$$

where i, j refer to the pixel position in the image. The SNR in decibel unit (dB) is expressed as $SNR =$

$$20 \log_{10} \left(\frac{\sqrt{\frac{1}{MN} \sum_{i=1}^{M} \sum_{j=1}^{N} I^2(i,j)}}{RMSE} \right) = 10 \log_{10} \left(\frac{\sum_{i=1}^{M} \sum_{j=1}^{N} I^2(i,j)}{\sum_{i=1}^{M} \sum_{j=1}^{N} [I(i,j) - \bar{I}(i,j)]^2} \right).$$
$$(1.4)$$

In case of an 8-bit image, the corresponding $PSNR$ in dB is computed as

$$PSNR = 20 \log_{10} \left(\frac{255}{RMSE} \right), \qquad (1.5)$$

where 255 is the maximum possible pixel value in 8 bits.

It should be noted that a lower $RMSE$ (or equivalently, higher SNR or $PSNR$) does not necessarily always indicate a higher subjective quality. These objective error metrics do not always correlate well with the subjective quality metrics. There are many cases where the PSNR of a reconstructed image can be reasonably high, but the subjective quality is really bad when visualized by human eyes. Hence the choice of the objective or subjective metrics to evaluate a compression and decompression algorithm often depends on the application criteria.

Similar objective quality metrics are used for audio and speech signals as well.

1.6.3   Coding Delay

Coding delay is another performance measure of the compression algorithms where interactive encoding and decoding is the requirement (e.g., interactive videoteleconferencing, on-line image browsing, real-time voice communication, etc.). The complex compression algorithm might provide a better amount of compression, but it could lead to increased coding delay, prohibiting the interactive real-time applications. The constraint to the coding delay often forces the compression system designer to use a less sophisticated algorithm for the compression system.

1.6.4   Coding Complexity

The coding complexity of a compression algorithm is often considered to be a performance measure where the computational requirement to implement the codec is an important criteria. The computational requirements are usually measured in terms of a number of arithmetic operations and memory requirements. Usually, the number of arithmetic operations is described by MOPS (millions of operations per second). But in the compression literature, the term MIPS (millions of instructions per second) is often used to measure the compression performance in a specific computing engine's architecture. Especially, the implementation of the compression schemes using special-purpose DSP (digital signal processor) architectures is common in communication systems. In portable systems, this coding complexity is an important criterion from the perspective of the low-power hardware implementation.

1.7   OVERVIEW OF IMAGE COMPRESSION

The general model of a still image compression framework can be described using a block diagram shown in Figure 1.3.

Statistical analysis of a typical image indicates that there is a strong correlation among the neighboring pixels. This causes redundancy of information in the image. The redundancy can be greatly removed by decorrelating the image with some sort of preprocessing in order to achieve compression. In general, still image compression techniques rely on two fundamental redundancy reduction principles—*spatial redundancy reduction* and *statistical redundancy reduction*. Spatial redundancy is the similarity of neighboring pixels in an image and it is reduced by applying decorrelation techniques such as *predictive coding, transform coding, subband coding*, etc. The statistical redundancy reduction is popularly known as *entropy encoding*. The *entropy encoding* further reduces the redundancy in the decorrelated data by using variable-length coding techniques such as Huffman Coding, Arithmetic Coding, etc. These entropy encoding techniques allocate the bits in the codewords in such a manner that the more probably appearing symbols are represented with a smaller number of bits compared to the less probably appearing pixels, which aids in achieving compression.

The *decorrelation* or *preprocessing* block in Figure 1.3 is the step for reducing the spatial redundancy of the image pixels due to strong correlation among the neighboring pixels. In lossless coding mode, this decorrelated image is directly processed by the entropy encoder to encode the decorrelated pixels using a variable-length coding technique. In the case of the lossy compression mode, the decorrelated image is subject to further preprocessing in order to mask or throw away irrelevant information depending on the nature of application of the image and its reconstructed quality requirements. This process of masking is popularly called *quantization* process. The decorrelated and quantized image pixels then go through the entropy encoding process to compactly represent them using variable-length codes to produce the compressed image.

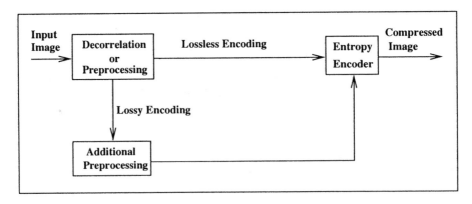

Fig. 1.3 A general image compression framework.

1.8   MULTIMEDIA DATA COMPRESSION STANDARDS

Multimedia data compression has become an integrated part of today's digital communications systems—digital telephony, facsimile, digital cellular communication, personal communication systems, videoconferencing, Internet, broadcasting, etc. Other applications are voice messaging systems, image archival systems, CD-quality audio, digital library, DVD, movie and video distribution, graphics, and film industry, to name a few. New results and research concepts are emerging every day throughout the world. The number of applications will continue to grow in the days to come. As a result, it is necessary to define standards for common data compression systems specifications to make them perfectly interoperable in different systems and manufacturable platforms. We mention here some of the data compression standards for various types of multimedia data—image, video, speech, audio, text, etc.

1.8.1   Still Image Coding Standard

The two main international bodies in the image compression area are the *International Organization for Standardization* (ISO) and *International Telecommunication Union—Telecommunications Sector* (ITU-T) formerly known as CCITT. ISO deals with information-processing related issues such as image storage and retrieval, whereas ITU-T deals with information transmission. JPEG (Joint Photographic Expert Group) is the standard jointly developed by ISO and ITU-T in 1992 for still images—for both continuous-tone grayscale and color images. JPEG is officially referred as **ISO/IEC IS** (International Standard) **10918-1:** *Digital Compression and Coding of Continuous-tone Still Images* and also **ITU-T Recommendation T.81**. There is a common misconception among many people that JPEG is a single algorithm for still image compression. Actually, the JPEG standard defines four modes of operations [13]. They are *sequential DCT-based mode, sequential lossless mode, progressive DCT-based mode*, and *hierarchical mode*. The widely used algorithm for image compression in the *sequential DCT-based mode* of the standard is called the **baseline JPEG**. The current JPEG system is targeted for compressing still images with bit-rate of 0.25–2 bits per pixel. Working group 1 in ISO is engaged in defining the next-generation still-picture coding standard JPEG2000 [17] to achieve lower bit-rates at much higher quality with many additional desirable features to meet newer challenges which current JPEG does not offer. The core coding system of the JPEG2000 (Part 1), its extension (Part 2), Motion JPEG2000 (Part 3), their conformance testing (Part 4), and some of the file formats have already been finalized as international standards. As of writing this book, the working group is currently engaged in defining some new parts of the standard.

Popular bi-level image compression standards are Group 3 and Group 4 (also called ITU-T Recommendation T.4 and T.6), developed by the *Interna-

tional Telecommunication Union (formerly known as CCITT) in 1980 for fax compression, and JBIG, developed by ISO in 1994 for black-and-white image compression. The working group in ISO recently defined a new bi-level image compression standard called JBIG2, in conjunction with JPEG2000 standard.

1.8.2   Video Coding Standards

MPEG (Moving Picture Expert Group) is the standard in ISO for a digital compression system to handle moving pictures (video) and associated audio. MPEG-1 (officially known as ISO 11172) is the first generation of digital compression standards for video and two-channel stereo audio to achieve bit-rate of about 1.5 Mbps (Mega bits per second) for storage in CD-ROMs [11]. MPEG-1 was standardized in 1994. ISO developed the second-generation standard MPEG-2 (officially known as ISO 13818) in 1995 to address the requirements of the digital compression systems for broadcast-quality video and audio at bit-rate of 6–10 Mbps [12]. ISO is now defining the next-generation video coding standard MPEG-4 to meet newer challenges of object-based video coding suitable for multimedia applications [14]. The MPEG committee is also currently working on a new work item called *Multimedia Content Description Interface*, or MPEG-7 [15]. There is a popular misconception that MPEG-7 will be another new video compression standard. The fact is that MPEG-7 will not define any new compression algorithm. It deals with the file format and metadata description of the compressed video in order to define a standard for description of various types of multimedia information coded with the standard codecs [15]. Another new work item has recently been initiated in the MPEG committee —*MPEG-21 Multimedia Framework*. The overall vision of MPEG-21 as it is described in its statement is "To enable transparent and augmented use of multimedia resources across a wide range of networks and devices." The requirements and purpose are still being defined in the committee.

In parallel with ISO, ITU plays the role of defining image sequence compression standards for telecommunication applications such as videoteleconferencing, etc. H.261 is a standard in ITU developed in 1990 for the video coding portion of the videoteleconferencing standard (H.320) to transmit video at the bit-rate of 56 Kbps–2 Mbps through the telecommunication channel. H.263 is the low bit-rate standard developed in 1995 for video coding to transmit video at a bit-rate below 28.8 Kbps through the telecommunication channel [18]. H.263L is under definition to meet the newer telecommunication requirements.

1.8.3   Audio Coding Standard

The standardization effort for digital audio was initiated in the audio layer of the MPEG video coding standard. The MPEG bitstream consists of audio and video signals that are synchronized at the decoder. MPEG-1 and MPEG-2 audio-coding standards are the first international standards in the field of high-quality digital audio compression. The MPEG-1 audio coding system operates in single-channel or two-channel stereo modes at sampling frequencies of 32 KHz, 44.1 KHz, and 48 KHz. The system was specified in three layers—I, II, and III— for different data rates. MPEG-1 Layer I provides high quality at a data-rate of 192 Kbps per channel, while Layer II provides high quality at data-rate of 128 Kbps, and Layer III provides data-rate of 64 Kbps. The MPEG-2 Advanced Audio Coding (MPEG-2 AAC) system operates at sampling frequencies between 8 and 96 KHz and supports up to 48 audio channels. MPEG-2 AAC is used as the kernel of the MPEG-4 audio standard at data-rates at or above 16 Kbps per channel. MPEG-4 coding of audio objects provides different compression tools for natural sounds as well as synthesized sound for a wide range of bit rates. Other audio coding tools of great interest are Dolby AC-3 [21], Philips DCC [22], etc. **MP3** is the term that Internet users most often use for searching music. However, MP3 is not a new audio coding standard; it is based on the MPEG-1 audio Layer III.

1.8.4 Text Compression

The basic philosophy of text compression differs from the transformation-based video, image, speech, and audio compression techniques. Text compression is by default a lossless coding [27]. Effective text compression schemes are basically dictionary-based coding. This dictionary could be static where a fixed dictionary is used to compress the text, or it could be dynamic in order to dynamically change the dictionary during the encoding and decoding process. The basic idea behind most of the dictionary-based robust lossless text compression schemes is to *parse* the source symbol string into a sequence of *phrases* or *substrings* and then generate the compressed codes of these phrases. The most popular and widely used text compression schemes belong to the Lempel-Ziv (LZ) family—LZ77 [23], LZ78 [24], LZZZ [26], LZW [25], LZC [27], LZWAJ [28], etc. For example LZSS, a variation of LZ77, is the text compression engine in *zip, gzip, pkzip, and winzip* compression utilities. The LZW algorithm, a variant of LZ78, is the core of the *Unix compress* utility.

Some people in the industry have a misconception that LZ coding techniques are applied in text compression only and they do not work for compressing any other multimedia data type. In lossless compression mode, the LZ coding techniques have been found to be effective to compress different kinds of images. For example, the popular image-compression algorithm GIF (Graphical Interchange Format) is an implementation of the LZW algorithm and very similar to the *Unix compress* utility. GIF is effective to compress computer-generated graphical images and pseudocolor or color-mapped images. TIFF (Tag Image File Format) is another industry standard. Some of the modes in TIFF have been developed based on LZ coding. This is useful for compressing *dithered binary images*, which simulate grayscale images through a variation in the density of black dots. The TIFF Revision 6.0 was released in 1992 and supports numerous data compression schemes such as LZW, CCITT Group 3 and Group 4, and JPEG.

1.9 SUMMARY

In this chapter, we introduced readers with the fundamentals of data and image compression. We discussed why data compression is important and how it became an integrated part of today's multimedia computing and communications systems. We discussed some fundamentals including information theory such as discrete memoryless model, entropy, noiseless source coding theorem, unique decipherability, etc., in order to aid the readers to understand the principles behind data compression. We discussed the concepts of classification of compression techniques, performance measures, etc. We also presented brief introduction of various international standards for digital compression techniques of various multimedia data types—image, video, text, audio, data, etc. Different source coding algorithms for data compression, the principles of image compression techniques, and details of JPEG and JPEG2000 image compression standards will be discussed in the following chapters.

REFERENCES

1. C. E. Shannon and W. Weaver, *The Mathematical Theory of Communication*. University of Illinois Press, Urbana, IL, 1949.

2. C. E. Shannon, "Certain Results in Coding Theory for Noisy Channels," *Information Control*, Vol. 1, No. 1, pp. 6–25, September 1957.

3. C. E. Shannon, "Coding Theorems for a Discrete Source with a Fidelity Criterion," *IRE National Convention Record*, Part 4, pp. 142–163, 1959.

4. B. McMillan, "The Basic Theorems of Information Theory," *Ann. Math. Statist.*, Vol. 24, pp. 196–219, 1953.

5. D. S. Hirschberg and D. A. Lelewer, "Efficient Decoding of Prefix Codes," *Comm. of the ACM*, Vol. 33, No. 4, pp. 449–459, April 1990.

6. R. M. Fano, *Transmission of Information*. MIT Press, Cambridge, MA, 1949.

7. D. Huffman, "A Method for the Construction of Minimum Redundancy codes," *Proc. IRE*, Vol. 40, pp. 1098–1101, 1952.

8. P. Elias, "Universal Codeword Sets and Representations of the Integers," *IEEE Trans. on Info. Theory*, Vol. 21, No. 2, pp. 194–203, March 1975.

9. I. H. Witten, R. M. Neal, and J. G. Cleary, "Arithmetic Coding for Data Compression," *Communications of the ACM*, Vol. 30, No. 6, June 1987.

10. A. N. Netravali and B. G. Haskell, *Digital Pictures*. Plenum Press, New York, 1988.

11. ISO/IEC 11172 (MPEG-1), "Information Technology—Coding of Moving Pictures and Associated Audio for Digital Storage Media at Up to About 1.5 Mbit/s."

12. ISO/IEC 13818 (MPEG-2), "Information Technology—Generic Coding of Moving Pictures and Associated Audio Information."

13. ISO/IEC 10918 (JPEG), "Information Technology—Digital Compression and Coding of Continuous-Tone Still Images."

14. R. Koenen, F. Pereira, and L. Chiariglione, "MPEG-4: Context and Objectives," *Image Communication Journal*, Vol. 9, No. 4, 1997.

15. MPEG-7: ISO/IEC JTC1/SC20/WG211, N2207, "Context and Objectives," March 1998.

16. G. Wallace, W. B. Pennebaker, and J. L. Mitchell, "Draft Proposal for the Joint Photographic Expert Group (JPEG)," JPEG-8-R6, June 24, 1990.

17. ISO/IEC WD15444 (V3.0), "JPEG2000 Lossless and Lossy Compression of Continuous-Tone and Bi-level Still Images," 1999.

18. ITU-T, "Draft ITU-T Recommendation H.263: Video Coding for Low Bit Rate Communication," December 1995.

19. ITU-T Recommendation G.729, "Coding of Speech at 8 Kbit/s Using Conjugate Structure Algebraic Code Excited Linear Prediction (CS-ACELP)," March 1996.

20. "Mandatory Speech Codec Speech Processing Functions—AMR Speech Codec; General Description (3GPP)," 3G TS 26.071 v3.0.0, June 1999.

21. United States Advanced Television Systems Committee (ATSC), Audio Specialist Group (T3/S7) Doc. A/52, "Digital Audio Compression Standard (AC-3)," November 1994.

22. A. Hoogendoorn, "Digital Compact Cassette," *Proc. IEEE*, Vol. 82, pp. 554–563, April 1994.

23. J. Ziv and A. Lempel, "A Universal Algorithm for Sequential Data Compression," *IEEE Trans. on Info. Theory*, IT-23, Vol. 3, pp. 337–343, May 1977.

24. J. Ziv and A. Lempel, "Compression of Individual Sequences via Variable-Rate Coding," *IEEE Trans. on Info. Theory*, IT-24, Vol. 5, pp. 530–536, September 1978.

25. T. Welch, "A Technique for High-Performance Data Compression," *IEEE Computer*, Vol. 17, No. 6, 1984.

26. J. A. Storer and T. G. Syzmanski, "Data Compression via Textual Substitution," *Journal of the ACM*, Vol. 29, pp. 928–951, 1982.

27. T. C. Bell, J. G. Cleary, and I. H. Witten, *Text Compression*. Prentice Hall, Englewood Cliffs, NJ, 1990.

28. T. Acharya and J. F. JáJá, "An On-line Variable-Length Binary Encoding of Text," *Information Sciences*, Vol. 94, pp. 1–22, 1996.

29. J. G. Cleary and I. H. Witten, "Data Compression Using Adaptive Coding and Partial String Matching," *IEEE Transactions on Communications*, Vol. 32, pp. 396–402, 1984.

30. A. Moffat, "Implementing the PPM Data Compression Scheme," *IEEE Transactions on Communications*, Vol. 38, pp. 1917–1921, 1990.

31. M. Burrows and D. J. Wheeler, "A Block-Sorting Lossless Data Compression Algorithm," Tech. Rep. 124, Digital Equipment Corporation, Palo Alto, California, May 1994.

2

Source Coding Algorithms

In this chapter, we present some of the popular source coding algorithms used for data compression. From an information theoretic perspective, *source coding* can mean both lossless and lossy compression. However, it is often reserved by researchers to indicate lossless coding only. In the signal processing community, the source coding is used to mean source model-based coding. We adopt this convention here and by source coding we mean lossless coding only. These algorithms can be used directly to compress any data losslessly. Depending on the characteristics of the data, each algorithm may give different compression performance. So selection of the particular algorithm will depend up characteristics of the data themselves. In lossy image compression mode, the source coding algorithms are usually applied in the entropy encoding step after transformation and quantization.

2.1 RUN-LENGTH CODING

The neighboring pixels in a typical image are highly correlated to each other. Often it is observed that the consecutive pixels in a smooth region of an image are identical or the variation among the neighboring pixels is very small. Appearance of runs of identical values is particularly true for binary images where usually the image consists of runs of 0's or 1's. Even if the consecutive pixels in grayscale or color images are not exactly identical but slowly varying, it can often be preprocessed and the consecutive processed pixel values become identical. If there is a long run of identical pixels, it is more economical to transmit the length of the run associated with the particular pixel value instead of encoding individual pixel values.

Run-length coding is a simple approach to source coding when there exists a long run of the same data, in a consecutive manner, in a data set. As an example, the data $d = $ 5 5 5 5 5 5 5 19 19 19 19 19 19 19 19 19 19 19 19 0 0 0 0 0 0 0 8 23 23 23 23 23 23 contains long runs of 5's, 19's, 0's, 23's, etc. Rather than coding each sample in the run individually, the data can be represented compactly by simply indicating the value of the sample and the length of its run when it appears. In this manner, the data d can be run-length encoded as (5 7) (19 12) (0 8) (8 1) (23 6). For ease of understanding, we have shown a pair in each parentheses. Here the first value represents the pixel, while the second indicates the length of its run.

In some cases, the appearance of runs of symbols may not be very apparent. But the data can possibly be preprocessed in order to aid run-length coding. Consider the data $d = $ 26 29 32 35 38 41 44 50 56 62 68 78 88 98 108 118 116 114 112 110 108 106 104 102 100 98 96. We can simply preprocess this data, by taking the sample difference $e(i) = d(i) - d(i - 1)$, to produce the processed data $\bar{e}= $ 26 3 3 3 3 3 3 6 6 6 6 10 10 10 10 10 −2 −2 −2 −2 −2 −2 −2 −2 −2 −2 −2. This preprocessed data can now be easily run-length encoded as (26 1) (3 6) (6 4) (10 5) (−2 11). A variation of this technique is applied in the baseline JPEG standard for still-picture compression [8]. The same technique can be applied to numeric databases as well.

On the other hand, binary (black-and-white) images, such as facsimile, usually consist of runs of 0's or 1's. As an example, if a segment of a binary image is represented as

$d = $ 00000000011111111111000000000000000011100000000000001001111111111,

it can be compactly represented as $c(d) = $ (9, 11, 15, 3, 13, 1, 2, 10) by simply listing the lengths of alternate runs of 0's and 1's. While the original binary data d requires 65 bits for storage, its compact representation $c(d)$ requires 32 bits only under the assumption that each length of run is being represented by 4 bits. The early facsimile compression standard (CCITT Group 3, CCITT Group 4) algorithms were developed based on this principle [3].

2.2 HUFFMAN CODING

From Shannon's *Source Coding Theory*, we know that a source can be coded with an average code length close to the entropy of the source. In 1952, D. A. Huffman [1] invented a coding technique to produce the shortest possible average code length given the source symbol set and the associated probability of occurrence of the symbols. Codes generated using this coding technique are popularly known as *Huffman codes*. Huffman coding technique is based on the following two observations regarding optimum prefix codes.

- The more frequently occurring symbols can be allocated with shorter codewords than the less frequently occurring symbols.

- The two least frequently occurring symbols will have codewords of the same length, and they differ only in the least significant bit.

Average length of these codes is close to entropy of the source.

Let us assume that there are m source symbols $\{s_1, s_2, \cdots, s_m\}$ with associated probabilities of occurrence $\{p_1, p_2, \cdots, p_m\}$. Using these probability values, we can generate a set of Huffman codes of the source symbols. The Huffman codes can be mapped into a binary tree, popularly known as the Huffman tree. We describe the algorithm to generate the Huffman tree and hence the Huffman codes of the source symbols below. We show a Huffman tree in Figure 2.1.

1. Produce a set $N=\{N_1, N_2, \cdots, N_m\}$ of m nodes as leaves of a binary tree. Assign a node N_i with the source symbol s_i, $i = 1, 2, \cdots, m$ and label the node with the associated probability p_i.
   (**Example:** As shown in Figure 2.1, we start with eight nodes N_0, N_1, N_2, N_3, N_4, N_5, N_6, N_7 corresponding to the eight source symbols a, b, c, d, e, f, g, h, respectively. Probability of occurrence of each symbol is indicated in the associated parentheses.)

2. Find the two nodes with the two lowest probability symbols from the current node set, and produce a new node as a parent of these two nodes.
   (**Example:** From Figure 2.1 we find that the two lowest probability symbols g and d are associated with nodes N_6 and N_3 respectively. The new node N_8 becomes the parent of N_3 and N_6.)

3. Label the probability of this new parent node as the sum of the probabilities of its two child nodes.
   (**Example:** The new node N_8 is now labeled by probability 0.09, which is the sum of the probabilities 0.06 and 0.03 of the symbols d and g associated with the nodes N_3 and N_6 respectively.)

4. Label the branch of one child node of the new parent node as 1 and the branch of the other child node as 0.
   (**Example:** The branch N_3 to N_8 is labeled by 1 and the branch N_6 to N_8 is labeled by 0.)

5. Update the node set by replacing the two child nodes with smallest probabilities by the newly generated parent node. If the number of nodes remaining in the node set is greater than 1, go to Step 2.
   (**Example:** The new node set now contains the nodes N_0, N_1, N_2, N_4, N_5, N_7, N_8 and the associated probabilities are 0.30, 0.10, 0.20, 0.09, 0.07, 0.15, 0.09, respectively. Since there are more than one node in

the node set, Steps 2 to 5 are repeated and the nodes N_9, N_{10}, N_{11}, N_{12}, N_{13}, N_{14} are generated in the next six iterations, until the node set consists only of N_{14}.)

6. Traverse the generated binary tree from the root node to each leaf node N_i, $i = 1, 2, \cdots, m$, to produce the codeword of the corresponding symbol s_i, which is a concatenation of the binary labels (0 or 1) of the branches from the root to the leaf node.
   (**Example:** The Huffman code of symbol h is 110, formed by concatenating the binary labels of the branches N_{14} to N_{13}, N_{13} to N_{11} and N_{11} to N_7.)

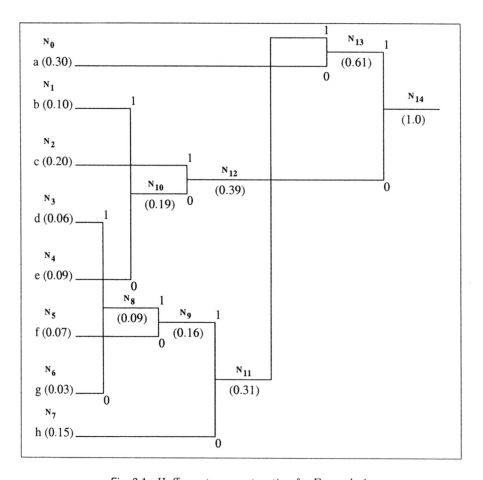

Fig. 2.1 Huffman tree construction for Example 1.

It is needless to mention that any ensemble of binary codes, which can be mapped into a binary tree, consists of prefix codes. Hence Huffman code is also a prefix code. The Huffman code generation process described above is a bottom-up approach, since we perform the code construction process on the two symbols with least probabilities.

2.2.0.1 **Example 1:** Assume the alphabet $S = \{a, b, c, d, e, f, g, h\}$ with 8 source symbols and their corresponding probabilities are $p(a) = 0.30$, $p(b) = 0.10$, $p(c) = 0.20$, $p(d) = 0.06$, $p(e) = 0.09$, $p(f) = 0.07$, $p(g) = 0.03$, and $p(h) = 0.15$ respectively. The Huffman tree generated by the Huffman Coding algorithm is shown in Figure 2.1 and the corresponding Huffman code table is shown in Table 2.1.

Let us consider a string M of 200 symbols generated from the above source, where the numbers of occurrences of a, b, c, d, e, f, g and h in M are 60, 20, 40, 12, 18, 14, 6 and 30 respectively. Size of the encoded message M using the Huffman codes in Table 2.1 will be 550 bits. Here it requires 2.75 bits per symbol on the average. On the other hand, the length of the encoded message M will be 600 bits if it is encoded by a fixed-length code of length 3 for each of the symbols. This simple example demonstrates how we can achieve compression using variable-length coding or source coding techniques.

Table 2.1 Huffman Code Table

Symbol	Probability	Huffman Code
a	0.30	1 0
b	0.10	0 0 1
c	0.20	0 1
d	0.06	1 1 1 1 1
e	0.09	0 0 0
f	0.07	1 1 1 0
g	0.03	1 1 1 1 0
h	0.15	1 1 0

2.2.1 Limitations of Huffman Coding

Although Huffman coding is a very efficient entropy coding technique, it has several limitations. Huffman code is optimal only if exact probability distribution of the source symbols is known. It is also clear that each symbol is encoded with integer number of bits. We have known from Shannon's theory that the optimal length of a binary codeword for a source symbol s from a discrete memoryless source is $-\log_2 p(s)$ where $p(s)$ is the probability of appearance of symbol s. This condition is exactly satisfied when the probabilities of the source symbols are negative integer powers of two (e.g., 2^{-1}, 2^{-2}, 2^{-3}, 2^{-4}, etc.). If the probabilities of the symbols significantly deviates from this ideal condition, encoding of these symbols can result in poor coding efficiency.

Redundancy of a source is defined by the average code length less the entropy. It can be shown that the redundancy of Huffman codes can be bounded by $p + 0.086$, where p is the probability of the most likely symbol [2]. As a result the redundancy will be very high if the probability of occurrence of a symbol is significantly greater compared to the others.

Huffman coding is not efficient to adapt with the changing source statistics. A predefined Huffman code can lead to data expansion when it is applied to encode data whose statistical characteristics are significantly different from the source statistics used to generate the Huffman code. In image compression applications, a Huffman code is developed using a set of typical images in practice. As a result, the Huffman coding is not necessarily optimal for a particular image unless the code is generated using the statistical distribution of that image.

Another limitation of Huffman coding is that length of the codes of the least probable symbol could be very large to store into a single word or basic storage unit in a computing system. In the worst-case scenario, if the probability distribution of the symbols generates a Huffman tree that is a skewed binary tree, the length of the longest two codes will be $n - 1$ if there are n source symbols. For example, consider four source symbols a, b, c and d with corresponding probabilities $p(a) = 0.60$, $p(b) = 0.25$, $p(c) = 0.10$, and $p(d) = 0.05$ respectively. The Huffman tree for this source will be a skewed binary tree and the Huffman codes of a, b, c and d can be 1, $0\,1$, $0\,0\,1$ and $0\,0\,0$ respectively. Usually the Huffman codes are stored in a table called the Huffman table. In its simplest form of implementation, usually each entry in the table contains a Huffman code. Since the Huffman code is a variable-length code, storage of each entry into the code table is usually determined by the length of the longest code. For an arbitrarily large code it is a limitation.

2.2.2   Modified Huffman Coding

For a large set of source symbols, it is often possible that most of the symbols have small probabilities of occurrence and a significantly smaller number of symbols are most probable. In this situation, the code length of these least probable symbols could be prohibitively high because of their large information content $- \log_2 p$. To avoid this, we can consider a reduced set of symbols consisting of the most probable symbols and a special symbol "$ESCAPE$." The Huffman code is generated for this reduced subset of symbols only. We can assume that the least probable symbols are all lumped into this $ESCAPE$ category. Whenever a symbol in this $ESCAPE$ category needs to be encoded, we transmit Huffman code of $ESCAPE$, followed by extra bits to identify the symbol. If the number of appearance of the symbols in the $ESCAPE$ category is significantly small, the increase in average bit rate will be very small while the storage requirement for the Huffman Table and the decoding complexity will be substantially reduced. *Modified Huffman Coding* has been adopted in the CCITT Group 3 International digital facsimile coding standards [3].

2.2.2.1 **Example 2:**   From the set of symbols in Example 1, if the least probable symbols d, e, f, and g are lumped together into a special *ESCAPE* category, the reduced subset of will be $\{a, b, c, h, ESCAPE\}$ and the probability distribution of these symbols changes to $p(a) = 0.30$, $p(b) = 0.10$, $p(c) = 0.20$, $p(h) = 0.15$, and $p(ESCAPE) = 0.25$ respectively. Construction of the corresponding Huffman tree using this reduced subset of source symbols is shown in Figure 2.2. We call this reduced Huffman tree a *modified Huffman tree*. From the modified Huffman tree, we derive the Huffman code table shown in Table 2.2. If we assign fixed-length code identifiers 0 0, 0 1, 1 0, and 1 1 for d, e, f, and g respectively, the *modified Huffman code* can be constructed as shown in Table 2.3.

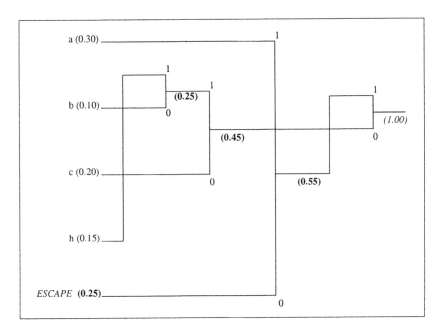

Fig. 2.2   Huffman Tree Construction for the reduced symbols in Example 2.

The first two bits 1 0 of the codeword for d in Table 2.3 is the Huffman code of the special symbol *ESCAPE* and the last two bits 0 0 represent the identifier for d. Similarly the other codewords have been defined. It is interesting to note in this example that length of the modified Huffman codes for the two least probable symbols d and g is now 4 compared to the original code length 5 of the original Huffman code in Table 2.1. This may not be true in other cases.

Table 2.2   Huffman Code for Reduced Alphabet

Reduced Symbol	Probability	Huffman Code
a	0.30	1 1
b	0.10	0 1 0
c	0.20	0 0
h	0.15	0 1 1
ESCAPE	0.25	1 0

Table 2.3   Modified Huffman Code

Symbol	Modified Huffman Code
a	1 1
b	0 1 0
c	0 0
h	0 1 1
d	1 0 0 0
e	1 0 0 1
f	1 0 1 0
g	1 0 1 1

2.3   ARITHMETIC CODING

Arithmetic coding   is a variable-length source encoding technique [4].   In traditional entropy encoding techniques such as Huffman coding, each input symbol in a message is substituted by a specific code specified by an integer number of bits. Arithmetic coding deviates from this paradigm. In arithmetic coding, a sequence of input symbols is represented by an interval of real numbers between 0.0 and 1.0. The longer the message, the smaller the interval to represent the message becomes, as will be evident in the following discussions. More probable symbols reduce the interval less than the less probable symbols and hence add fewer bits in the encoded message. As a result, the coding result can reach to Shannon's entropy limit for a sufficiently large sequence of input symbols as long as the statistics are accurate.

Arithmetic coding offers superior efficiency and more flexibility compared to the popular Huffman coding. It is particularly useful when dealing with sources with small alphabets such as binary alphabets and alphabets with highly skewed probabilities. Huffman coding cannot achieve any compression for a source of binary alphabets. As a result arithmetic coding is highly efficient for coding bi-level images. However, arithmetic coding is more complicated and is intrinsically less error resilient compared to the Huffman coding. The arithmetic coding requires significantly higher computation because of the requirement of multiplication to compute the intervals. However, several multiplication-free arithmetic coding techniques have been developed for binary image compression [5, 6, 7].

2.3.1 Encoding Algorithm

The arithmetic coding algorithm is explained here with an example. We consider a four-symbol alphabet $A = \{a, b, c, d\}$ with the fixed symbol probabilities $p(a) = 0.3$, $p(b) = 0.2$, $p(c) = 0.4$, and $p(d) = 0.1$ respectively. The symbol probabilities can be expressed in terms of partition of the half-open range $[0.0, 1.0)$ as shown in Table 2.4.

Table 2.4 Probability Model

Index	Symbol	Probability	Cumulative Probability	Range
1	a	0.3	0.3	$[0.0, 0.3)$
2	b	0.2	0.5	$[0.3, 0.5)$
3	c	0.4	0.9	$[0.5, 0.9)$
4	d	0.1	1.0	$[0.9, 1.0)$

The algorithm for arithmetic coding is presented below. In this algorithm, we consider N is the length of the message (i.e., total number of symbols in the message); $F(i)$ is the cumulative probability of ith source symbol as shown in Table 2.4.

Algorithm : Arithmetic Coding
begin
    $L = 0.0$;
    $H = 1.0$;
    $F(0) = 0$;
    for $(j = 1$ to $N)$ {
        $i =$ index of Symbol(j);
        $L = L + (H - L) * F(i - 1)$;
        $H = L + (H - L) * F(i)$;
    }
    Output $(\frac{L+H}{2})$;
end

2.3.1.1 **Example:**   We would like to encode a message "$c\,a\,c\,b\,a\,d$" using the above fixed model of probability estimates. At the beginning of both encoding and decoding processes, the range for the message is the entire half-open interval [0.0, 1.0), which can be partitioned into disjoint subintervals or ranges [0.0, 0.3), [0.3, 0.5), [0.5, 0.9), and [0.9, 1.0) corresponding to the symbols a, b, c, and d respectively, as shown by the range $R(start)$ in Figure 2.3 in terms of the vertical bar with ticks representing the symbol probabilities stipulated by the probability model. As each symbol in the message is processed, the range is narrowed down by the encoder as explained in the algorithm.

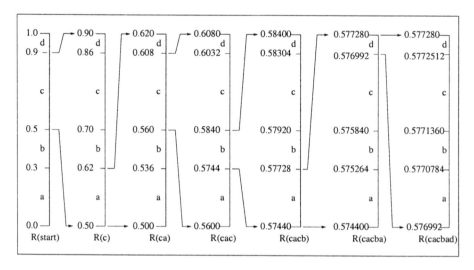

Fig. 2.3 Arithmetic coding technique: an example.

Since the first symbol of the message is c, the range is first narrowed down to the half-open interval $R(c)=[0.5, 0.9)$. This range is further partitioned into exactly the same proportions as the original one, yielding the four half-open disjoint intervals [0.5, 0.62), [0.62, 0.70), [0.70, 0.86), and [0.86, 0.9) corresponding to a, b, c and d respectively as shown in Figure 2.3. As a result, the range is narrowed down to $R(ca)=[0.5, 0.62)$ when the second symbol a in the message is processed. This new range [0.5, 0.62) is now partitioned into four disjoint intervals [0.5, 0.536), [0.536, 0.560), [0.560, 0.608), and [0.608, 0.62). After processing the third symbol, c, the range is accordingly narrowed down to $R(cac)=[0.560, 0.608)$. This is again partitioned into [0.560, 0.5744), [0.5744, 0.5840), [0.5840, 0.6032), and [0.6032, 0.608) in order to process the next symbol in the message. After processing the fourth symbol, b, the range is now narrowed down to $R(cacb)=[0.5744, 0.5840)$. This is again partitioned into four intervals [0.5744, 0.57728), [0.57728. 0.57920), [0.57920, 0.58304), and [0.58304, 0.584) corresponding to the symbols a, b, c, and d respectively. After processing the fifth symbol, a, the range is now narrowed down to $R(cacba)=[0.5744, 0.57728)$. This is further partitioned into the disjoint intervals [0.5744, 0.575264), [0.575264, 0.575840), [0.575840, 0.576992), and [0.576992, 0.57728). The last symbol in the message is d and hence the final range for the message becomes $R(c\,a\,c\,b\,a\,d) = [0.576992, 0.57728)$. As a result, the message "$c\,a\,c\,b\,a\,d$" can be encoded by any number in the range $[0.576992, 0.57728)$ because it is not necessary for the decoder to know both ends of the range produced by the encoder. If we use the midpoint of the interval, the encoded value will be 0.577136. Assuming that we choose 0.577, the decoding processing is explained below using the same probability model in Figure 2.3 used in the encoding process.

2.3.2   Decoding Algorithm

Both the encoder and the decoder have the same probability model. Initially the decoder starts with the range $[0.0, 1.0)$, which is partitioned into four intervals $[0.0, 0.3)$, $[0.3, 0.5)$, $[0.5, 0.9)$, and $[0.9, 1.0)$ corresponding to the symbols a, b, c, and d in the alphabet. As soon as the decoder receives an encoded number 0.577, it can immediately decode that the first symbol of the message is c because the number 0.577 belongs to the range $[0.5, 0.9)$ and the range is narrowed down to $[0.5, 0.9)$ and partitioned into $[0.5, 0.62)$, $[0.62, 0.70)$, $[0.70, 0.86)$, and $[0.86, 0.9)$ in a similar fashion as the encoder. Since the number 0.577 belongs to the range $[0.5, 0.62)$, it can immediately decode the second symbol to be a. The range is now narrowed down to $[0.5, 0.62)$ and partitioned into $[0.5, 0.536)$, $[0.536, 0.560)$, $[0.560, 0.608)$, and $[0.608, 0.62)$. Since the number 0.577 belongs to the range $[0.560, 0.608)$, the decoder can decode the third symbol to be c. The range is now narrowed down to $[0.560, 0.608)$ and partitioned into the four subintervals $[0.560, 0.5744)$, $[0.5744, 0.584)$, $[0.584, 0.6032)$, and $[0.6032, 0.608)$. Since the number 0.577 belongs in the range $[0.5744, 0.584)$, the decoder deduces that the next symbol is b and narrows the range down to be $[0.5744, 0.584)$. The range is now subdivided into $[0.5744, 0.57728)$, $[0.57728, 0.5792)$, $[0.5792, 0.58304)$, and $[0.58304, 0.584)$. Since the number 0.577 belongs within the range $[0.5744, 0.57728)$, the next symbol decoded is a and the range is narrowed down to $[0.5744, 0.57728)$ and partitioned into four subintervals $[0.5744, 0.575264)$, $[0.575264, 0.575840)$, $[0.575840, 0.576992)$, and $[0.576992, 0.57728)$. Since 0.577 belongs to the range $[0.576992, 0.57728)$, it is very natural that the decoder decodes the next symbol to be d and narrows the range down to $[0.576992, 0.5770784)$, $[0.5770784, 0.577136)$, $[0.577136, 0.5772512)$, and $[0.5772512, 0.57728)$ respectively. Hence the decoder could uniquely decode the message "$c\,a\,c\,b\,a\,d$" until this step. If the decoder is aware of the length of the message, it can stop decoding here. Otherwise, it can continue decoding the next symbol to be a because 0.577 belongs to the range $[0.576992, 0.5770784)$ and so on indefinitely. Hence the decoder faces the problem of detecting the end of the message in order to stop. To resolve the ambiguity, we can ensure that each message ends with a special terminating symbol known to both encoder and decoder. In this example, if we assume that d is the special terminating symbol, the decoder will effectively stop after decoding the message "$cacbad$." Otherwise the length of the original message needs to be known to the decoder in order to stop decoding effectively.

The arithmetic coding algorithm described above suffers from the following limitations.

- The encoded value is not unique because any value within the final range can be considered as the encoded message. It is desirable to have a unique binary code for the encoded message.

- The encoding algorithm does not transmit anything until encoding of the entire message has been completed. As a result, the decoding algorithm cannot start until it has received the complete encoded data. The above two limitations can be overcome by using the binary arithmetic coding which will be described in the next section.

- The precision required to represent the intervals grows with the length of the message. A fixed-point arithmetic implementation is desirable, which can again be achieved using the binary arithmetic coding by restricting the intervals using a scaling approach. We can replace the initial range $[0.0, 1.0)$ with a large range of $[0, MAX\_VALUE)$, where MAX_VALUE is the largest integer number that a computer can handle. For a 16-bit integer arithmetic, the initial range will be $[0, 2^{16} - 1)$. Rather than defining the cumulative probabilities in the range of $[0,1)$, we can define cumulative frequencies of the symbols within the range $[0, 2^{16} - 1)$. This resolves the precision problem.

- Use of the multiplications in the encoding and decoding process, in order to compute the ranges in every step, may be prohibitive for many real-time fast applications.

- The algorithm is very sensitive to transmission errors. A minor change in the encoded data could represent a completely different message after decoding.

2.4 BINARY ARITHMETIC CODING

Binary arithmetic coding is an incremental encoding and decoding process; that is, the encoder need not wait till the end of the encoding of the last symbol of the message before it can output or transmit the encoded data. Similarly, the decoder need not wait to receive all the encoding bits before it can start decoding. Also binary arithmetic coding helps to resolve the issue of the precision of the final result that we discussed in arithmetic coding; that is, if the number of symbols in the alphabet is large, the intervals of individual symbols could be very small, and coding large numbers of symbols in data with these small intervals can make the final range too small beyond the allowed precision of a digital computer. The incremental encoding and decoding process in binary arithmetic coding resolves this issue. The four general observations or rules behind binary arithmetic coding are as follows:

- **Case 1:** If the present range $[LOW, HIGH)$ entirely belongs to the lower half of the interval $[0.0, 1.0)$ (i.e., $HIGH < 0.5$), the encoder outputs or transmits a binary bit 0 and rescales the range by a factor 2 as $[2 * LOW, 2 * HIGH)$.

- **Case 2:** If the present range $[LOW, HIGH)$ entirely belongs to the upper half of the interval $[0.0, 1.0)$ (i.e., $LOW \geq 0.5$), the encoder outputs or transmits a binary bit 1 and rescales the range by subtracting 0.5 from both LOW and $HIGH$ and multiplying the results by a factor 2 as $[2 * (LOW - 0.5), 2 * (HIGH - 0.5))$.

- **Case 3:** If the present range $[LOW, HIGH)$ entirely belongs to the second and third quarters of the interval $[0.0, 1.0)$ (i.e., $LOW \geq 0.25$ and $HIGH < 0.75$), we keep track of this situation by incrementing a special counter $SPCL\_COUNT$ and rescale the range by subtracting 0.25 from both LOW and $HIGH$ and multiplying the results by a factor 2 as $[2 * (LOW - 0.25), 2 * (HIGH - 0.25))$. Whenever case 1 or 2 arises, the encoder checks the value of $SPCL\_COUNT$. If it is greater than 0, those many binary 1's (or 0's) are output or transmitted after it outputs the binary bit 0 (or 1) as described in case 1 (or 2). After all the binary bits are output, the $SPCL\_COUNT$ is reset to count 0.

- For any other cases, there is no need to output or transmit any binary bit and also no need to rescale the range. This is a significant part of the binary arithmetic coding that leads to low bit rate.

We describe the binary arithmetic coding algorithm using the same example as in the previous section. We consider the same probability model and show how we can generate a unique binary code incrementally for the same message "$c\,a\,c\,b\,a\,d$." Consider LOW and $HIGH$ represent the low and high values of the present half-open range. The changes in the range and output of the binary bits are shown in Figure 2.4.

We begin with the half-open interval $R0 = [0.0, 1.0)$ (i.e., $LOW = 0.0$ and $HIGH = 1.0$). The special counter $SPCL\_COUNT$ is initialized to count 0. The first symbol in the message is c which represents the range $R1 = [0.5, 0.9)$ shown in Figure 2.4. Since the new range $[0.5, 0.9)$ entirely belongs to the upper half of the interval $[0.0, 1.0)$, we output the binary code 1 and rescale the interval to $R2 = [0.0, 0.8)$. Since $SPCL\_COUNT = 0$, no other binary bit is output.

The second symbol in the message is a and the corresponding range is $R3 = [0.0, 0.24)$. Since this range entirely belongs to the lower half of the interval $[0.0, 1.0)$, we output the binary code 0 and rescale the range to $R4 = [0.0,$

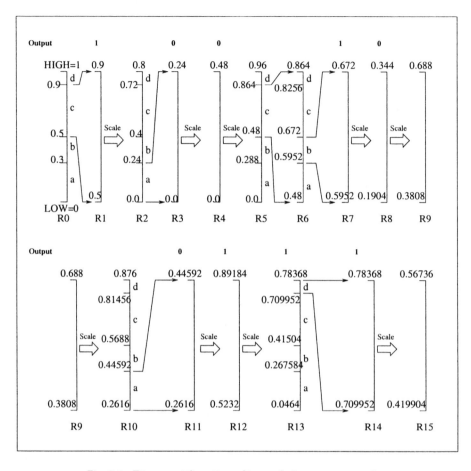

Fig. 2.4 Binary arithmetic coding technique: an example.

0.48). This again entirely belongs to the lower half of the interval [0.0, 1.0). Hence, we output the binary code 0 and rescale the range to R5 = [0.0, 0.96).

The third symbol in the message is *c* and the corresponding range is R6 = [0.48, 0.864). This does not require us to output any binary bit nor is the range rescaled.

The fourth symbol in the message is *b* and the corresponding range is R7 = [0.5952, 0.672). Since this range entirely belongs to the upper half of the interval [0.0, 1.0), we output the binary code 1 and rescale the range to R8 = [0.1904, 0.344). The new range now entirely belongs to the lower half of the interval [0.0, 1.0). Hence, we output the binary code 0 and rescale the range to R9 = [0.3808, 0.688). Now this range entirely belongs to the second and third quarter of the interval [0.0, 1.0) because $LOW = 0.3808 > 0.25$ and $HIGH = 0.688 < 0.75$. Hence we increment the special counter to $SPCL\_COUNT = 1$ and rescale the range to R10=[0.2616, 0.876).

The fifth symbol in the message is a and the corresponding range is R11 = [0.2616, 0.44592) which entirely belongs to the lower half of the interval [0.0, 1.0). Hence we output the binary code 0 and rescale the range to R12 = [0.5232, 0.89184). Since the value of the special counter is greater than 0 ($SPCL\_COUNT$ = 1), we output one more binary bit 1. Now the new range R12 = [0.5232, 0.89184) entirely belongs to the upper half of the interval [0.0, 1.0). As a result, we output the binary bit 1 and rescale the range to R13 = [0.0464, 0.78368).

The last symbol is d and the corresponding range is R14 = [0.709952, 0.78368). As a result we rescale the range to R15 = [0.419904, 0.56736) and output the binary bit 1. At this point, we can stop encoding by sending the binary representation of any value in the final interval. In this case we can conveniently choose the value 0.5. The binary representation of 0.5 is 0.1000.... Thus, we transmit a 1 followed by as many as 0's required by the word length used in the implementation. Hence the unique binary code for the message "$c a c b a d$" is 1 0 0 1 0 0 1 1 1 1 0 0 0 0 0 0. It should be noted that the first 9 bits, 1 0 0 1 0 0 1 1 1, represent the binary codes generated by the above incremental binary arithmetic coding procedure. The last 7 bits, 1 0 0 0 0 0 0, represent 0.5 chosen from the final range [0.419904, 0.56736), assuming a 16-bit word for implementation.

Let us describe how to decode the binary code 1 0 0 1 0 0 1 1 1 1 0 0 0 0 0 0 generated using the above incremental encoding process. We do not need to wait for the entire binary code before we can start the decoding process. The decoding can be done in incremental fashion as well. To decode the first symbol, we need to wait to receive the number of bits that is enough to represent the shortest interval of the probability model. But to properly handle the situation that arises due to case 3 in the encoder, we need more bits to take care of the look-ahead bits. As a result we start with twice the number of minimum bits required to represent the shortest interval of the probability model. The length of the shortest interval [0.9, 1.0) is 0.1 and the condition of minimum number of bits (say k) to represent 0.1 is $2^{-k} < 0.1$ or $k = 4$. Hence we start with 8 bits.

As soon as the first eight bits, 1 0 0 1 0 0 1 1, are available as a codeword C, we can start decoding. Since $C = 1 0 0 1 0 0 1 1$ represents the fraction 0.57421875, we can immediately deduce that that first symbol of the message is c because 0.57421875 belongs in the range R1 = [0.5, 0.9) as shown in Figure 2.4. Since range R1 entirely belongs to the upper half of the interval [0.0, 1.0), it is scaled to R2 = [0.0, 0.8). We shift the most-significant bit (MSB) 1 of codeword C out and append a new bit at the least significant bit (LSB) position of the codeword C to form the new codeword $C = 0 0 1 0 0 1 1 1$.

Now the new codeword $C = 0 0 1 0 0 1 1 1$ represents the fraction 0.15234375, which belongs to the range R3 = [0.0, 0.24) for symbol a and hence the decoded symbol is a. Since R3 entirely belongs to the lower half of the interval [0.0, 1.0), it is scaled to R4 = [0.0, 0.48). We shift out the MSB 0 of C and append a new bit 1 to form the codeword $C = 0 1 0 0 1 1 1 1$. Still the range R4 entirely belongs to the lower half of the interval [0.0, 1.0) and hence R4 is scaled to R5 = [0.0, 0.96) and forms the new codeword $C = 10011110$ after shifting the MSB 0 out and appending a new bit 0 at the LSB. The new codeword now represents the fraction 0.61718750 and belongs to the range R6 = [0.48, 0.864) for symbol c and hence the symbol c is decoded.

The range R6 does not entirely belong to upper half or lower half of the interval [0.0, 1.0). It does not entirely belong to the second and third quarter [0.25, 0.75) either. Hence we do not need any scaling of the range. Now the fraction represented by the codeword belongs to the range R7 = [0.5952, 0.672), which represents the symbol b and hence the symbol b is decoded. The new range entirely belongs to the upper half of the interval [0.0, 1.0) and hence it is scaled to R8 = [0.1904, 0.344). Accordingly, we output the MSB 1 from codeword C and form a new codeword $C = 00111100$ after appending the new bit 0 in the LSB. The range R8 now entirely belongs to the lower half of the interval [0.0, 1.0) and hence it is scaled to R9 = [0.3808, 0.688). Accordingly, new codeword is $C = 01111000$ is formed.

Now the new range R9 entirely belongs to the second and third quarter [0.25, 0.75) of the interval [0.0, 1.0). Hence we increment the special counter to $SPCL\_COUNT = 1$ and rescale the range to R10=[0.2616, 0.876). Since this range does not need any scaling, we drop $SPCL\_COUNT = 1$ bits adjacent to the MSB of the codeword shown in bold in $C = 01111000$ to form the new codeword $C = 01110000$.

The codeword $C = 01110000$ represents the fraction 0.4375, which belongs to the range R11 = [0.2616, 0.44592) to represent the symbol a and hence the symbol a is now decoded. The range R11 now entirely belongs to the lower half of the interval [0.0, 1.0) and hence is scaled to R12 = [0.5232, 0.89184) and the new codeword $C = 11100000$ after shifting the MSB 0 and inserting 0 at the LSB. The range R12 now entirely belongs to the upper half of the interval [0.0, 1.0) and hence is scaled further to R13 = [0.0464, 0.78368) and the new codeword is $C = 11000000$. The codeword C now represents the fraction 0.75 which belongs to the range R14=[0.709952, 0.78368) to represent the symbol d. Hence the decoded symbol is now d. We can stop the decoding process here because the final symbol is d.

We can further proceed to verify the validity of the last codeword and the decoding procedure. Since R14 = [0.709952, 0.78368) entirely belongs to the upper half of the interval [0.0, 1.0), it can be scaled further to R15 = [0.419904, 0.56736). Accordingly, the codeword can be modified to $C = 10000000$. The value of this codeword is 0.5, which matches the final value that the encoder transmitted during the encoding processing.

2.4.1   Implementation with Integer Mathematics

The precision required to represent the intervals grows with the length of the message. If we continue encoding a large number of symbols in the message, the final range may even become smaller than the precision of any computer, to define such a range. In binary arithmetic coding, we can replace the initial range $[0.0, 1.0)$ by $[0, MAX\_VALUE)$, where MAX_VALUE is the largest integer number that a computer can handle. For a 16-bit integer, $MAX\_VALUE = 2^{16} - 1 = 65535$ and hence the initial range will be $[0, 2^{16} - 1)$. Rather than defining the cumulative probabilities of the symbols in the range of $[0.0, 1.0)$, we can define their cumulative frequencies scaled up within the range $[0, 2^{16} - 1)$. This resolves the precision problem.

Since we are going to do the integer arithmetic, we need to replace the cumulative probability $F(i)$ of the symbol with index i by an integer expression. We can replace this by the cumulative frequency $Cum\_Frequency(i)$. Define N_i as the number of times the symbol with index i occurs in a sequence of length $Total\_Count$. Then $Cum\_Frequency(i)$ and $F(i)$ can be expressed as

$$\left. \begin{aligned} Cum\_Frequency(i) &= \sum_{k=1}^{i} N_k \\ F(i) &= \frac{\sum_{k=1}^{i} N_k}{Total\_Count} = \frac{Cum\_Frequency(i)}{Total\_Count} \end{aligned} \right\}.$$

As a result, the ranges can be updated by the following expressions

$$\left. \begin{aligned} LOW &= LOW + \frac{(HIGH - LOW + 1) * Cum\_Frequency(i-1)}{Total\_Count} \\ HIGH &= LOW + \frac{(HIGH - LOW + 1) * Cum\_Frequency(i)}{Total\_Count} - 1 \end{aligned} \right\}.$$

If $LOW \geq \frac{MAX\_VALUE+1}{2}$, the range $[LOW, HIGH)$ entirely belongs to the upper half of the interval $[0, MAX\_VALUE)$. If $HIGH < \frac{MAX\_VALUE+1}{2}$, the range $[LOW, HIGH)$ entirely belongs to the lower half of the interval $[0, MAX\_VALUE)$.

Details of the integer arithmetic implementation of the binary arithmetic algorithm and the source code in C have been presented in [4]. The binary arithmetic coding became particularly useful for encoding binary images. Q-coder is a popular implementation of an adaptive binary arithmetic coding technique for coding bilevel images (i.e., the source symbols are 0 and 1 only) without requiring any multiplication [5]. The Q-coder approximates the intervals in such a way that it can avoid the multiplications and adjustment of the intervals in successive coding steps. It does not achieve optimum coding efficiency, but evidence shows that it can achieve coding efficiency within 2 to 6% of the ideal results. A variation of this technique called QM-coder has been adopted for entropy encoding in a mode of JPEG image compression standard [8]. The upcoming JPEG2000 standard uses another variation called the MQ-coder, a context-based adaptive arithmetic coder [9].

2.4.2   The QM-Coder

The QM-coder [8] is an enhancement of the Q-coder [5]. The QM-coder is the adaptive binary arithmetic coding algorithm used in the JBIG (Joint Bi-level

Image Processing Group) standard for bi-level image compression. Although it follows the same principle of arithmetic coding, QM-coder is designed for simplicity and speed. The input symbols to the QM-coder are single bits of the bi-level image and it is free from multiplications by approximating the computation of intervals by fixed-precision integer arithmetic operations (addition, subtraction, and shift operations only).

The main idea behind the QM-coder is to map the input bits into *more probable symbol* (MPS) and *less probable symbol* (LPS). This can be explained in terms of a black-and-white image. If bits 0 and 1 represent the black and white pixels respectively, then in a mostly black region 0 will be mapped to MPS and 1 will be mapped to LPS, whereas in a mostly white region 1 will be mapped to MPS and 0 will be mapped to LPS. Before the next bit is input, the QM-coder determines which bit is MPS (the other bit is LPS) and compresses this information instead of the input bit directly. During the decoding process, the QM-decoder decodes whether the bit just decoded is MPS or LPS and then converts this information to actual binary pixel value. Hence the QM-coder assigns the intervals to the MPS and LPS symbols instead of the 0 or 1 input bit. If the probability estimate of LPS is Q, then the probability estimate of MPS is $(1 - Q)$ because there are only two symbols in the alphabet. For interval A, the QM-coder divides the interval into two subintervals according to the value of Q. The sizes of the subintervals assigned to LPS and MPS are AQ and $A(1 - Q)$ respectively as shown in Figure 2.5.

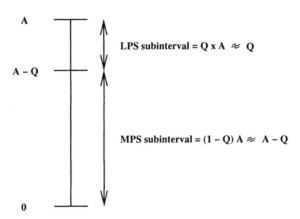

Fig. 2.5 Subinterval assignment in QM-coder.

In QM-coder, the value of A is always assumed to maintain close to 1. As a result, the subintervals of LPS and MPS can be approximated to $AQ \approx Q$ and $A(1 - Q) \approx A - Q$ respectively and hence the multiplication is avoided. The subinterval of LPS is placed above the subinterval of MPS as shown in Figure 2.5. Accordingly, the MPS and LPS are assigned the subintervals $[0, A - Q)$ and $[A - Q, A)$ respectively. Actually the value of A is always maintained within the range $1.5 > A \geq 0.75$. Whenever the value of A drops below

0.75 during the encoding process, the *renormalization* is done by repeated doubling (shifting left) A until it is greater than or equal to 0.75. Whenever we renormalize A, we need to apply the same renormalization to C as well to keep these two parameters in sync.

We denote the output code stream of the QM-coder by C. Ideally C can be any value within the current interval as we explained in the arithmetic coding algorithm in the previous section. However, for simplicity of implementation, the QM-coder points C at the bottom of the current interval. If the current input is MPS (or LPS), C is updated by adding the bottom of the MPS (or LPS) subinterval to the current value of C. Since the bottom of MPS subinterval is 0, C actually remains unchanged when MPS is encoded. During encoding of LPS, C is updated by adding $A - Q$ to the current value of C since $A - Q$ is the bottom of the LPS subinterval as shown in Figure 2.5. It should be noted that the encoder is initialized with the $A = 1$ at the beginning of the encoding process. Hence the encoding algorithm can be described as follows.

When MPS is encoded:

> **begin**
> > C is unchanged;
> > $A = A - Q$;
> > **if** $(C < 0.75)$ **then**
> > > Renormalize A and C;
> > **endif**;
> **end**

When LPS is encoded:

> **begin**
> > $C = C + (A - Q)$;
> > $A = Q$;
> > Renormalize A and C;
> **end**

The probability estimation in QM-coder is accomplished by using a pre-determined table of Q values. The value of Q of the LPS is updated each time a renormalization occurs during the encoding. The table consists of a preset ordered list of the Q values. For every renormalization, Q is updated by the next lower or next higher Q value in the table, depending on whether the renormalization takes place because of encoding of an LPS or MPS during the encoding process. An important issue in QM-coder is called the problem of *interval inversion*. This problem happens when the size of the subinterval assigned to MPS becomes smaller than the size of the LPS subinterval because of the result of approximation of A and C. This problem occurs when LPS

actually occurs more frequently than the MPS due to some peculiar characteristics of the input bits. As a result, it is possible that the value of Q becomes
of the order of 0.5 and as a result the size of the subinterval assigned to MPS
can be as small as 0.25. In this situation, the problem is solved by reversing the assignment of the two subintervals whenever the LPS subinterval is
greater than the MPS subinterval. This is known as the *conditional exchange*.
The term *conditional* is used due to the fact that the subinterval reassignment
takes place only when the LPS probability occupies more than half of the total interval A. Thus the condition for interval inversion is $Q > A - Q$. Since
$Q \leq 0.5$, we get $0.5 \geq Q > A - Q$. As a result, both the subintervals Q
and $A - Q$ are less than 0.75 and this necessitates renormalization of A and
C. That's why the conditional exchange is performed only after the encoder
detects that renormalization is needed.

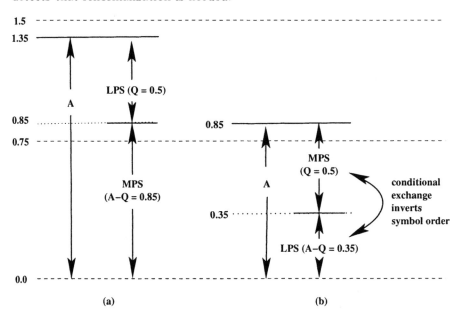

Fig. 2.6 Subinterval assignment in QM-coder, (a) without conditional exchange and
(b) with conditional exchange.

We have demonstrated the situation of a *conditional exchange* as an example in Figure 2.6. We assume that the current value of A is 1.35, which is less
than 1.5 as shown in Figure 2.6(a). Assuming that $Q = 0.5$, the subintervals
$[0.0, 0.85)$ and $[0.85, 1.35)$ are assigned to MPS and LPS respectively as shown
in Figure 2.6(a). Now if the value of A is changed to $A = A - Q = 0.85$ in the
next coding cycle, the symbol orders are inverted and accordingly subintervals assigned to LPS and MPS are exchanged as shown in Figure 2.6(b). The
subintervals assigned to LPS and MPS after conditional exchange are $[0.0,
0.35)$ and $[0.35, 0.85)$ respectively, as shown in Figure 2.6(b).

Incorporating the process of handling the *conditional exchange*, the encoding algorithm thus becomes as follows.

QM-Coder: The Encoding Algorithm

When MPS is encoded:

```
begin
        C is unchanged;
        A = A − Q;
        if (C < 0.75) then
            if (A < Q) then
                C = C + A;
                A = Q;
            endif;
            Renormalize A and C;
        endif;
end
```

When LPS is encoded:

```
begin
        A = A − Q;
        if (A ≥ Q) then
            C = C + A;
            A = Q;
        endif;
        Renormalize A and C;
end
```

2.4.2.1 *The QM-Decoder* The decoder decodes an MPS or LPS by determining which subinterval the value of the code stream belongs to. The QM-decoder is just the reverse of the encoder. For simplicity we ignore the *conditional exchange* situation here. The matching decoding algorithm is as follows.

QM-Decoder: The Decoding Algorithm

```
begin
    if (C ≥ Q) then
        (MPS is decoded)
        C = C − Q;
        A = A − Q;
    else
        (LPS is decoded)
        A = Q;
    endif;
```

if $(A < 0.75)$ **then**
    Renormalize A and C;
  endif;
end.

Another variation of Q-coder, called the MQ-coder, has been used for adaptive binary arithmetic coding in JPEG2000 encoding. The details of this algorithm will be discussed in Section 7.3.3 in Chapter 7.

2.5 ZIV-LEMPEL CODING

Dictionary-based coding techniques are often used for data compression. Most of the popular text compression algorithms use the dictionary-based coding approach. In dictionary coding, groups of consecutive input symbols can be replaced by an index into some dictionary. The simplest example is to express (or encode) the words "Sunday," "Monday," ..., "Saturday" by the indexes 1, 2, ..., 7. Another dictionary coding that we use every day is to replace "January," "February," ..., "December" by 1, 2, ..., 12. These are examples of *static* dictionary coding because the dictionary is predefined and does not change during either the encoding or the decoding process. A *dynamic dictionary coding*, however, builds a *dictionary* dynamically using the same message being encoded or decoded.

There is a misconception that Ziv-Lempel coding is a single, well-defined algorithm. Jacob Ziv and Abraham Lempel described dynamic dictionary encoders, popularly known as LZ77 [10] and LZ78 [11], by replacing the phrases with a pointer to where they have occurred earlier in the text. Since then many other people have developed dynamic dictionary coding algorithms based on the work by Ziv and Lempel, resulting in a family of compression algorithms. This family is popularly called the Ziv-Lempel coding, abbreviated LZ coding. The reversal of the initials in the abbreviation *LZ* instead of *ZL* is a historical aberration that people chose to perpetuate and we follow the same convention in this book. **LZW** (Lempel-Ziv-Welch) [12] is a very popular algorithm in the LZ family. This is used in the *compress* command in Unix operating system and many others.

There is a mistaken impression that the LZ coding works for text compression only. In lossless mode, compressing images can be the same as compressing text. The popular image format, **TIFF (Tag Image File Format)**, supports LZ coding. LZ coding techniques are widely used in dithered binary images as well.

2.5.1 The LZ77 Algorithm

LZ77 is the first form of Ziv-Lempel coding proposed by Ziv and Lempel in 1977 [10]. In this approach, a fixed-size buffer containing a previously encoded character sequence that precedes the current coding position can be considered as a dictionary. The encoder matches the input sequence through a sliding window as shown in Figure 2.7. The window is divided into two parts: a *search window* that consists of an already encoded character sequence and a *lookahead buffer* that contains the character sequence to be encoded.

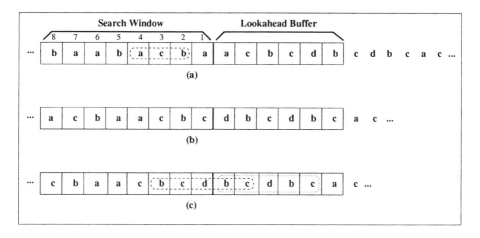

Fig. 2.7   LZ77 coding: An example with sliding window.

To encode the sequence in the lookahead buffer, the *search window* is searched to find the longest match with a prefix of the lookahead buffer. The match can overlap with the lookahead buffer, and obviously cannot be the buffer itself. Once the longest match is found, it is coded into a triple $<$*offset, length, C(char)* $>$, where *offset* is the distance of the first character of the longest match in the search window from the lookahead buffer, *length* is the length of the match, and *C(char)* is the codeword of the symbol *char* that follows the match in the lookahead buffer. The window is shifted left by *length* + 1 symbols to begin the next search.

2.5.1.1 **Example—LZ77 Algorithm:**   Consider the sequence to be encoded is $\cdots baabacbaacbcdbcdbcac \cdots$. We assume that the size of the *search window* is 8 and that of the *lookahead buffer* is 6. Assume that the substring $baabacba$ in the search window has already been encoded and the substring $acbcdb$ in the lookahead buffer is to be encoded as shown in Figure 2.7(a). After searching the search window, we find that the longest match found is the substring acb of length 3 at distance 4 from the lookahead buffer. The character following the prefix acb in lookahead buffer is c. Hence the triple to output is $< 4, 3, C(c) >$, where $C(c)$ is the codeword for the character c. Since the match length is 3, we shift the window left by 4 characters.

Now the first character in the lookahead buffer is d as shown in Figure 2.7(b) and there is no match for d in the search window. Hence we output the triple $< 0, 0, C(d) >$ and shift the sliding window by one.

Now the longest match in the sliding window is the substring $bcdbc$ as shown in Figure 2.7(c). It should be noted that the matching substring starts in character position 3 in the search window and overlaps with the first two characters $\underline{bc}dbc$ in the lookahead buffer. Hence we output the triple $< 3, 5, C(a) >$ and shift the sliding window left by 6 characters and continue.

There are many variations of LZ77 coding. The popular compression softwares Zip and PKZip both use a variation of the LZ77 coding scheme called the LZSS coding scheme [13]. Use of the codeword for an explicit character in a triple in LZ77 is wasteful in practice because it could often be included as part of the next pointer. This inefficiency has been reduced by the LZSS coding scheme simply by adding a flag bit to indicate whether what follows the pointer is the codeword of a single character. As a result, we need to send only a pair of values corresponding to the *offset* and the *length* of the match instead of the triple.

2.5.2 The LZ78 Algorithm

LZ78 is the other key algorithm in the LZ family proposed by Ziv and Lempel in 1978 [11]. Instead of using the previously encoded sequence of symbols (or string) in the sliding window as the implicit dictionary, the LZ78 algorithm explicitly builds a dictionary of patterns dynamically at both the encoder and the decoder. The encoder searches this dictionary to find the longest pattern that matches with the prefix of the input string and encodes it as a pair $< i, C(S) >$, where i is the index of the matched pattern in the dictionary and $C(S)$ is the codeword of the first symbol following the matched portion of the input. A new entry is then added in the dictionary. The new entry is the matched pattern concatenated by the symbol S. The codeword $C(S)$ is usually a Huffman-type variable-length code of the symbol S.

In order to achieve further compression, the index i in the output pair can be encoded using some Huffman-type variable-length binary encoding in order to achieve better compression by exploiting the statistics of the indexes. But for the sake of simplicity of explanation, we avoid it here.

2.5.2.1 **Example—LZ78 Encoding:**   Consider the following sequence:

$$S = bacababbaabbabbaaacbbc$$

Initially the dictionary is empty. Since the first input symbol b has no match in the dictionary, the encoder outputs the pair $< 0, C(b) >$ and inserts the first entry b into the dictionary with index 1 as shown in Table 2.5.

Similarly, the next input symbol a has no match in the dictionary and hence the encoder outputs the pair $< 0, C(a) >$ and inserts new entry a at index 2 in the dictionary as shown in Table 2.6.

Table 2.5 Dictionary After Step 1

Encoder Output	Index	Entry
$< 0, C(b) >$	1	b

Table 2.6 Dictionary After Step 2

Encoder Output	Index	Entry
$< 0, C(b) >$	1	b
$< 0, C(a) >$	2	a

Similarly, the next input symbol c has no match in the dictionary and hence the encoder outputs the pair $< 0, C(c) >$ and inserts the new entry c at index 3 as shown in Table 2.7.

Table 2.7 Dictionary After Step 3

Encoder Output	Index	Entry
$< 0, C(b) >$	1	b
$< 0, C(a) >$	2	a
$< 0, C(c) >$	3	c

The next input symbol a matches with entry 2 in the dictionary, but ab does not have any match. So the encoder outputs the pair $< 2, C(b) >$ and inserts new entry ab at index 4 in the dictionary as shown in Table 2.8.

Table 2.8 Dictionary After Step 4

Encoder Output	Index	Entry
$< 0, C(b) >$	1	b
$< 0, C(a) >$	2	a
$< 0, C(c) >$	3	c
$< 2, C(b) >$	4	ab

The next two symbols ab match with entry 4 in the dictionary, but abb does not have any match. So the encoder outputs the pair $< 4, C(b) >$ and inserts a new entry abb at index 5 in the dictionary as shown in Table 2.9.

Table 2.9 Dictionary After Step 5

Encoder Output	Index	Entry
$< 0, C(b) >$	1	b
$< 0, C(a) >$	2	a
$< 0, C(c) >$	3	c
$< 2, C(b) >$	4	ab
$< 4, C(b) >$	5	abb

Continuing the above procedure, the encoder generates the output pairs $< 2, C(a) >$, $< 1, C(b) >$, $< 5, C(a) >$, $< 6, C(c) >$, and $< 7, C(c) >$ and builds the dictionary accordingly. The final dictionary is shown in Table 2.10 below.

Table 2.10 Final Dictionary

Encoder Output	Index	Entry
$< 0, C(b) >$	1	b
$< 0, C(a) >$	2	a
$< 0, C(c) >$	3	c
$< 2, C(b) >$	4	ab
$< 4, C(b) >$	5	abb
$< 2, C(a) >$	6	aa
$< 1, C(b) >$	7	bb
$< 5, C(a) >$	8	$abba$
$< 6, C(c) >$	9	aac
$< 7, C(c) >$	10	bbc

As a result, the sequence $S = bacababbaabbabbaaacbbc$ is encoded as $< 0, C(b) >$, $< 0, C(a) >$, $< 0, C(c) >$, $< 2, C(b) >$, $< 4, C(b) >$, $< 2, C(a) >$, $< 1, C(b) >$, $< 5, C(a) >$, $< 6, C(c) >$, $< 7, C(c) >$.

2.5.2.2 Example—LZ78 Decoding: We now decode the encoded data to explain how the LZ78 decoding process works. As with the encoder, the decoder also dynamically builds the dictionary. This dictionary is the same as the one built by the encoder. Initially the dictionary contains nothing. Since the first input pair to the decoder is $< 0, C(b) >$, the decoder first decodes the symbol b from the codeword $C(b)$. Since the decoded index is 0, it outputs the symbol b and inserts the first entry $< 1, b >$ in the dictionary same as shown in Table 2.5.

The next input pair to the decoder is $< 0, C(a) >$. As result, the decoder outputs the symbol a and inserts the next entry $< 2, a >$ in the dictionary, same as shown in Table 2.6. The following input pair is $< 0, C(c) >$ and hence the decoder outputs the symbol c and inserts the next entry $< 3, c >$ in the dictionary, same as shown in Table 2.7.

The next input pair is $< 2, C(b) >$, which indicates that the new output is the pattern for entry 2 in the dictionary concatenated by the decoded symbol b. Since entry 2 represents a, the output will be $a\,b$. A new pattern $a\,b$ is now inserted at index 4 in the dictionary.

The following input pair is $< 4, C(b) >$. As a result the decoder outputs the string $a\,b\,b$ and inserts it in the dictionary in entry 5. The decoder similarly reads the next pair $< 2, C(a) >$ and generates the output $a\,a$ and inserts it in the dictionary in entry 6. Continuing in the similar fashion, the following decoder outputs are $b\,b$, $a\,b\,b\,a$, $a\,a\,c$, and $b\,b\,c$ respectively. The final dictionary should also be identical to the one in Table 2.10. Hence the final decoder output is $b\,a\,c\,a\,b\,a\,b\,b\,a\,a\,b\,b\,a\,b\,b\,a\,a\,a\,c\,b\,b\,c$ and it exactly matches with the original input sequence.

There are a number of variations of the LZ78 algorithm. The most popular variation of LZ78 is the algorithm by Welch [12], popularly known as LZW algorithm.

2.5.3   The LZW Algorithm

In the LZ78 encoding algorithm, inclusion of the explicit codeword $C(S)$ of the symbol S along with the index i in the output $< i, C(S) >$ is often very wasteful. In LZW algorithm, this inefficiency has been overcome by removing the inclusion of $C(S)$ and transmitting the index i only. This is accomplished by initializing the dictionary with a list of single symbol patterns to include all the symbols of the source alphabet. In each step, the index of the longest match from the input in the dictionary is output and a new pattern is inserted in the dictionary. The new pattern is formed by concatenating the longest match with the next character in the input stream. As a result, the last symbol (or character) of this new pattern is encoded as the first character of the next one.

2.5.3.1 Example—LZW Encoding: The LZW encoding algorithm is explained below with an example to encode the string $b\,a\,b\,a\,c\,b\,a\,b\,a\,b\,a\,b\,c\,b$.

The dictionary generation is shown in Table 2.11. Initially, the dictionary consists of single symbol (or character) patterns a, b, and c from the input alphabet $\{a, b, c\}$. The indexes of the patterns in the dictionary are 1, 2, and 3 respectively.

After receiving the first character b, the encoder finds the match at index 2. But the pattern ba with first two characters does not have a match in

Table 2.11   LZW Dictionary

Index	Pattern	Derived as
1	a	
2	b	initial
3	c	
4	ba	$2 + a$
5	ab	$1 + b$
6	bac	$4 + c$
7	cb	$3 + b$
8	bab	$4 + b$
9	$baba$	$8 + a$
10	abc	$5 + c$

the current dictionary. Hence the encoder outputs index 2 to encode the first character b and inserts the new pattern ba to index 4 in the dictionary.

The second input character a has a match in the dictionary to index 1, but ab formed by the second and third characters does not have a match. As a result the encoder outputs index 1 to encode a and inserts the new pattern ab in the dictionary to index 5.

Now the next two characters ba match with the pattern to index 4, but bac does not have a match. Hence the encoder outputs index 4 to encode ba and inserts the new pattern bac in the dictionary to index 6.

The next character c now matches with index 3, but cb does not. Hence the encoder outputs index 3 to encode c and inserts cb in the dictionary to index 7.

The next two characters ba have a match at index 4, but bab does not. Hence the encoder outputs the index 4 to encode ba and inserts the new pattern bab in the dictionary to index 8.

The next three characters bab have a match in the dictionary to index 8, but $baba$ does not. Hence the encoder now outputs the index 8 to encode bab and inserts the new pattern $baba$ in the dictionary to index 9.

The next two characters ab now match with the pattern at index 5 in the dictionary, but abc does not. Hence the encoder outputs index 5 to encode ab and inserts the new pattern abc in the dictionary to index 10.

The next two characters cb have a match at index 7 in the dictionary. Hence the encoder outputs the index 7 to encode cb and stops.

As a result the output of the encoder is 2 1 4 3 4 8 5 7.

2.5.3.2 Example—LZW Decoding:

In this example, we take the same encoder output from the previous example and decode using LZW decoding algorithm. The input to the decoder is 2 1 4 3 4 8 5 7.

Like the encoder, the decoder starts with the initial dictionary with three entries for a, b, c with indexes 1, 2, 3. After visiting the first index 2, the decoder outputs the corresponding pattern b from the dictionary.

The next output is a corresponding to the second input index 1. At this point, the decoder inserts a new pattern $b\,a$ in the dictionary to index 4. This new pattern $b\,a$ is formed by concatenating the first character (a) of the current output pattern (a) at the end of the last output pattern (b).

The next input index is 4, which corresponds to the pattern ba in the dictionary. Hence the decoder outputs $b\,a$ and inserts the new pattern $a\,b$ in the dictionary to index 5. The new pattern $a\,b$ is again formed by concatenating the first character (b) of the current output pattern $b\,a$ at the end of the last output pattern a.

The next input index is 3, which corresponds to c in the current dictionary. The decoder hence outputs c and inserts a new pattern $b\,a\,c$ in the dictionary to index 6. This pattern $b\,a\,c$ has been formed by concatenating c at the end of the previous output or matching pattern $b\,a$.

The next output of the decoder is $b\,a$ because of the input index 4. The decoder now inserts the new pattern $c\,b$ in the dictionary to index 7. This pattern is again formed by concatenating the first character b of the current output ba at the end of the previous output c. At this point, the dictionary has only 7 entries, as shown in Table 2.12. So far the decoding process was straightforward.

Table 2.12   LZW Dictionary

Index	Pattern	Derived as
1	a	
2	b	initial
3	c	
4	$b\,a$	$2 + a$
5	$a\,b$	$1 + b$
6	$b\,a\,c$	$4 + c$
7	$c\,b$	$3 + b$

The next input to the decoder is index 8. But the dictionary does not have any pattern with index 8. This tricky situation arises during decoding if a pattern has been encoded using the pattern immediately preceding it during the encoding process. As a result, the last character of the pattern is the same as the first character in this tricky situation. If we carefully examine the encoding steps in the previous example, we find that index 8 corresponds to the pattern $b\,a\,b$, which has been encoded using the immediately preceding pattern $b\,a$. And we get $b\,a\,b$ by appending the first character b of $b\,a$ with itself.

Hence after the decoder receives the input index 8, it discovers that the index and a corresponding pattern does not exist in the current dictionary. It also recognizes that this tricky situation will happen because of the scenario that we discussed above. Hence the decoder creates the output by concatenating the first character of the previous output with the previous output itself. Since the previous output was ba, the decoder outputs the bab in the current decoding step and inserts this new pattern in the dictionary to index 8. The following input index 5 corresponds to the pattern ab and hence the decoder outputs ab and inserts the new pattern $baba$ in the dictionary to index 9. This pattern $baba$ is formed by concatenating the first character a of the current output ab at the end of the previous output bab.

The next input index 7 corresponds to the pattern cb. The decoder outputs cb and obviously inserts the new pattern abc in the dictionary and stops. At this point the final dictionary is exactly identical to the final dictionary that was formed during the encoding process, as shown in Table 2.11 in the previous example.

2.6 SUMMARY

In this chapter, we presented some of the key source coding algorithms widely used in data and image compression. First we described the run-length coding scheme with an example. We described the popular Huffman coding scheme that is used in various image and data compression techniques. We discussed the modified Huffman coding scheme to enhance its efficiency. Arithmetic coding is an alternative approach for an efficient entropy encoding and it achieves compression efficiency very close to the entropy limit. We discussed the basic principles of arithmetic coding with an example and the implementation issues. We described the binary arithmetic coding with an example. Binary arithmetic coding is a key algorithm for bilevel image compression. Variations of adaptive implementation of binary arithmetic coding algorithm have been adopted in different image compression standards—JBIG, JBIG2, JPEG, JPEG2000. We discussed the QM-coder algorithm for implementation of an adaptive binary arithmetic coding, which has been adopted in the JBIG standard for bilevel image compression and also in a mode of JPEG standard. A variation of QM-coder called the MQ-coder is the basis of the entropy encoding of the new JPEG2000 standard for still picture compression. We also described dictionary-based coding, especially the key algorithms in the popular Ziv-Lempel family of algorithms that are mainly used in text compression.

REFERENCES

1. D. A. Huffman, "A Method for the Construction of Minimum-Redundancy Codes," *Proceedings of the IRE*, Vol. 40, No. 9, pp. 1098–1101, 1952.

2. R. G. Gallagher, "Variations on a Theme by Huffman," *IEEE Transactions on Information Theory*, IT-24, Vol.6, pp. 668–674, November 1978.

3. R. Hunter and A. H. Robinson, "International Digital Facsimile Standard," *Proceedings of IEEE*, Vol. 68, No. 7, pp. 854–867, 1980.

4. I. H. Witten, R. M. Neal, and J. G. Cleary, "Arithmetic Coding for Data Compression," *Communications of the ACM*, Vol. 30, No. 6, June 1987.

5. W. B. Pennebaker, J. L. Mitchell, G. G. Langdon, Jr., and R. B. Arps, "An Overview of the Basic Principles of the Q-Coder Adaptive Binary Arithmetic Coder," *IBM Journal of Research and Development*, Vol. 32, pp. 717–726, November 1988.

6. S. Lei, "Efficient Multiplication-Free Arithmetic Codes," *IEEE Transactions on Communications*, Vol. 43, No. 12, December 1995.

7. B. Fu and K. K. Parhi, "Generalized Multiplication-Free Arithmetic Codes," *IEEE Transactions on Communications*, Vol. 45, No. 5, May 1997.

8. W. B. Pennebaker and J. L. Mitchell, *JPEG Still Image Data Compression Standard.* Chapman & Hall, New York, 1993.

9. ISO/IEC JTC 1/SC 29/WG 1 WG1N1878, "JPEG2000 Verification Model 8.5 (Technical Description)," September 13, 2000.

10. J. Ziv and A. Lempel, "A Universal Algorithm for Sequential Data Compression," *IEEE Trans. on Info. Theory*, IT-23, Vol. 3, pp. 337–343, May, 1977.

11. J. Ziv and A. Lempel, "Compression of Individual Sequences Via Variable-rate Coding," *IEEE Trans. on Info. Theory*, IT-24, Vol. 5, pp. 530–536, September 1978.

12. T. Welch, "A Technique for High-Performance Data Compression," *IEEE Computer*, Vol. 17, No. 6, 1984.

13. J. A. Storer and T. G. Syzmanski, "Data Compression via Textual Substitution," *Journal of the ACM*, Vol. 29, pp. 928–951, 1982.

3

JPEG: Still Image Compression Standard

3.1 INTRODUCTION

JPEG is the first international image compression standard for continuous-tone still images—both grayscale and color images [1]. JPEG is the acronym for *Joint Photographic Experts Group*. This image compression standard is a result of collaborative efforts by the International Telecommunication Union (ITU), International Organization for Standardization (ISO), and International Electrotechnical Commission (IEC). The JPEG standard is officially referred to as **ISO/IEC IS** (International Standard) **10918-1**: *Digital Compression and Coding of Continuous-tone Still Images* and also **ITU-T Recommendation T.81**. The goal of this standard is to support a variety of applications for compression of continuous-tone still images of most image sizes in any color space in order to achieve compression performance at or near the state-of-the-art with user-adjustable compression ratios and with very good to excellent reconstructed quality. Another goal of this standard is that it would have manageable computational complexity for widespread practical implementation. JPEG defines four modes of operations:

1. *Sequential Lossless Mode*: Compress the image in a single scan and the decoded image is an exact replica of the original image.

2. *Sequential DCT-based Mode*: Compress the image in a single scan using DCT-based lossy compression technique. As a result, the decoded image is not an exact replica, but an approximation of the original image.

3. *Progressive DCT-based Mode*: Compress the image in multiple scans and also decompress the image in multiple scans with each successive scan producing a better-quality image.

4. *Hierarchical Mode*: Compress the image at multiple resolutions for display on different devices.

The three DCT-based modes (2, 3, and 4) in JPEG provide lossy compression because precision limitation to digitally compute DCT (and its inverse) and the quantization process introduce distortion in the reconstructed image. For sequential lossless mode of compression, predictive coding is used instead of the DCT-based transformation, and also there is no quantization involved in this mode. The hierarchical mode uses extensions of either the DCT-based coding or predictive coding techniques. The simplest form of the sequential DCT-based JPEG algorithm is called the **baseline JPEG** algorithm, which is based on Huffman coding for entropy encoding. The other form of sequential DCT-based JPEG algorithm is based on arithmetic coding for entropy encoding. The baseline JPEG algorithm is widely used in practice. We shall describe the JPEG lossless algorithm and the baseline JPEG algorithm in greater detail in this chapter.

People often mention *Motion JPEG* for compression of moving pictures. This is not really a standard. Although it is not specifically defined as part of the standard, JPEG can be used to compress image sequence in video on the basis that video clips can be considered as a sequence of still image frames and each image frame can be compressed independently using the JPEG algorithm. This process of image sequence compression is popularly known as *Motion JPEG* in the industry.

JPEG standard does not specify any inherent file format. It defines only the syntax of the compressed bitstream. This caused creation of a number of file formats to store the JPEG compressed images such as JFIF (JPEG File Interchange Format), JPEG extension to TIFF 6.0, FlashPix, etc. But none of them is considered to be an official international standard defined under the auspices of an international standards committee.

3.2   THE JPEG LOSSLESS CODING ALGORITHM

The lossless JPEG compression is based on the principles of predictive coding. Since the adjacent pixels in a typical image are highly correlated, it is possible to extract a great deal of information about a pixel from its neighboring pixel values. Predictive coding is a simple method for spatial redundancy reduction. In this method, a pixel value is predicted by a set of previously encoded adjacent pixels using a suitable prediction model. For an ideal prediction model, the predicted value of the pixel can be equal to the actual value. But that is not the case in reality. Using an effective prediction model, we can predict the pixel value, which is very close to its actual value and hence error of prediction can be very small.

A practical approach to the prediction model is to take a linear combination of the previously encoded immediate neighboring adjacent pixels. The reason for taking the previously encoded pixel values is that the same values will be available to the decoder when it decodes the pixels in the same order they were encoded by the encoder. The difference between the actual pixel value and the predicted value is called the *differential* or the *prediction error* value. The *prediction error* is then entropy encoded using a variable-length encoding technique to generate compressed image. This method is popularly known as *Differential Pulse Code Modulation* (DPCM).

In lossless JPEG algorithm, the value of a pixel in any pixel location in the image is first predicted by using one or more of the previously encoded adjacent pixels A, B, and C as shown in Figure 3.1(a) to predict pixel X. It then encodes the difference between the pixel and its predicted value, usually called the *prediction error* or *prediction residual*, by either Huffman coding or arithmetic coding.

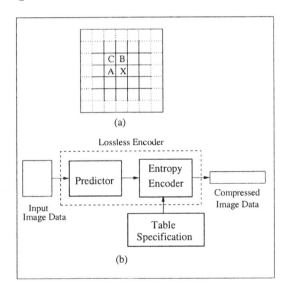

Fig. 3.1 (a) Three-pixel prediction neighborhood. (b) Encoder diagram in lossless mode.

There are eight possible options for prediction as shown in Table 3.1. The **No prediction** option 0 in Table 3.1 is available only for differential coding in the JPEG hierarchical mode. We briefly discuss the essence of the hierarchical mode of coding later in this chapter. Options 1 to 3 are one-dimensional predictors and options 4 to 7 are two-dimensional predictors. Depending on the nature of the image, one predictor may yield better compression results compared to any other predictor. However, experimental results for various kinds of images show that on the average their performances are relatively close to each other [2]. The chosen option for prediction is indicated in the header of the compressed file so that both the encoder and decoder use the same function for prediction.

Table 3.1   Prediction Functions in Lossless JPEG

Option	Prediction Function	Type of Prediction
0	No prediction	Differential Coding
1	$X_p = A$	1-D Horizontal Prediction
2	$X_p = B$	1-D Vertical Prediction
3	$X_p = C$	1-D Diagonal Prediction
4	$X_p = A + B - C$	2-D Prediction
5	$X_p = A + \frac{1}{2}(B - C)$	2-D Prediction
6	$X_p = B + \frac{1}{2}(A - C)$	2-D Prediction
7	$X_p = \frac{1}{2}(A + B)$	2-D Prediction

In lossless mode, the standard allows precision (P) of the input source image to be 2 bits to 16 bits wide. Since there is no previously encoded pixel known to the encoder when it encodes the very first pixels in the very first row of the image, it is handled differently. For a given input precision P and a point transform parameter P_t, the predicted value for the first pixel in the first line is 2^{P-P_t-1}. By default, we can assume $P_t = 0$. For details of the point transform parameter, the reader is advised to consult the JPEG standard [1].

For all other pixels (except the first one) in the first line, we use option 1 for prediction function. Except for the first line, option 2 is used to predict the very first pixel in all other lines. For all other pixels, we select one of the eight options for the prediction function from Table 3.1. Once a predictor is selected, it is used for all other pixels in the block.

In lossless JPEG standard, the prediction error values are computed modulo 2^{16} in order to take consideration of the full precision allowed in this mode. These error values are not directly encoded using Huffman codes. They are first represented as a pair of symbols ($CATEGORY$, $MAGNITUDE$). The first symbol $CATEGORY$ represents the category of the error value. The second symbol $MAGNITUDE$ represents the variable-length integer (VLI) for the prediction error value. The category represents the number of bits to encode the $MAGNITUDE$ in terms of VLI. All the possible prediction error values modulo 2^{16} and their corresponding categories are shown in Table 3.2. Only the $CATEGORY$ in the symbol pair for each prediction error value is Huffman coded. The codeword for the symbol pair ($CATEGORY$, $MAGNITUDE$) is formed in two steps. First it assigns the Huffman code of the $CATEGORY$. This Huffman code is then appended with additional

Table 3.2 Categories of Prediction Error Values

Category	Prediction Error Value
0	0
1	-1, +1
2	-3, -2, +2, +3
3	-7, ..., -4, +4, ..., +7
4	-15, ..., -8, +8, ..., +15
5	-31, ..., -16, +16, ..., +31
6	-63, ..., -32, +32, ..., +63
7	-127, ..., -64, +64, ..., +127
8	-255, ..., -128, +128, ..., +255
9	-511, ..., -256, +256, ..., +511
10	-1023, ..., -512, +512, ..., +1023
11	-2047, ..., -1024, +1024, ..., +2047
12	-4095, ..., -2048, +2048, ..., +4095
13	-8191, ..., -4096, +4096, ..., +8191
14	-16383, ..., -8192, +8192, ..., +16383
15	-32767, ..., -16384, +16384, ..., +32767
16	+32768

CATEGORY number of bits to represent the *MAGNITUDE* in VLI. If the prediction error value is positive, the *MAGNITUDE* is directly binary represented by a VLI using *CATEGORY* number of bits and hence it starts with bit 1. If the error value is negative, the VLI is one's complement of its absolute value and hence it starts with bit 0. For example, the prediction error value 25 is represented by the pair (5, 25) because the number 25 belongs to category 5 in Table 3.2 and hence 25 is represented by a 5-bit VLI. If the Huffman code for category 5 is 011, then the binary codeword for the error value 25 will be 01111001. The first three bits correspond to the Huffman code 011 for category 5 and the next 5 bits, 11001, is the VLI for 25. Similarly, the prediction error value -25 will be represented as 01100110 where the last 5 bits, 00110, is the 1's complement of 11001 to represent -25, and since -25 belongs to the same category 5, the first three bits of the codeword corresponds to the Huffman code of category 5. Use of the category table greatly simplifies the Huffman coder. Without this categorization, we would need to use a Huffman table with 2^{16} entries for all the 2^{16} possible symbols of prediction error values, which definitely complicates the implementation of the Huffman coder both in software and hardware, if it is not rendered impossible for all practical purposes.

Detailed information for implementation of the JPEG lossless coding for both the Huffman coding mode and the arithmetic coding mode can be found in Annex H of the JPEG standard [1].

3.3   BASELINE JPEG COMPRESSION

The baseline JPEG compression algorithm is widely used among the four modes in JPEG family. This is defined for compression of continuous-tone images with 1 to 4 components. Number of components for grayscale images is 1, whereas a color image can have up to four color components. The baseline JPEG allows only 8-bit samples within each component of the source image. An example of a four-component color image is a CMYK (Cyan, Magenta, Yellow, and Black) image, which is used in many applications such as printing, scanning, etc. A color image for display has three color components, RGB (Red, Green, and Blue), though. In a typical color image, the spatial intercomponent correlation between the red, green, and blue color components is significant. In order to achieve good compression performance, correlation between the color components is first reduced by converting the RGB image into a decorrelated color space. In baseline JPEG, a three-color RGB image is first transformed into a luminance–chrominance (L–C) color space such as YCbCr, YUV, CIELAB, etc. The advantage of converting the image into luminance–chrominance color space is that the luminance and chrominance components are very much decorrelated between each other. Moreover, the chrominance channels contain much redundant information and can easily be subsampled without sacrificing any visual quality for the reconstructed image.

3.3.1   Color Space Conversion

In this book, we consider color space conversion from RGB to YCbCr and vice versa only. There are several ways to convert from RGB to YCbCr color space. In this book, we adopt the CCIR (International Radio Consultative Committee) Recommendation 601-1. This is the typical method for color conversion used in baseline JPEG compression. According to the CCIR 601-1 Recommendation, the transformation from RGB to YCbCr is done based on the following mathematical expression:

$$
\begin{pmatrix} Y \\ Cb \\ Cr \end{pmatrix} = \begin{pmatrix} 0.299000 & 0.587000 & 0.114000 \\ -0.168736 & -0.331264 & 0.500002 \\ 0.500000 & -0.418688 & -0.081312 \end{pmatrix} \begin{pmatrix} R \\ G \\ B \end{pmatrix}.
$$

Color space conversion from RGB to YCbCr using the above transformation may result in negative numbers for Cb and Cr, while Y is always positive. In order to represent Cb and Cr in unsigned 8-bit integers, they are level shifted by adding 128 to each sample followed by rounding and saturating the value in the range [0, 255]. Hence the above transformation can be expressed as

$$
\begin{pmatrix} Y \\ Cb \\ Cr \end{pmatrix} = \begin{pmatrix} 0.29900 & 0.58700 & 0.11400 \\ -0.16874 & -0.33126 & 0.50000 \\ 0.50000 & -0.41869 & -0.08131 \end{pmatrix} \begin{pmatrix} R \\ G \\ B \end{pmatrix} + \begin{pmatrix} 0 \\ 128 \\ 128 \end{pmatrix}
$$

in order to produce 8-bit unsigned integers for each of the components in the YCbCr domain. Accordingly, the inverse transformation from YCbCr to RGB is done as

$$
\begin{pmatrix} R \\ G \\ B \end{pmatrix} = \begin{pmatrix} 1.0 & 0.0 & 1.40210 \\ 1.0 & -0.34414 & -0.71414 \\ 1.0 & 1.77180 & 0.0 \end{pmatrix} \begin{pmatrix} Y \\ Cb \\ Cr \end{pmatrix} - \begin{pmatrix} 0 \\ 128 \\ 128 \end{pmatrix}.
$$

After the color space conversion, most of the spatial information of the image is contained in the luminance component (Y). The chrominance components (Cb and Cr) contain mostly redundant color information and we lose little information by subsampling these components both horizontally and/or vertically. We can subsample the chrominance components by simply throwing away every other sample in each row and/or in each column if desired. If we subsample the redundant chrominance components both horizontally and vertically, the amount of data required to represent the color image is reduced to half because the size of each chrominance component (Cb and Cr) is one-fourth of the original size. This color format is called the 4:2:0 color subsampling format. Baseline JPEG also supports 4:2:2 and 4:4:4 color formats. Each chrominance component, in 4:2:2 color format, has the same vertical resolution as the luminance component, but the horizontal resolution is halved by dropping alternate samples in each row. In 4:4:4 format, both the chrominance components Cb and Cr have identical vertical and horizontal resolution as the luminance component. Hence no subsampling is done in 4:4:4 format. The subsampling operation to generate in 4:2:0 or 4:2:2 color format is the first lossy step. For a grayscale image there is only one component and obviously no color transformation is required.

3.3.2 Source Image Data Arrangement

In the previous section, we have seen that the dimension of each of the color components Y, Cb, and Cr could be different depending on the color subsampling format. Each color component is divided into 8 × 8 nonoverlapping blocks, and we can form what is called a *minimum coded unit* (MCU) in JPEG by selecting one or more data blocks from each of the color components. The standard defines the arrangement of the data blocks in interleaved or noninterleaved scanning order of the color components. In noninterleaved scan, the data blocks in each color component are stored and processed separately in raster scan order, left-to-right and top-to-bottom. In interleaved order, data blocks from all the color components appear in each MCU. Definition of the MCUs for 4:4:4, 4:2:2, and 4:2:0 formats of YCbCr images in interleaved scan is shown in Figure 3.2.

Each dot in Figure 3.2 represents a 8 × 8 data block. In 4:4:4 format interleaved scan, each MCU consists of a data block from each of the Y, Cb, and Cr components as shown in Figure 3.2(a). The order of processing these blocks is in the scan order from left to right and top to bottom. For example,

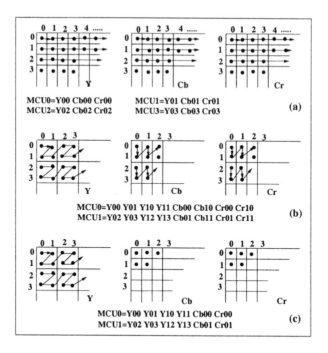

Fig. 3.2 (a) YCbCr 4:4:4, (b) YCbCr 4:2:2, (c) YCbCr 4:2:0.

the first MCU consists of the first data blocks Y00 from the Y component followed by the first data blocks Cb00 from the Cb component followed by Cr00 from the Cr component as shown in Figure 3.2(a). The next MCU consists of Y01, Cb01 and Cr01 respectively. After all the MCUs consisting of the 8 × 8 data blocks from the first row, as shown in Figure 3.2(a), are encoded the second row of 8 × 8 blocks are scanned in the similar fashion. This procedure is continued until the last 8 × 8 block in the raster scan is encoded. In 4:2:2 format, each MCU consists of a 2 × 2 unit of four data blocks from the Y component, a 2 × 1 unit of two data blocks from each of the Cb and Cr components, and the corresponding order of processing is shown in Figure 3.2(b). In 4:2:0 format, each MCU consists of 2 × 2 units of four data blocks from the Y component, one from each of the Cb and Cr components, and the corresponding order of processing is shown in Figure 3.2(c).

3.3.3   The Baseline Compression Algorithm

The baseline JPEG algorithm follows the principles of block-based transform coding. Block diagram of the baseline JPEG algorithm for a grayscale image with a single component is shown in Figure 3.3. For a color image, the same algorithm is applied in each 8 × 8 data block based on the source image data arrangement as described in the previous section.

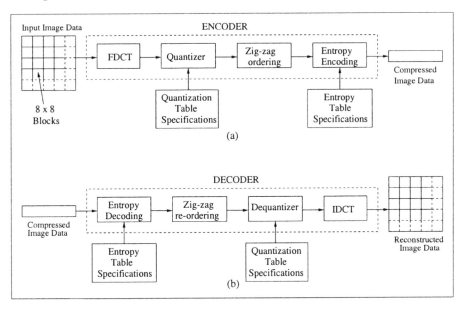

Fig. 3.3   Baseline JPEG: (a) compression, (b) decompression.

The image component is first divided into non-overlapping 8 × 8 blocks in the raster scan order left-to-right and top-to-bottom as shown in Figure 3.3(a). Each block is then encoded separately by the ENCODER shown in the broken box in Figure 3.3(a). The first step is to level shift each pixel in the block to convert into a signed integer by subtracting 128 from each pixel. Each level-shifted pixel in the 8 × 8 block is then transformed into frequency domain via forward discrete cosine transform (FDCT). The FDCT of an 8 × 8 block of pixels $f(x, y)$ for $(x, y = 0, 1, \cdots, 7)$ is defined by:

$$F(u, v) = \frac{1}{4}C(u)C(v) \sum_{x=0}^{7} \sum_{y=0}^{7} f(x, y) \cos\left[\frac{\pi(2x + 1)u}{16}\right] \cos\left[\frac{\pi(2y + 1)u}{16}\right]$$

for $u = 0, 1, \ldots, 7$ and $v = 0, 1, \ldots, 7$, where

$$C(k) = \begin{cases} \frac{1}{\sqrt{2}} & \text{for } k = 0 \\ 1 & \text{otherwise.} \end{cases}$$

We discuss discrete cosine transform in further detail in the following section.

3.3.4   Discrete Cosine Transform

Discrete Cosine Transform (DCT) is the basis for many image and video compression algorithms, especially the still image compression standard JPEG in lossy mode and the video compression standards MPEG-1, MPEG-2, and MPEG-4. Since an image is a two-dimensional signal, the two-dimensional DCT is relevant in terms of still image and video compression. The two-dimensional DCT can be computed using the one-dimensional DCT horizontally and then vertically across the signal because DCT is a separable function.

The one-dimensional forward Discrete Cosine Transform (1-D FDCT) of N samples is formulated by

$$F(u) = \sqrt{\frac{2}{N}} C(u) \sum_{x=0}^{N-1} f(x) \cos\left[\frac{\pi(2x+1)u}{2N}\right]$$

for $u = 0, 1, \ldots, N-1$, where

$$C(u) = \begin{cases} \frac{1}{\sqrt{2}} & \text{for } u = 0 \\ 1 & \text{otherwise.} \end{cases}$$

The function $f(x)$ represents the value of the xth sample of the input signal. $F(u)$ represents a Discrete Cosine Transformed coefficient for $u = 0, 1, \cdots, N-1$.

The one-dimensional inverse Discrete Cosine Transform (1-D IDCT) is formulated in a similar fashion as follows,

$$f(x) = \sqrt{\frac{2}{N}} \sum_{u=0}^{N-1} C(u) F(u) \cos\left[\frac{\pi(2x+1)u}{2N}\right]$$

for $x = 0, 1, \ldots, N-1$.

The two-dimensional forward Discrete Cosine Transform (2-D FDCT) of a block of $M \times N$ samples of a two-dimensional signal $F(x, y)$ is formulated as

$$F(u, v) = \frac{2}{\sqrt{MN}} C(u) C(v) \sum_{x=0}^{N-1} \sum_{y=0}^{M-1} f(x, y) \cos\left[\frac{\pi(2x+1)u}{2N}\right] \cos\left[\frac{\pi(2y+1)u}{2M}\right]$$

for $u = 0, 1, \ldots, N-1$ and $v = 0, 1, \ldots, M-1$, where

$$C(k) = \begin{cases} \frac{1}{\sqrt{2}} & \text{for } k = 0 \\ 1 & \text{otherwise.} \end{cases}$$

The function $f(x, y)$ represents the value of the xth sample in the yth row of a two-dimensional signal. $F(u, v)$ is a two-dimensional transformed coefficient for $u = 0, 1, \ldots, N-1$ and $v = 0, 1, \ldots, M-1$.

The above expression for 2-D FDCT is clearly a separable function because we can express the formula as follows:

$$F(u, v) = \sqrt{\frac{2}{M}} C(v) \sum_{y=0}^{M-1} \left\{ \sqrt{\frac{2}{N}} C(u) \sum_{x=0}^{N-1} f(x, y) \cos\left[\frac{\pi(2x+1)u}{2N}\right] \right\} \cos\left[\frac{\pi(2y+1)u}{2M}\right].$$

As a result we can accomplish the 2-D FDCT of a two-dimensional signal by applying 1-D FDCT first row-wise followed by 1-D FDCT column-wise in two steps. First, the 1-D FDCT is applied row-wise in all the rows independently to obtain $F(u, y)$, where

$$F(u, y) = \sqrt{\frac{2}{N}} C(u) \sum_{x=0}^{N-1} f(x, y) \cos \left[\frac{\pi(2x+1)u}{2N} \right]$$

for $u = 0, 1, \ldots, N - 1$.

In the second step, the same 1-D FDCT is applied column-wise in all the columns of $F(u, y)$ to obtain the result $F(u, v)$, where

$$F(u, v) = \sqrt{\frac{2}{M}} C(v) \sum_{y=0}^{M-1} F(u, y) \cos \left[\frac{\pi(2y+1)v}{2M} \right]$$

for $v = 0, 1, \ldots, M - 1$.

The two-dimensional inverse Discrete Cosine Transform (2-D IDCT) is computed in the similar fashion. The 2-D IDCT of $F(u, v)$ is formulated as

$$f(x, y) = \frac{2}{\sqrt{MN}} \sum_{u=0}^{N-1} \sum_{v=0}^{M-1} C(u)C(v)F(u, v) \cos \left[\frac{\pi(2x+1)u}{2N} \right] \cos \left[\frac{\pi(2y+1)u}{2M} \right]$$

for $x = 0, 1, \ldots, N - 1$ and $y = 0, 1, \ldots, M - 1$.

The above function is again a separable function similar to what we have shown for the 2-D FDCT. As a result, the 2-D IDCT can be computed in exactly the opposite way of the 2-D FDCT. The 2-D IDCT is computed in two steps: by first applying 1-D IDCT column-wise followed by the 1-D IDCT row-wise. After column-wise computation of 1-D IDCT in every column of the input signal $F(u, v)$, we obtain $F(u, y)$, where

$$F(u, y) = \sqrt{\frac{2}{M}} \sum_{v=0}^{M-1} C(v)F(u, v) \cos \left[\frac{\pi(2y+1)v}{2M} \right]$$

for $v = 0, 1, \ldots, M - 1$.

In the second step, the same 1-D IDCT is applied row-wise in all the rows of $F(u, y)$ to obtain the two-dimensional signal $f(x, y)$, where

$$f(x, y) = \sqrt{\frac{2}{N}} \sum_{u=0}^{N-1} C(u)F(u, y) \cos \left[\frac{\pi(2x+1)u}{2N} \right]$$

for $u = 0, 1, \ldots, N - 1$.

Computational complexity of the direct implementation of the above 1-D DCT algorithm is $O(N^2)$. For DCT-based transform coding algorithms, the images are usually divided into 8 × 8 blocks and the 2-D DCT is applied on this 8 × 8 block. A brute-force implementation of the 2-D DCT of an 8 × 8 block without row-wise and column-wise computation requires approximately 4096 multiply-accumulate operations.

As we have discussed, the 2-D DCT is a separable function and the computation can be done in two steps, by applying one-dimensional DCT row-wise and then column-wise instead of the direct computation. Every one-dimensional FDCT or IDCT requires eight multiplications and seven additions for each sample using the direct method. Since there are 64 samples in an 8 × 8 block, the 2-D DCT will require 64×8 multiplications and 64×7 additions in each direction. As a result, it requires 2×64×8 = 1024 multiplications and 896 additions for each 8 × 8 block. Although the computational requirement using this method is only 25% of the brute-force method, still the computational requirement is very high. Reduction of such a huge computational requirement is highly desirable for any practical implementation.

Since DCT belongs to the family of *Discrete Fourier Transform* (DFT), there are fast DCT algorithms of computational complexity $O(N \log_2 N)$ similar to the *Fast Fourier Transform* (FFT). There are many fast DCT algorithms proposed in the literature [5, 6, 7]. Developers of the DCT-based image compression algorithms have explored various techniques to implement the 8 × 8 DCT in computationally efficient ways both for software and hardware implementation. Lee's algorithm [6] for fast DCT computation of an 8 × 8 block requires only 192 multiplications and 464 additions. The fast algorithm proposed by Cho and Lee requires only 96 multiplications and 466 additions for 8 × 8 DCT computation [7]. There are many other algorithms especially suitable for 8 × 8 DCT computation. Each of the fast algorithms has its own merits for implementation.

3.3.5   Coding the DCT Coefficients

The transformed 8 × 8 block now consists of 64 DCT coefficients. The first coefficient $F(0,0)$ is the DC component of the block and other 63 coefficients are AC components $AC_{u,v} = F(u,v)$ of the block as shown in Figure 3.4. The DC component $F(0,0)$ is essentially sum of the 64 pixels in the input 8 × 8 pixel block multiplied by the scaling factor $\frac{1}{4}C(u)C(v) = \frac{1}{8}$ as shown in the expression for $F(u,v)$.

The next step in the compression process is to quantize the transformed coefficients. This step is primarily responsible for losing the information and hence introduces distortion in the reconstructed image. That's why baseline JPEG is a lossy compression. Each of the 64 DCT coefficients are uniformly quantized. The 64 quantization step-size parameters for uniform quantization of the 64 DCT coefficients form an 8 × 8 *Quantization Matrix*. Each element in the quantization matrix is an integer between 1 and 255. Each DCT coefficient $F(u,v)$ is divided by the corresponding quantizer step-size parameter $Q(u,v)$

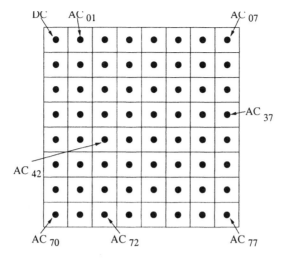

Fig. 3.4   DC and AC components of the transformed block.

in the quantization matrix and rounded to the nearest integer as

$$F_q(u,v) = Round\left(\frac{F(u,v)}{Q(u,v)}\right).$$

The standard does not define any fixed quantization matrix. It is prerogative of the user's choice to select a quantization matrix. There are two quantization matrices provided in Annex K of the JPEG standard for reference, but not as a requirement. These two quantization matrices are shown in Tables 3.3 and 3.4 respectively.

Table 3.3   Luminance Quantization Matrix

16	11	10	16	24	40	51	61
12	12	14	19	26	58	60	55
14	13	16	24	40	57	69	56
14	17	22	29	51	87	80	62
18	22	37	56	68	109	103	77
24	35	55	64	81	104	113	92
49	64	78	87	103	121	120	101
72	92	95	98	112	100	103	99

Table 3.3 is the *luminance quantization matrix* for quantizing the transformed coefficients of the luminance component of an image. Table 3.4 is the *chrominance quantization matrix* for quantizing the transformed coefficients of the chrominance components of the image. These two quantization tables have been designed based on the psychovisual experiments by Lohscheller [3]

Table 3.4   Chrominance Quantization Matrix

17	18	24	47	99	99	99	99
18	21	26	66	99	99	99	99
24	26	56	99	99	99	99	99
47	66	99	99	99	99	99	99
99	99	99	99	99	99	99	99
99	99	99	99	99	99	99	99
99	99	99	99	99	99	99	99
99	99	99	99	99	99	99	99

to determine the visibility thresholds for 2-D basis functions. These tables may not be suitable for all kinds of images, but they provide reasonably good results for most of the natural images with 8-bit precision for luminance and chrominance samples. If the elements in these tables are divided by 2, we get perceptually lossless compression—the reconstructed image is indistinguishable from the original one by human eyes. If the quantization tables are designed based on the perceptual masking properties of human eyes, many of the small DCT coefficients and mainly high-frequency samples are zeroed out to aid significant compression. This is done by using larger quantization step-size parameters for higher-frequency AC components as shown in Tables 3.3 and 3.4. Quality of the reconstructed image and the achieved compression can be controlled by a user by selecting a quality factor Q_JPEG to tune the elements in the quantization tables as proposed by the *Independent JPEG Group* and implemented in their software [4]. The value of Q_JPEG may vary from 1 to 100. The quantization matrices in Tables 3.3 and 3.4 have been set for $Q\_JPEG = 50$. For other Q_JPEG values, each element in both the tables is simply scaled by the factor alpha (α) as defined in [4], where

$$
\alpha = \begin{cases} \frac{50}{Q\_JPEG} & \text{if } 1 \leq Q\_JPEG \leq 50 \\[2ex] 2 - \frac{Q\_JPEG}{50} & \text{if } 50 \leq Q\_JPEG \leq 100, \end{cases}
$$

subject to the condition that the minimum value of the scaled quantization matrix elements, $\alpha Q(u, v)$ is 1. For the best reconstructed quality, Q_JPEG is set to 100.

After quantization of the DCT coefficients, the quantized DC coefficient is encoded by differential encoding. The DC coefficient DC_i of the current block is subtracted by the DC coefficient DC_{i-1} of the previous block and the difference $DIFF = DC_i - DC_{i-1}$ is encoded as shown in Figure 3.5(b). This is done to exploit the spatial correlation between the DC values of the adjacent blocks. Encoding of the AC coefficients is not straightforward. Instead of encoding each AC coefficient in the block, only the significant (nonzero) coefficients are encoded by an efficient manner such that the runs of zeros

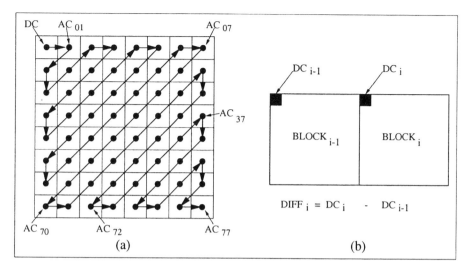

Fig. 3.5 (a) Zig-zag ordering of AC coefficients; (b) differential coding of DC.

preceding a nonzero value are embedded into the encoding. Usually there are few significant low-frequency AC coefficients in the whole 8×8 block and most of the higher-frequency coefficients are quantized to 0's. In order to exploit this property, the AC coefficients are ordered in a particular irregular order sequence as shown in Figure 3.5(a). This irregular ordering of the AC coefficients is called *zig-zag ordering*. This is done to keep the low-frequency coefficients together and form long runs of 0's corresponding to the higher-frequency quantized coefficients. This zig-zag sequence is then broken into runs of zeros ending in a nonzero value. Before we explain the entropy encoding procedure, let us show the results of level shifting, DCT, quantization, and zig-zag ordering with an example 8×8 block extracted from a natural image.

Example: A Sample 8×8 Data Block

110	110	118	118	121	126	131	131
108	111	125	122	120	125	134	135
106	119	129	127	125	127	138	144
110	126	130	133	133	131	141	148
115	116	119	120	122	125	137	139
115	106	99	110	107	116	130	127
110	91	82	101	99	104	120	118
103	76	70	95	92	91	107	106

The 8 × 8 Data Block After Level Shifting

−18	−18	−10	−10	−7	−2	3	3
−20	−17	−3	−6	−8	−3	6	7
−22	−9	1	−1	−3	−1	10	16
−18	−2	2	5	5	3	13	20
−13	−12	−9	−8	−6	−3	9	11
−13	−22	−29	−18	−21	−12	2	−1
−18	−37	−46	−27	29	−24	−8	−10
−25	−52	−58	−33	−36	−37	−21	−22

DCT Coefficients of the Above 8 × 8 Block

−89.00	−63.47	18.21	−6.85	7.50	13.45	−7.00	0.13
74.14	−2.90	−19.93	−21.04	−17.88	−10.81	8.29	5.26
−63.65	3.10	5.08	14.82	10.12	9.33	1.31	−0.62
3.73	2.85	6.67	8.99	−3.38	1.54	1.04	−0.62
2.50	0.57	−4.46	0.52	3.00	−2.89	−0.32	1.33
7.52	−1.80	−0.63	−0.10	0.41	−3.21	−2.74	−2.07
−3.40	0.43	0.81	0.28	−0.40	−0.19	−0.58	−1.09
−2.26	−0.88	1.73	0.23	−0.21	−0.12	1.23	1.61

Results of DCT Coefficients Quantized by Luminance Quantization Matrix

−6	−6	2	0	0	0	0	0
6	0	−1	−1	−1	0	0	0
−5	0	0	1	0	0	0	0
0	0	0	0	0	0	0	0
0	0	0	0	0	0	0	0
0	0	0	0	0	0	0	0
0	0	0	0	0	0	0	0
0	0	0	0	0	0	0	0

After the DC coefficient is differentially encoded, the AC coefficients are ordered in the zig-zag sequence and the sequence is subsequently broken into a number of runs of zeros ending in a nonzero coefficient. The entropy encoding procedure for differentially encoded DC coefficient is identical to the entropy encoding of the prediction error values that we explained for lossless JPEG. For 8-bit images in baseline JPEG, the DCT coefficients fall in the range $[-1023, +1023]$. Since the DC coefficient is differentially encoded, the differential values of DC fall in the range $[-2047, +2047]$. Assuming that the DC coefficient of the previous block is -4 as an example, the differential DC value of the present block is -2. From Table 3.2, we find that this belongs to category 2 and hence -2 is described as $(2, 01)$. If the Huffman code of category 2 is 011, then -2 is coded as 01101, where last two bits 01 represent the variable-length integer (VLI) code of -2. There are two Huffman tables (Table K.3 and K.4) for encoding the DC coefficients in Annex K of the baseline JPEG standard for reference. But the user can choose any table and add them as part of the header of the compressed file [1]. Table K.3 is supplied for coding the luminance DC differences as a reference. Table K.4 is supplied for chrominance DC differences.

After zig-zag ordering of the AC coefficients in the example, the resulting sequence is -6 6 -5 0 2 0 -1 0 0 0 0 0 -1 0 0 -1 1 0 0 0 0 0 0 0 0 0 0 0 0 0 0 0 0 0 0 0 0 0 0 0 0 0 0 0 0 0 0 0 0 0 0 0 0 0 0 0 0 0 0 0 0 0 0 0 0. This sequence of AC coefficients can be mapped into an *intermediate sequence* of a combination of two symbols, $symbol_1$ and $symbol_2$. $symbol_1$ is represented by a pair $(RUNLENGTH, CATEGORY)$, where $RUNLENGTH$ is the number of consecutive zeros preceding the nonzero AC coefficient being encoded and $CATEGORY$ is the number of bits to represent the VLI code of this nonzero AC coefficient; $symbol_2$ is a single piece of information designated $(AMPLITUDE)$ that is encoded by the VLI code of the nonzero AC coefficient. Accordingly, the zig-zag sequence in the example can be compactly represented as:

$(0, 3)(-6)$, $(0, 3)(6)$, $(0, 3)(-5)$, $(1, 2)(2)$, $(1, 1)(-1)$, $(5, 1)(-1)$, $(2, 1)(-1)$, $(0, 1)(1)$, $(0,0)$.

The first significant (nonzero) AC coefficient in the zig-zag sequence is -6. It is represented as $(0, 3)(-6)$ because it precedes with no run of zeros (i.e., $RUNLENGTH = 0$) and the $AMPLITUDE = -6$ belongs to $CATEGORY = 3$. Similarly, the following two nonzero coefficients 6 and -5 are represented as $(0, 3)(6)$ and $(0, 3)(-5)$ respectively. The next significant coefficient 2 is represented by $(1, 2)(2)$ because it precedes a 0 coefficient (i.e., $RUNLENGTH = 1$) and $AMPLITUDE = 2$ belongs to $CATEGORY = 2$. Similarly, the next significant symbol is represented as $(1, 1)(-1)$. The following significant coefficient -1 is represented as $(5, 1)(-1)$ because it precedes five 0's (i.e., $RUNLENGTH = 5$) and $AMPLITUDE = -1$ belongs to $CATEGORY = 1$. Following the same procedure, the next two nonzero coefficients -1 and 1 are represented by $(2, 1)(-1)$ and $(0, 1)(1)$ respectively. There are no other nonzero coefficients in the remainder of the zig-zag sequence. It is represented by a special symbol $(0,0)$ to indicate that the remaining elements in the zig-zag block are all zeros. Each $(RUNLENGTH,$

CATEGORY) pair is encoded using a Huffman code and the corresponding *AMPLITUDE* is encoded by the VLI code.

There are two special symbols in encoding the zig-zag sequence of AC coefficients—(0,0) and (15, 0). The first special symbol is (0,0), and it is referred to as EOB (end-of-block), to indicate that the remaining elements in the zig-zag block are zeros. The other special symbol is (15, 0) and it is also referred to as ZRL (zero-run-length) to indicate a run of 16 zeros. Maximum length of a run of zeros allowed in baseline JPEG is 16. If there are more than 16 zeros, then the run is broken into the number of runs of zeros of length 16. For example, consider 57 zeros before a nonzero coefficient, say -29. This will be represented by (15, 0) (15, 0) (15, 0), (9, 5)(-29). The first three (15, 0) pairs represent 48 zeros and (9, 5)(-29) represents 9 zeros followed by the coefficient -29 which belongs to the category 5.

The baseline JPEG allows maximum four Huffman tables—two for encoding AC coefficients and two for encoding DC coefficients. In luminance–chrominance image data, usually two Huffman tables (one for AC and one for DC) are used for encoding luminance data and similarly two for encoding chrominance data. The Huffman tables used during the compression process are stored as header information in the compressed image file in order to uniquely decode the coefficients during the decompression process. There are two Huffman tables (Table K.5 and K.6) for encoding the AC coefficients and two others (Table K.3 and K.4) for encoding the DC coefficients in Annex K of the baseline JPEG standard for reference. The users can choose any table of their choice and store it as part of the header of the compressed file [1]. Tables K.3 and K.5 are recommended for luminance DC differences and AC coefficients. Tables K.4 and K.6 are recommended for corresponding chrominance channels.

Let us now allocate the variable-length codes in the last example. The codewords for (0, 0), (0, 1), (0, 3), (1, 1), (1, 2), (2, 1), and (5, 1) from Table K.5 are 1010, 00, 100, 1100, 11011, 11100, and 1111010 respectively. VLI codes for the nonzero AC coefficients 1, -1, 2, -5, 6 and -6 are 1, 0, 10, 010, 110, and 001 respectively. Codeword for the differential DC value is 01101. The compressed bitstream for the 8 × 8 block is shown below, and it requires only 52 bits as opposed to 512 bits required by the original 8 × 8 block of 8-bit pixels,

01101 100001 100110 100010 1101110 11000 11110100 111000 001 1010

where the first five bits, 01101, represent the DC coefficient and the other 47 bits represent the AC coefficients. Hence, we achieved approximately 10:1 compression using baseline JPEG to compress the block as shown above.

3.3.6   Decompression Process in Baseline JPEG

Decompression is the inverse process to decode the compressed bit-stream in order to properly reconstruct the image. The inverse functions in the decompression process are obvious and the corresponding block diagram of the baseline decompression algorithm is shown in Figure 3.3(b). During the decompression process, the system first parses the header of the compressed file in order to retrieve all the relevant information—image type, number of components, format, quantization matrices, and the Huffman tables that were used to compress the original image, etc. After parsing the header information, the decompression algorithm is applied on the compressed bitstream as shown in Figure 3.3(b). The *entropy decoding* step in Figure 3.3(b) decodes the bitstream of the compressed data using the Huffman tables that were used during the compression process. The purpose of this step is to regenerate the zig-zag-ordered sequence of the quantized DCT coefficients. This zig-zag sequence is then reordered by the *zig-zag reordering* step to create the 8 × 8 block of quantized DCT coefficients. Each DCT coefficient in the quantized block is then dequantized as

$$F'(u, v) = F_q(u, v) \times Q(u, v),$$

where $Q(u, v)$ is the quantization step-size parameter from the same quantization table that was used during the compression process. After dequantization, the DCT coefficients $F'(u, v)$ are inverse transformed to spatial domain data via inverse DCT (IDCT). IDCT of the 8 × 8 block $F'(u, v)$ for $(u, v = 0, 1, \cdots, 7)$ is defined by:

$$f(x, y) = \frac{1}{4} \sum_{u=0}^{7} \sum_{v=0}^{7} C(u)C(v)F'(u, v) \cos \left[\frac{\pi(2x + 1)u}{16} \right] \cos \left[\frac{\pi(2y + 1)v}{16} \right]$$

for $x = 0, 1, \ldots, 7$ and $y = 0, 1, \ldots, 7$.

After decompression of all the MCUs from the compressed bitstream, the image components are reconstructed and stored. For grayscale image, there is only one component and no color transformation is required. For color image, the reconstructed Y, Cb, and Cr components are inverse transformed to RGB color space. We show a picture of the famous "Peppers" image in Figure 3.6(a). The color version of Figure 3.6 is provided in the color figures page. The image is compressed using the baseline JPEG algorithm with quality factor $Q\_JPEG = 75$ and the reconstructed image is perceptually almost identical to the original image. This is shown in Figure 3.6(b). When we compress the same image with quality factor $Q\_JPEG = 10$, we can see prominent artifacts in the image as shown in Figure 3.6(c). The nature of artifacts that is caused by lossy JPEG compression/decompression is called *blocking* artifacts. This happens because of the discontinuities created at the 8 × 8 block boundaries, since the blocks are compressed and decompressed independently. The new JPEG2000 standard solves this problem by using Discrete Wavelet Transform over the whole image. Figure 3.6(d) shows the result of the JPEG2000 standard compressing the image with the same bit-rate (0.24 bits per pixel). The details of this new standard will be discussed in Chapter 6.

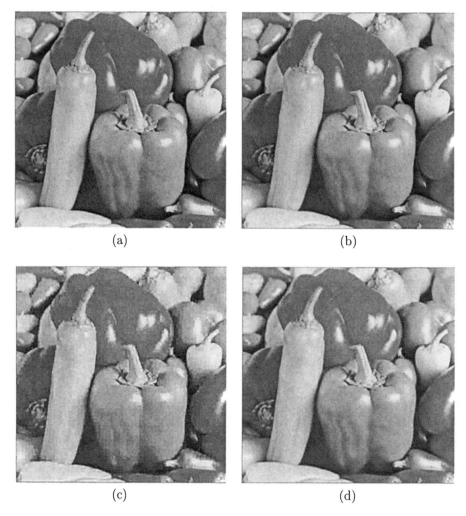

Fig. 3.6 (a) Original Pepper image, (b) compressed with baseline JPEG using quality factor 75 (1.57 bit/pixel), (c) compressed with baseline JPEG using quality factor 10 (0.24 bit/pixel), and (d) compressed with the new JPEG2000 standard using the same bit rate (0.24 bit/pixel).

3.4 PROGRESSIVE DCT-BASED MODE

One of the major disadvantages of the single scan sequential DCT-based mode (baseline JPEG) of compression is that the entire image cannot be rendered or viewed until the whole compressed bitstream is received and decoded. This is not desirable for many applications such as image browsing applications. In image browsing applications, the user is not expected to wait until the whole bitstream is decoded before viewing the entire image. It is desirable to the user that one can browse an initial appearance of the image and then choose to continue for finer detail or stop. This is possible in progressive DCT-based mode in JPEG.

In progressive DCT-based mode, the image is coded sequentially in multiple scans. Idea of this mode is to transmit a coarser version of the image in the first scan and then progressively improve the reconstructed quality at the receiver by transmitting more compressed bits in successive scans. In progressive coding mode, the DCT blocks of the entire image are computed first before entropy encoding of a block can start. Hence implementation of this mode requires the availability of a buffer that can contain all the DCT coefficients of the whole image. The entropy encoding method then selectively encodes the DCT coefficients and transmits. There are two complementary ways to achieve this partial encoding of the DCT blocks—*spectral selection* and *successive approximation*. Examples of these two methods have been shown in Figure 3.7.

In the spectral selection mode of progressive coding, all the DCT coefficients in an 8×8 data block are not encoded in one scan. Instead it encodes sets of DCT coefficients starting from lower frequencies and moving progressively to higher frequencies. For example, we can encode all the DC coefficients of all the 8×8 DCT blocks in the first scan as shown in Figure 3.7(a). In the second scan we can encode and transmit the first three AC coefficients of the zig-zag sequence of all the DCT blocks. We can transmit the next three AC coefficients in the third scan, and so on. The last three AC coefficients can be transmitted in the 21st scan as shown in Figure 3.7(a). The number of coefficients in each scan could be different and user selectable. This progressive coding scheme is simple to implement. The result of this method is that reconstructed images at the earlier scans are blurred and the image gets sharper in the successive scans.

In successive approximation mode of progressive coding, a certain number of most significant bits (say N_1) of all the DCT coefficients of all the blocks are encoded and transmitted in the first scan. In the second scan, the following N_2 most significant bits are encoded and transmitted and so on. We show this method in Figure 3.7(b) as an example. In this figure, the most significant three bits of all the DCT coefficients are encoded and transmitted in the first scan. Then we can choose to encode and transmit the next 1 bit of all the DCT coefficients in each of the successive scans and continue until the least significant bit of all the coefficients is encoded. Usually the successive approx-

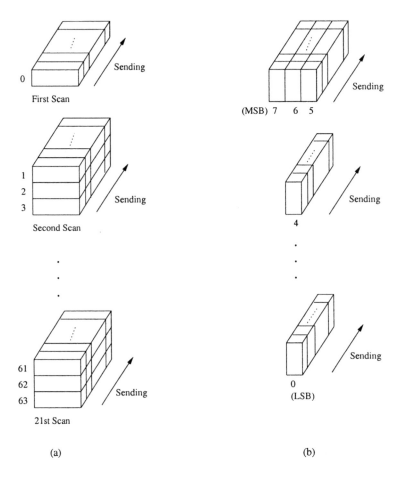

Fig. 3.7 Progressive encoding: (a) spectral selection; (b) successive approximation.

imation offers better reconstructed quality in the earlier scans compared to the spectral selection method.

Eight DCT-based progressive coding methodologies have been defined in JPEG standard [1].

3.5   HIERARCHICAL MODE

In hierarchical mode, JPEG provides a progressive coding with increasing spatial resolution in a number of stages. This is particularly suitable for applications where a higher-resolution image is viewed on a lower-resolution display device and other similar kinds of applications. The *pyramidal* multiresolution approach for implementation of the hierarchical mode of coding is shown in Figure 3.8.

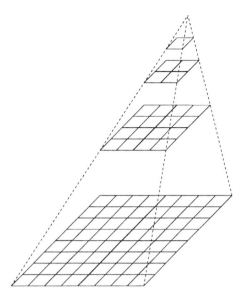

Fig. 3.8   Hierarchical multiresolution encoding.

In this mode, the original image is filtered and down-sampled by required multiples of two for the target resolution and the lower-resolution image is encoded using any of the other three JPEG modes. The compressed lower-resolution image is then decoded and interpolated for upsampling by the same interpolation method that will be used at the decoder. The interpolated image is then subtracted from the next-higher-resolution image. The difference is then encoded by one of the other three JPEG modes (lossless or lossy). This procedure of the hierarchical encoding process is continued until it encodes all the resolutions.

Fourteen different methods for encoding the difference images in the hierarchical mode have been explained in greater detail in JPEG standard [1].

3.6   SUMMARY

In this chapter, we described the JPEG standard for still image compression. We discussed the details of the algorithm for lossless JPEG. We also discussed in great detail the principles and algorithms for the baseline JPEG standard. Baseline JPEG is the most widely used algorithm among all different modes in the JPEG standard for still image compression. We presented some results of baseline JPEG and compared them with the new JPEG2000 standard. The features, concepts, and principles behind the algorithms for the JPEG2000 standard will be elaborated on in great details in Chapters 6, 7, 8, and 10. We also summarized the progressive mode and hierarchical mode of operation of the JPEG standard in this chapter with examples.

REFERENCES

1. W. B. Pennebaker and J. L. Mitchell, *JPEG Still Image Data Compression Standard.* Chapman & Hall, New York, 1993.

2. T. Acharya and A. Mukherjee, "High-Speed Parallel VLSI Architectures for Image Decorrelation," *International Journal of Pattern Recognition and Artificial Intelligence*, Vol. 9, No. 2, pp. 343–365, 1995.

3. H. Lohscheller, "A Subjectively Adapted Image Communication System," *IEEE Transactions on Communications*, COM-32, Vol. 12, pp. 1316–1322, 1984.

4. The independent JPEG Group, "The Sixth Public Release of the Independent JPEG Group's Free JPEG Software," *C source code of JPEG Encoder research 6b*, March 1998 (ftp://ftp.uu.net/graphics/jpeg/).

5. K. R. Rao and P. Yip, *Discrete Cosine Transform—Algorithms, Advantages, Applications.* Academic Press, San Diego, 1990.

6. B. G. Lee, "FCT—A Fast Cosine Transform," *Proc. of the Intl. Conf. on Acoustics, Speech, and Signal Processing*, pp. 28A.3.1–28A.3.3, San Diego, March 1984.

7. N. I. Cho and S. U. Lee, "Fast Algorithm and Implementation of 2D Discrete Cosine Transform," *IEEE Trans. on Circuits and Systems*, Vol. 38, pp. 297–305, March 1991.

8. "Information Technology—JPEG2000 Image Coding System," Final Committee Draft Version 1.0, ISO/IEC JTC 1/SC 29/WG 1 N1646R, March 2000.

4

Introduction to Discrete Wavelet Transform

4.1 INTRODUCTION

Although the "wavelet" has become very popular and is widely used as a versatile signal analysis function, its concepts were hidden in the works of mathematicians even more than a century ago. In 1873, Karl Weierstrass mathematically described how a family of functions can be constructed by superimposing scaled versions of a given basis function [1]. Mathematically a "wave" is expressed as a sinusoidal (or oscillating) function of time or space. Fourier analysis expands an arbitrary signal in terms of infinite number of sinusoidal functions of its harmonics and has been well studied by the signal processing community for decades. Fourier representation of signals is known to be very effective in analysis of time-invariant (stationary) periodic signals. In contrast to a sinusoidal function, a wavelet is a small wave whose energy is concentrated in time. The term *wavelet* was originally used in the field of seismology to describe the disturbances that emanate and proceed outward from a sharp seismic impulse [2]. In 1982, Morlet et al. first described how the seismic wavelets could be effectively modelled mathematically [3]. In 1984, Grossman and Morlet extended this work to show how an arbitrary signal can be analyzed in terms of scaling and translation of a single *mother wavelet* function (basis) [4, 5]. Properties of wavelets allow both time and frequency analysis of signals simultaneously because of the fact that the energy of wavelets is concentrated in time and still possesses the wave-like (periodic) characteristics. As a result, wavelet representation provides a versatile mathematical tool to analyze transient, time-variant (nonstationary) signals that may not be statistically predictable especially at the region of discontinuities — a special feature that is typical of images having discontinuities at the edges.

In 1989, Mallat proposed the theory of signal analysis based on "multiresolution decomposition" of signals using wavelets in time-scale space and proposed the popular *pyramid algorithm* [6]. For historical perspectives of wavelets and the underlying mathematical foundation of wavelet transform, the reader is referred to the treatise by Ives Meyer [7].

4.2   WAVELET TRANSFORMS

Wavelets are functions generated from one single function (basis function) called the *prototype* or *mother wavelet* by *dilations* (scalings) and *translations* (shifts) in time (frequency) domain. If the mother wavelet is denoted by $\psi(t)$, the other wavelets $\psi_{a,b}(t)$ can be represented as

$$\psi_{a,b}(t) = \frac{1}{\sqrt{|a|}} \psi\left(\frac{t-b}{a}\right) \tag{4.1}$$

where a and b are two arbitrary real numbers. The variables a and b represent the parameters for *dilations* and *translations* respectively in the time axis. From Eq. 4.1, it is obvious that the mother wavelet can be essentially represented as

$$\psi(t) = \psi_{1,0}(t). \tag{4.2}$$

For any arbitrary $a \neq 1$ and $b = 0$, we can derive that

$$\psi_{a,0}(t) = \frac{1}{\sqrt{|a|}} \psi\left(\frac{t}{a}\right). \tag{4.3}$$

As shown in Eq. 4.3, $\psi_{a,0}(t)$ is nothing but a time-scaled (by a) and amplitude-scaled (by $\sqrt{|a|}$) version of the mother wavelet function $\psi(t)$ in Eq. 4.2. The parameter a causes contraction of $\psi(t)$ in the time axis when $a < 1$ and expansion or stretching when $a > 1$. That's why the parameter a is called the *dilation* (scaling) parameter. For $a < 0$, the function $\psi_{a,b}(t)$ results in time reversal with dilation.

Mathematically, we can substitute t in Eq. 4.3 by $t-b$ to cause a translation or shift in the time axis resulting in the wavelet function $\psi_{a,b}(t)$ as shown in Eq. 4.1. The function $\psi_{a,b}(t)$ is a shift of $\psi_{a,0}(t)$ in right along the time axis by an amount b when $b > 0$ whereas it is a shift in left along the time axis by an amount b when $b < 0$. That's why the variable b represents the *translation* in time (*shift* in frequency) domain.

In Figure 4.1, we have shown an illustration of a mother wavelet and its dilations in the time domain with the dilation parameter $a = \alpha$. For the mother wavelet $\psi(t)$ shown in Figure 4.1(a), a contraction of the signal in

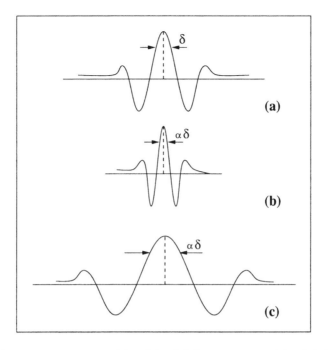

Fig. 4.1   (a) A *mother wavelet* $\psi(t)$,   (b) $\psi(t/\alpha)$: $0 < \alpha < 1$,   (c) $\psi(t/\alpha)$: $\alpha > 1$.

the time axis when $\alpha < 1$ is shown in Figure 4.1(b) and expansion of the signal in the time axis when $\alpha > 1$ is shown in Figure 4.1(c). Based on this definition of wavelets, the *wavelet transform* (WT) of a function (signal) $f(t)$ is mathematically represented by

$$W(a,b) = \int_{-\infty}^{+\infty} \psi_{a,b}(t) f(t)\, dt \tag{4.4}$$

The inverse transform to reconstruct $f(t)$ from $W(a,b)$ is mathematically represented by

$$f(t) = \frac{1}{C} \int_{a=-\infty}^{+\infty} \int_{b=-\infty}^{+\infty} \frac{1}{|a|^2} W(a,b)\psi_{a,b}(t) da\, db \tag{4.5}$$

where

$$C = \int_{-\infty}^{+\infty} \frac{|\Psi(\omega)|^2}{|\omega|} d\omega$$

and $\Psi(\omega)$ is the Fourier transform of the mother wavelet $\psi(t)$.

If a and b are two continuous (nondiscrete) variables and $f(t)$ is also a continuous function, $W(a,b)$ is called the *continuous wavelet transform* (CWT). Hence the CWT maps a one-dimensional function $f(t)$ to a function $W(a,b)$ of two continuous real variables a (dilation) and b (translation).

4.2.1   Discrete Wavelet Transforms

Since the input signal (e.g., a digital image) is processed by a digital computing machine, it is prudent to define the discrete version of the wavelet transform. Before we define the *discrete wavelet transform*, it is essential to define the wavelets in terms of discrete values of the *dilation* and *translation* parameters a and b instead of being continuous. There are many ways we can discretize a and b and then represent the *discrete wavelets* accordingly. The most popular approach of discretizing a and b is using Eq. 4.6,

$$a = a_0^m, \qquad b = nb_0 a_0^m \qquad\qquad (4.6)$$

where m and n are integers. Substituting a and b in Eq. 4.1 by Eq. 4.6, the discrete wavelets can be represented by Eq. 4.7.

$$\psi_{m,n}(t) = a_0^{-m/2} \psi\left(a_0^{-m}t - nb_0\right). \qquad\qquad (4.7)$$

There are many choices to select the values of a_0 and b_0. We select the most common choice here: $a_0 = 2$ and $b_0 = 1$; hence, $a = 2^m$ and $b = n2^m$. This corresponds to sampling (discretization) of a and b in such a way that the consecutive discrete values of a and b as well as the sampling intervals differ by a factor of two. This way of sampling is popularly known as *dyadic sampling* and the corresponding decomposition of the signals is called the *dyadic decomposition*. Using these values, we can represent the discrete wavelets as in Eq. 4.8, which constitutes a family of orthonormal basis functions.

$$\psi_{m,n}(t) = 2^{-m/2}\psi\left(2^{-m}t - n\right). \qquad\qquad (4.8)$$

In general, the wavelet coefficients for function $f(t)$ are given by

$$c_{m,n}(f) = a_0^{-m/2} \int f(t)\psi\left(a_0^{-m}t - nb_0\right)\, dt \qquad\qquad (4.9)$$

and hence for dyadic decomposition, the wavelet coefficients can be derived accordingly as

$$c_{m,n}(f) = 2^{-m/2} \int f(t)\psi\left(2^{-m}t - n\right)\, dt. \qquad\qquad (4.10)$$

This allows us to reconstruct the signal $f(t)$ in from the discrete wavelet coefficients as

$$f(t) = \sum_{m=-\infty}^{\infty} \sum_{n=-\infty}^{\infty} c_{m,n}(f)\psi_{m,n}(t). \qquad\qquad (4.11)$$

The transform shown in Eq. 4.9 is called the *wavelet series*, which is analogous to the *Fourier series* because the input function $f(t)$ is still a continuous function whereas the transform coefficients are discrete. This is often called the *discrete time wavelet transform* (DTWT). For digital signal or image processing applications executed by a digital computer, the input signal $f(t)$

needs to be discrete in nature because of the digital sampling of the original data, which is represented by a finite number of bits. When the input function $f(t)$ as well as the wavelet parameters a and b are represented in discrete form, the transformation is commonly referred to as the *discrete wavelet transform* (DWT) of signal $f(t)$ [6, 11].

The *discrete wavelet transform* (DWT) became a very versatile signal processing tool after Mallat [6] proposed the multiresolution representation of signals based on wavelet decomposition. The method of multiresolution is to represent a function (signal) with a collection of coefficients, each of which provides information about the position as well as the frequency of the signal (function). The advantage of the DWT over Fourier transformation is that it performs multiresolution analysis of signals with localization both in time and frequency, popularly known as time-frequency localization. As a result, the DWT decomposes a digital signal into different subbands so that the lower frequency subbands have finer frequency resolution and coarser time resolution compared to the higher frequency subbands. The DWT is being increasingly used for image compression due to the fact that the DWT supports features like progressive image transmission (by quality, by resolution), ease of compressed image manipulation, region of interest coding, etc. Because of these characteristics, the DWT is the basis of the new JPEG2000 image compression standard [8].

4.2.2 Concept of Multiresolution Analysis

There were a number of orthonormal wavelet basis functions of the form $\psi_{m,n}(t) = 2^{-m/2}\psi(2^{-m}t - n)$ discovered in 1980s. The theory of *multiresolution analysis* presented a systematic approach to generate the wavelets [6, 9, 10]. The idea of multiresolution analysis is to approximate a function $f(t)$ at different levels of resolution.

In multiresolution analysis, we consider two functions: the mother wavelet $\psi(t)$ and the *scaling function* $\phi(t)$. The dilated (scaled) and translated (shifted) version of the scaling function is given by $\phi_{m,n}(t) = 2^{-m/2}\phi(2^{-m}t - n)$. For fixed m, the set of scaling functions $\phi_{m,n}(t)$ are orthonormal. By the linear combinations of the scaling function and its translations we can generate a set of functions

$$f(t) = \sum_n \alpha_n \phi_{m,n}(t). \qquad (4.12)$$

The set of all such functions generated by linear combination of the set $\{\phi_{m,n}(t)\}$ is called the span of the set $\{\phi_{m,n}(t)\}$, denoted by $\text{Span}\{\phi_{m,n}(t)\}$. Now consider V_m to be a vector space corresponding to $\text{Span}\{\phi_{m,n}(t)\}$. Assuming that the resolution increases with decreasing m, these vector spaces describe successive approximation vector spaces, $\cdots \subset V_2 \subset V_1 \subset V_0 \subset V_{-1} \subset V_{-2} \subset \cdots$, each with resolution 2^m (i.e., each space V_{j+1} is contained in the next resolution space V_j). In multiresolution analysis, the set of subspaces satisfies the following properties:

1. $V_{m+1} \subset V_m$, for all m: This property states that each subspace is contained in the next resolution subspace.

2. $\overline{\bigcup V_m} = L^2(\mathcal{R})$: This property indicates that the union of subspaces is dense in the space of square integrable functions $L^2(\mathcal{R})$; $\mathcal{R}$ indicates a set of real numbers (*upward completeness* property).

3. $\bigcap V_m = 0$ (an empty set): This property is called *downward completeness* property.

4. $f(t) \in V_0 \leftrightarrow f(2^{-m}t) \in V_m$: Dilating a function from resolution space V_0 by a factor of 2^m results in the lower resolution space V_m (*scale* or *dilation invariance* property).

5. $f(t) \in V_0 \leftrightarrow f(t-n) \in V_0$: Combining this with the scale invariance property above, this property states that translating a function in a resolution space does not change the resolution (*translation invariance* property).

6. There exists a set $\{\phi(t-n) \in V_0: n$ is an integer$\}$ that forms an orthonormal basis of V_0.

The basic tenet of multiresolution analysis is that whenever the above properties are satisfied, there exists an orthonormal wavelet basis $\psi_{m,n}(t) = 2^{-m/2}\phi(2^{-m}t - n)$ such that

$$P_{m-1}(f) = P_m(f) + \sum c_{m,n}(f)\psi_{m,n}(t) \qquad (4.13)$$

where P_j is the orthogonal projection of ψ onto V_j. For each m, consider the wavelet functions $\psi_{m,n}(t)$ span a vector space W_m. It is clear from Eq. 4.13 that the wavelet that generates the space W_m and the scaling function that generates the space V_m are not independent. W_m is exactly the orthogonal complement of V_m in V_{m-1}. Thus, any function in V_{m-1} can be expressed as the sum of a function in V_m and a function in the wavelet space W_m. Symbolically, we can express this as

$$V_{m-1} = V_m \oplus W_m. \qquad (4.14)$$

Since m is arbitrary,

$$V_m = V_{m+1} \oplus W_{m+1}. \qquad (4.15)$$

Thus,

$$V_{m-1} = V_{m+1} \oplus W_{m+1} \oplus W_m. \qquad (4.16)$$

Continuing in this fashion, we can establish that

$$V_{m-1} = V_k \oplus W_k \oplus W_{k-1} \oplus W_{k-2} \oplus \cdots W_m \qquad (4.17)$$

for any $k \geq m$.

Thus, if we have a function that belongs to the space V_{m-1} (i.e., the function can be exactly represented by the scaling function at resolution $m-1$), we can decompose it into a sum of functions starting with lower-resolution approximation followed by a sequence of functions generated by dilations of the wavelet that represent the loss of information in terms of details. Let us consider the representation of an image with fewer and fewer pixels at successive levels of approximation. The wavelet coefficients can then be considered as the additional detail information needed to go from a coarser to a finer approximation. Hence, in each level of decomposition the signal can be decomposed into two parts, one is the coarse approximation of the signal in the lower resolution and the other is the detail information that was lost because of the approximation. The wavelet coefficients derived by Eq. 4.9 or 4.10, therefore, describe the information (detail) lost when going from an approximation of the signal at resolution 2^{m-1} to the coarser approximation at resolution 2^m.

4.2.3   Implementation by Filters and the Pyramid Algorithm

It is clear from the theory of multiresolution analysis in the previous section that multiresolution analysis decomposes a signal into two parts — one approximation of the original signal from finer to coarser resolution and the other detail information that was lost due to the approximation. This can be mathematically represented as

$$f_m(t) = \sum_n a_{m+1,n}\phi_{m+1,n} + \sum_n c_{m+1,n}\psi_{m+1,n} \qquad (4.18)$$

where $f_m(t)$ denotes the value of input function $f(t)$ at resolution 2^m, $c_{m+1,n}$ is the detail information, and $a_{m+1,n}$ is the coarser approximation of the signal at resolution 2^{m+1}. The functions, $\phi_{m+1,n}$ and $\psi_{m+1,n}$ are the dilation and wavelet basis functions (orthonormal).

In 1989, Mallat [6] proposed the multiresolution approach for wavelet decomposition of signals using a pyramidal filter structure of *quadrature mirror filter* (QMF) pairs. Wavelets developed by Daubechies [9, 10], in terms of discrete-time perfect reconstruction filter banks, correspond to FIR filters. In multiresolution analysis, it can be proven that decomposition of signals using the discrete wavelet transform can be expressed in terms of FIR filters [6, 10] and the all the discussions on multiresolution analysis boils down to the following algorithm (Eq. 4.19) for computation of the wavelet coefficients for the signal $f(t)$. For details see the original paper by Mallat [6].

$$\left. \begin{array}{l} c_{m,n}(f) = \sum_k g_{2n-k}\, a_{m-1,k}(f) \\[2mm] a_{m,n}(f) = \sum_k h_{2n-k}\, a_{m-1,k}(f) \end{array} \right\} \qquad (4.19)$$

where g and h are the high-pass and low-pass filters, $g_i = (-1)^i h_{-i+1}$ and $h_i = 2^{1/2} \int \phi(x-i)\phi(2x)\,dx$. Actually, $a_{m,n}(f)$ are the coefficients characterizing the projection of the function $f(t)$ in the vector subspace V_m (i.e., approximation of the function in resolution 2^m), whereas $c_{m,n}(f) \in W_m$ are the wavelet coefficients (detail information) at resolution 2^m. If the input signal $f(t)$ is in discrete sampled form, then we can consider these samples as the highest order resolution approximation coefficients $a_{0,n}(f) \in V_0$ and Eq. 4.19 describes the multiresolution subband decomposition algorithm to construct $a_{m,n}(f)$ and $c_{m,n}(f)$ at level m with a low-pass filter h and high-pass filter g from $c_{m-1,n}(f)$, which were generated at level $m-1$. These filters are called the *analysis* filters. The recursive algorithm to compute DWT in different levels using Eq. 4.19 is popularly called Mallat's *Pyramid Algorithm* [6]. Since the synthesis filters h and g have been derived from the orthonormal basis functions ϕ and ψ, these filters give exact reconstruction

$$a_{m-1,i}(f) = \sum_n h_{2n-i}\, a_{m,n}(f) + \sum_n g_{2n-i}\, c_{m,n}(f) \qquad (4.20)$$

Most of the orthonormal wavelet basis functions have infinitely supported ψ and accordingly the filters h and g could be with infinitely many taps. However, for practical and computationally efficient implementation of the DWT for image processing applications, it is desirable to have finite impulse response filters (FIR) with a small number of taps. It is possible to construct such filters by relaxing the orthonormality requirements and using biorthogonal basis functions. It should be noted that the wavelet filters are orthogonal when $(h', g') = (h, g)$, otherwise it is biorthogonal. In such a case the filters (h' and g', called the *synthesis* filters) for reconstruction of the signal can be different than the *analysis* filters (h and g) for decomposition of the signals. In order to achieve exact reconstruction, we can construct the filters such that it satisfies the relationship of the synthesis filter with the analysis filter [12] as shown in Eq. 4.21:

$$\left. \begin{aligned} g'_n &= (-1)^n h_{-n+1} \\[2mm] g_n &= (-1)^n h'_{-n+1} \\[2mm] \sum_n h_n h'_{n+2k} &= \delta_{k,0} \end{aligned} \right\} . \qquad (4.21)$$

If $(h', g') = (h, g)$, the wavelet filters are called *orthogonal*, otherwise they are called *biorthogonal*. The popular $(9, 7)$ wavelet filter adopted in JPEG2000 is one example of such a biorthogonal filter [8]. The signal is still decomposed using Eq. 4.19, but the reconstruction equation is now done using the synthesis filters h' and g' as shown in Eq. 4.22:

$$a_{m-1,i}(f) = \sum_n a_{m,n}(f) h'_{2n-i} + \sum_n c_{m,n}(f) g'_{2n-i}. \qquad (4.22)$$

Let's summarize the DWT computation here in terms of simple digital FIR filtering. Given the input discrete signal $x(n)$ (shown as $a(0, n)$ in Figure 4.2),

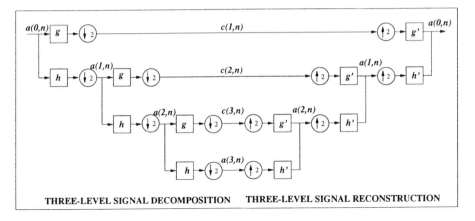

THREE-LEVEL SIGNAL DECOMPOSITION   THREE-LEVEL SIGNAL RECONSTRUCTION

Fig. 4.2 Three-level multiresolution wavelet decomposition and reconstruction of signals using pyramidal filter structure.

it is filtered parallelly by a low-pass filter (h) and a high-pass filter (g) at each transform level. The two output streams are then subsampled by simply dropping the alternate output samples in each stream to produce the low-pass subband y_L (shown as $a(1,n)$ in Figure 4.2) and high-pass subband y_H (shown as $c(1,n)$ in Figure 4.2). The above arithmetic computation can be expressed as follows:

$$y_L(n) = \sum_{i=0}^{\tau_L-1} h(i)x(2n-i), \quad y_H(n) = \sum_{i=0}^{\tau_H-1} g(i)x(2n-i) \qquad (4.23)$$

where τ_L and τ_H are the lengths of the low-pass (h) and high-pass (g) filters respectively. Since the low-pass subband $a(1,n)$ is an approximation of the input signal, we can apply the above computation again on $a(1,n)$ to produce the subbands $a(2,n)$ and $c(2,n)$ and so on. This multiresolution decomposition approach is shown in Figure 4.2 for three levels of decomposition. During the inverse transform to reconstruct the signal, both $a(3,n)$ and $c(3,n)$ are first upsampled by inserting zeros between two samples, and then they are filtered by low-pass (h') and high-pass (g') filters respectively. These two filtered output streams are added together to reconstruct $a(2,n)$ as shown in Figure 4.2. The same continues until we reconstruct the original signal $a(0,n)$.

4.3   EXTENSION TO TWO-DIMENSIONAL SIGNALS

The two-dimensional extension of DWT is essential for transformation of two-dimensional signals, such as a digital image. A two-dimensional digital signal can be represented by a two-dimensional array $X[M,N]$ with M rows and N columns, where M and N are nonnegative integers. The simple approach for two-dimensional implementation of the DWT is to perform the one-dimensional DWT row-wise to produce an intermediate result and then perform the same one-dimensional DWT column-wise on this intermediate result to produce the final result. This is shown in Figure 4.3(a). This is possible because the two-dimensional scaling functions can be expressed as separable functions which are the product of two one-dimensional scaling functions such as $\phi_2(x,y) = \phi_1(x)\phi_1(y)$. The same is true for the wavelet function $\psi(x,y)$ as well. Applying the one-dimensional transform in each row, we produce two subbands in each row. When the low-frequency subbands of all the rows (L) are put together, it looks like a thin version (of size $M \times \frac{N}{2}$) of the input signal as shown in Figure 4.3(a). Similarly we put together the high-frequency subbands of all the rows to produce the H subband of size $M \times \frac{N}{2}$, which contains mainly the high-frequency information around discontinuities (edges in an image) in the input signal. Then applying a one-dimensional DWT column-wise on these L and H subbands (intermediate result), we produce four subbands LL, LH, HL, and HH of size $\frac{M}{2} \times \frac{N}{2}$ respectively, as shown in Figure 4.3(a). LL is a coarser version of the original input signal. LH, HL, and HH are the high-frequency subband containing the detail information. It should be noted that we could have applied the one-dimensional DWT column-wise first and then row-wise to achieve the same result. To comprehend the idea visually, we show a block diagram with a sketch of a house in Figure 4.4 as an example.

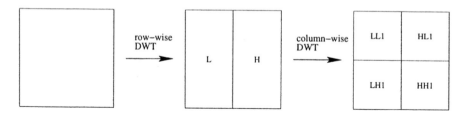

(a) First level of decomposition

(b) Second level decomposition

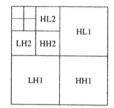

(c) Third level decomposition

Fig. 4.3 Row-Column computation of two-dimensional DWT.

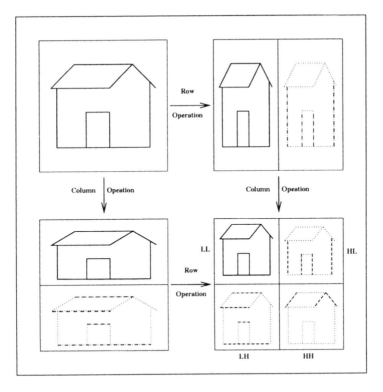

Fig. 4.4   Extension of DWT in two-dimensional signals.

We demonstrate the multiresolution decomposition approach in the two-dimensional signal in Figures 4.3(b) and (c). After the first level of decomposition, it generates four subbands LL1, HL1, LH1, and HH1 as shown in Figure 4.3(a). Considering the input signal is an image, the LL1 subband can be considered as a 2:1 subsampled (both horizontally and vertically) version of the original image. The other three subbands HL1, LH1, and HH1 contain higher frequency detail information. These spatially oriented (horizontal, vertical or diagonal) subbands mostly contain information of local discontinuities in the image and the bulk of the energy in each of these three subbands is concentrated in the vicinity of areas corresponding to edge activities in the original image. Since LL1 is a coarser approximation of the input, it has similar spatial and statistical characteristics to the original image. As a result, it can be further decomposed into four subbands LL2, HL2, LH2, and HH2 as shown in Figure 4.3(b) based on the principle of multiresolution analysis. Accordingly the image is decomposed into 10 subbands LL3, HL3, LH3, HH3, HL2, LH2, HH2, HL1, LH1, and HH1 after three levels of pyramidal multiresolution subband decomposition, as shown in Figure 4.3(c). The same computation can continue to further decompose LL3 into higher levels.

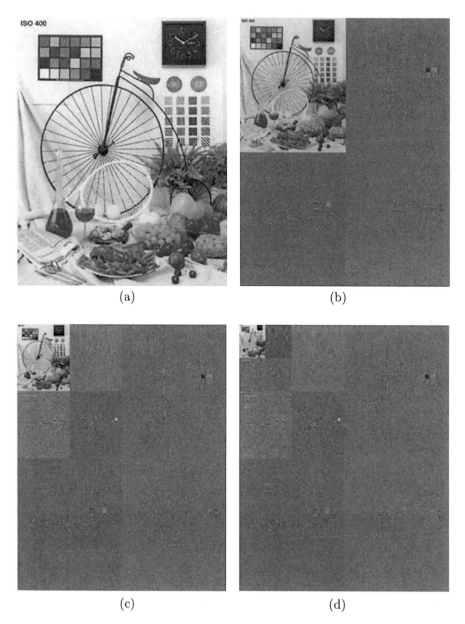

Fig. 4.5   (a) Original BIKE image and subbands; (b) after level 1, (c) after level 2, (d) after level 3 decomposition.

We have decomposed one of the ISO/IEC test images (BIKE image) provided by the JPEG2000 standard committee as shown in Figure 4.5(a). In Figures 4.5(b), (c), and (d), we show the subbands after one, two, and three levels of decomposition respectively. The subbands in this figure have been normalized to 8 bits for the purpose of display.

4.4   LIFTING IMPLEMENTATION OF THE DISCRETE WAVELET TRANSFORM

The DWT has been traditionally implemented by convolution or FIR filter bank structures. The DWT implementation is basically a frame-based as opposed to the block-based implementation of *discrete cosine transforms* (DCT) or similar transformations. Such an implementation requires both a large number of arithmetic computations and a large memory for storage — features that are not desirable for either high-speed or low-power image and video processing applications. Recently, a new mathematical formulation for wavelet transformation has been proposed by Swelden [13] based on spatial construction of the wavelets and a very versatile scheme for its factorization has been suggested in [14]. This new approach is called the lifting-based wavelet transform, or simply *lifting*. The main feature of the lifting-based DWT scheme is to break up the high-pass and low-pass wavelet filters into a sequence of smaller filters that in turn can be converted into a sequence of upper and lower triangular matrices, which will be discussed in the subsequent section. This scheme often requires far fewer computations compared to the convolution-based DWT [13, 14], and its computational complexity can be reduced up to 50%. It has several other advantages, including "in-place" computation of the DWT, integer-to-integer wavelet transform (IWT), symmetric forward and inverse transform, requiring no signal boundary extension, etc. As a result, lifting-based hardware implementations provide an efficient way to compute wavelet transforms compared to traditional approaches. So it comes as no surprise that lifting has been suggested for implementation of the DWT in the upcoming JPEG2000 standard [8].

In a traditional forward DWT using a filter bank, the input signal (x) is filtered separately by a low-pass filter $(\tilde{h})$ and a high-pass filter $(\tilde{g})$ at each transform level. The two output streams are then subsampled by simply dropping the alternate output samples in each stream to produce the low-pass (y_L) and high-pass (y_H) subbands as shown in Figure 4.6. These two filters $(\tilde{h}, \tilde{g})$ form the *analysis* filter bank. The original signal can be reconstructed by a *synthesis* filter bank (h, g) starting from y_L and y_H as shown in Figure 4.6. We have adopted the discussion on lifting from the celebrated paper by Daubechies and Sweldens [14]. It should also be noted that we adopted the notation $(\tilde{h}, \tilde{g})$ for the analysis filter and (h, g) as the synthesis filter in this section and onward in this chapter. Given a discrete signal $x(n)$, arithmetic computation of above can be expressed as follows:

$$y_L(n) = \sum_{i=0}^{\tau_L-1} \tilde{h}(i)x(2n-i), \quad y_H(n) = \sum_{i=0}^{\tau_H-1} \tilde{g}(i)x(2n-i) \qquad (4.24)$$

where τ_L and τ_H are the lengths of the low-pass ($\tilde{h}$) and high-pass ($\tilde{g}$) filters respectively. During the inverse transform to reconstruct the signal, both y_L and y_H are first upsampled by inserting zeros between two samples and then they are filtered by low-pass (h) and high-pass (g) filters respectively. These two filtered output streams are added together to obtain the reconstructed signal (x') as shown in Figure 4.6.

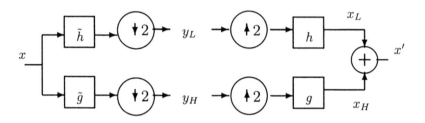

Fig. 4.6   Signal analysis and reconstruction in DWT.

4.4.1   Finite Impulse Response Filter and Z-transform

A digital *filter* $h = \{\cdots, h_{k-1}, h_k, h_{k+1}, \ldots\}$ is a linear time-invariant operator which can be completely defined by its *impulse* response $\{h_k \in R \,|\, k \in Z\}$. These *impulse* responses (h_k) are popularly called filter *coefficients*. If the number of nonzero coefficients in a digital filter is infinite, then the filter is called an *infinite impulse response* (IIR) filter. On the other hand, the number of non-zero coefficients h_k in a *finite impulse response* (FIR) is finite. The Z-transform of an FIR filter h is expressed as a Laurent polynomial $h(z)$ as shown in Eq. 4.25,

$$h(z) = \sum_{i=m}^{n} h_i z^{-i} \qquad (4.25)$$

where m and n are positive integers. The degree of the above Laurent polynomial is defined as $|h(z)| = n - m$. Thus the length of the FIR filter h is $n - m + 1$ (i.e., the degree of the associated Laurent polynomial plus one).

   The difference of the Laurent polynomial from an arbitrary polynomial is that an arbitrary polynomial can have negative exponents whereas the exponents in the Laurent polynomial are always positive. The sum or difference of two Laurent polynomials is a Laurent polynomial. The product of two Laurent polynomials $a(z)$ and $b(z)$ is a Laurent polynomial of degree $|a(z)|+|b(z)|$. Let us assume that $b(z) \neq 0$ and $|a(z)| \geq |b(z)|$. In general, exact division of $a(z)$ by $b(z)$ is not possible. However, division with remainder is possible although this division is not unique. There always exists a quotient $q(z)$ and a remainder $r(z)$ (not necessarily unique) with $|q(z)| = |a(z)| - |b(z)|$ and $|r(z)| < |b(z)|$ so that

$$a(z) = b(z)q(z) + r(z). \tag{4.26}$$

4.4.2 Euclidean Algorithm for Laurent Polynomials

The Euclidean algorithm can be used to find the *greatest common divisor* (gcd) of two Laurent polynomials $a(z)$ and $b(s)$. If $b(z) \neq 0$ and $|a(z)| \geq |b(z)|$, we can state the algorithm as follows. By operations '/' and '%' in the algorithm, we mean to find the quotient and remainder of the division.

> **begin**
> $k = 0$;
> $a_k(z) = a(z)$;
> $b_k(z) = b(z)$;
>   **while** $b_k(z) \neq 0$ **do**
>   {
> $a_{k+1} = b_k(z)$;
> $b_{k+1} = a_k(z)\%b_k(z)$;
> $q_{k+1} = a_k(z)/b_k(z)$;
> $k = k + 1$
>   }
> $gcd = a_k(z)$;
> **end.**

¿From the above algorithm, it is clear that the greatest common divisor (gcd) of $a(z)$ and $b(z)$ is a_n, where n is the smallest integer for which $b_n(z) = 0$. The number of iterations by the **while** loop in the above algorithms is bounded by $n \leq |n(z)| + 1$. From the above algorithm, we can establish that

$$\begin{bmatrix} a_{i+1}(z) \\ b_{i+1}(z) \end{bmatrix} = \begin{bmatrix} 0 & 1 \\ 1 & -q_i(z) \end{bmatrix} \begin{bmatrix} a_i(z) \\ b_i(z) \end{bmatrix} \tag{4.27}$$

which can be rewritten as

$$\begin{bmatrix} a_i(z) \\ b_i(z) \end{bmatrix} = \begin{bmatrix} q_i(z) & 1 \\ 1 & 0 \end{bmatrix} \begin{bmatrix} a_{i+1}(z) \\ b_{i+1}(z) \end{bmatrix}. \tag{4.28}$$

Thus,

$$\begin{bmatrix} a_0(z) \\ b_0(z) \end{bmatrix} = \begin{bmatrix} q_0(z) & 1 \\ 1 & 0 \end{bmatrix} \begin{bmatrix} a_1(z) \\ b_1(z) \end{bmatrix} = \begin{bmatrix} q_0(z) & 1 \\ 1 & 0 \end{bmatrix} \begin{bmatrix} q_1(z) & 1 \\ 1 & 0 \end{bmatrix} \begin{bmatrix} a_2(z) \\ b_2(z) \end{bmatrix}.$$
(4.29)

Since $a_0(z) = a(z)$ and $b_0(z) = b(z)$, we obtain the following factorization after iterating the above equation:

$$\begin{bmatrix} a(z) \\ b(z) \end{bmatrix} = \prod_{k=1}^{n} \begin{bmatrix} q_i(z) & 1 \\ 1 & 0 \end{bmatrix} \begin{bmatrix} a_n(z) \\ 0 \end{bmatrix}.$$
(4.30)

The above factorization algorithm will be used in Section 4.4.4.3 to show how the polyphase matrix for a filter pair can be factorized into lifting sequences.

4.4.3   Perfect Reconstruction and Polyphase Representation of Filters

For any practical signal transformation technique from one domain to another, the transformation should be reversible. For example, the Fourier transform converts a signal from the time domain to the frequency domain. When inverse Fourier transform is applied on the signal in frequency domain, the signal is converted back to the time domain. Ideally, if there is no additional processing or manipulation done in the frequency domain data after the transformation (i.e., if there is no loss of data or information at any form), the reconstructed signal after inverse Fourier transform should be an exact replica of the original one. The same principle applies for the DWT as well. Hence we need to choose the filter bank for DWT in such a way that perfect reconstruction is achieved. For the filter bank in Figure 4.6, the conditions for perfect reconstruction of a signal [14] are given by

$$\left. \begin{array}{l} h(z)\tilde{h}(z^{-1}) + g(z)\tilde{g}(z^{-1}) = 2 \\[2mm] h(z)\tilde{h}(-z^{-1}) + g(z)\tilde{g}(-z^{-1}) = 0 \end{array} \right\}$$
(4.31)

where $h(z)$ is the Z-transform of the FIR filter h.

The *polyphase* representation of a filter h is expressed as

$$h(z) = h_e(z^2) + z^{-1}h_o(z^2)$$
(4.32)

where h_e contains the even filter coefficients and h_o contains the odd filter coefficients of the FIR filter h. In general by *polyphase* representation, we mean to split a sequence into several subsequences for possible parallel processing of the subsequences. From Eq. 4.32, we can intuitively split the filter into two smaller filters — one (h_e) with the even filter coefficients and the other (h_o) with the odd filter coefficients delayed by a clock cycle, whose Z-transform can be expressed as

$$h_e(z) = \sum_k h_{2k} z^{-k}, \quad h_o(z) = \sum_k h_{2k+1} z^{-k} \tag{4.33}$$

and we can define a *polyphase matrix* for the filter h as

$$P(z) = \begin{bmatrix} h_e(z) & g_e(z) \\ h_o(z) & g_o(z) \end{bmatrix}. \tag{4.34}$$

Based on the discussion above, the polyphase representation of the filters $g(z)$, $\tilde{h}(z)$, and $\tilde{g}(z)$ is expressed as follows:

$$\left. \begin{aligned} g(z) &= g_e(z^2) + z^{-1} g_o(z^2) \\ \tilde{h}(z) &= \tilde{h}_e(z^2) + z^{-1}\tilde{h}_o(z^2) \\ \tilde{g}(z) &= \tilde{g}_e(z^2) + z^{-1}\tilde{g}_o(z^2) \end{aligned} \right\} \tag{4.35}$$

Based on the above formulation, we can define two *polyphase matrices* as follows:

$$\tilde{P}(z) = \begin{bmatrix} \tilde{h}_e(z) & \tilde{h}_o(z) \\ \tilde{g}_e(z) & \tilde{g}_o(z) \end{bmatrix}, \quad P(z) = \begin{bmatrix} h_e(z) & g_e(z) \\ h_o(z) & g_o(z) \end{bmatrix} \tag{4.36}$$

Often the polyphase matrix $P(z)$ is called the *dual* of the polyphase matrix $\tilde{P}(z)$. For perfect reconstruction, these two polyphase matrices $P(z)$ and $\tilde{P}(z)$ satisfy the following relation in Eq. 4.37,

$$P(z)\tilde{P}(z^{-1})^T = I \tag{4.37}$$

where I is the 2×2 *identity* matrix. Now based on the above formulation, the wavelet transform in terms of the polyphase matrix can be expressed as

$$\begin{bmatrix} y_L(z) \\ y_H(z) \end{bmatrix} = \tilde{P}(z) \begin{bmatrix} x_e(z) \\ z^{-1} x_o(z) \end{bmatrix} \tag{4.38}$$

for the forward DWT and

$$\begin{bmatrix} x_e(z) \\ z^{-1} x_o(z) \end{bmatrix} = P(z) \begin{bmatrix} y_L(z) \\ y_H(z) \end{bmatrix} \tag{4.39}$$

for the inverse DWT.

If the determinant of the polyphase matrix $P(z)$ is unity (i.e., $|P(z)| = h_e(z)g_o(z) - g_e(z)h_o(z) = 1$), then the matrix $P(z)$ is invertible. Hence we can apply the Cramer's rule [14] in Eq. 4.37 as follows:

$$\tilde{P}(z^{-1}) = P(z)^{-1} = \frac{\begin{bmatrix} g_o(z) & -g_e(z) \\ -h_o(z) & h_e(z) \end{bmatrix}}{|P(z)|} = \begin{bmatrix} g_o(z) & -g_e(z) \\ -h_o(z) & h_e(z) \end{bmatrix}. \tag{4.40}$$

From Eq. 4.36, we find that

$$\tilde{P}(z^{-1}) = \begin{bmatrix} \tilde{h}_e(z^{-1}) & \tilde{h}_o(z^{-1}) \\ \tilde{g}_e(z^{-1}) & \tilde{g}_o(z^{-1}) \end{bmatrix}. \tag{4.41}$$

From Eqs. 4.40 and 4.41, we can conclude that

$$\left. \begin{aligned} \tilde{h}_e(z) &= g_o(z^{-1}), \\ \tilde{h}_o(z) &= -g_e(z^{-1}), \\ \tilde{g}_e(z) &= -h_o(z^{-1}), \\ \tilde{g}_o(z) &= h_e(z^{-1}) \end{aligned} \right\} \tag{4.42}$$

which implies that

$$\tilde{h}(z) = -z^{-1}g(-z^{-1}), \qquad \tilde{g}(z) = z^{-1}h(-z^{-1}) \tag{4.43}$$

and hence

$$h(z) = -z^{-1}\tilde{g}(-z^{-1}), \qquad g(z) = z^{-1}\tilde{h}(-z^{-1}). \tag{4.44}$$

When the determinant of $P(z)$ is unity, the synthesis filter pair (h,g) is called *complementary* and so is the analysis filter pair $(\tilde{h},\tilde{g})$. When $(h,g)=(\tilde{h},\tilde{g})$, the wavelet transformation is called orthogonal; otherwise it is biorthogonal.

When $h(z) = \tilde{h}(z) = g(z) = \tilde{g}(z) = 1$, the DWT simply splits an input signal $(x = \{x_k \mid k \in Z\})$ into two subsequences, one with all the odd samples (x_{2i+1}) and the other with all the even sequences (x_{2i}). This is called the *lazy* wavelet transform [13].

4.4.4 Lifting

There are two types of lifting. One is called *primal lifting* and the other is called *dual lifting*. We define these two types of lifting based on the mathematical formulations shown in the previous section.

4.4.4.1 Primal Lifting According to the lifting theorem [14], if the wavelet filter pair $(h,\ g)$ is complementary then any other FIR filter g^{new} that is complementary to h is of the form

$$g^{new}(z) = g(z) + h(z)s(z^2) \tag{4.45}$$

where $s(z^2)$ is a Laurent polynomial.

Proof: Expanding $g^{new}(z)$ in polyphase representation, we get

$$\begin{aligned} g^{new}(z) &= g(z) + h(z)s(z^2) \\ &= \{g_e(z^2) + z^{-1}g_o(z^2)\} + \{h_e(z^2) + z^{-1}h_o(z^2)\}s(z^2) \\ &= \{g_e(z^2) + h_e(z^2)s(z^2)\} + z^{-1}\{g_o(z^2) + h_o(z^2)s(z^2)\}. \end{aligned} \tag{4.46}$$

We know that
$$h(z) = h_e(z^2) + z^{-1}h_o(z^2). \tag{4.47}$$

Hence the new polyphase matrix can be defined as

$$P^{new}(z) = \begin{bmatrix} h_e(z) & g_e(z) + h_e(z)s(z) \\ h_o(z) & g_o(z) + h_o(z)s(z) \end{bmatrix}$$

$$= \begin{bmatrix} h_e(z) & g_e(z) \\ h_o(z) & g_o(z) \end{bmatrix} \begin{bmatrix} 1 & s(z) \\ 0 & 1 \end{bmatrix} \tag{4.48}$$

$$= P(z) \begin{bmatrix} 1 & s(z) \\ 0 & 1 \end{bmatrix}.$$

It can be easily verified that the determinant of $P^{new}(z)$ is 1 and hence it proves Eq. 4.45. From Eq. 4.37 we know that

$$P^{new}(z)\tilde{P}^{new}(z^{-1})^T = I. \tag{4.49}$$

Thus, we can derive that

$$\tilde{P}^{new}(z^{-1}) = [P(z)]^{-1} \begin{bmatrix} 1 & s(z) \\ 0 & 1 \end{bmatrix}^{-1} = \tilde{P}(z^{-1}) \begin{bmatrix} 1 & 0 \\ -s(z) & 1 \end{bmatrix}. \tag{4.50}$$

Consequently

$$\tilde{P}^{new}(z) = \tilde{P}(z) \begin{bmatrix} 1 & 0 \\ -s(z^{-1}) & 1 \end{bmatrix}. \tag{4.51}$$

Hence, the lifting created a new low-pass filter

$$\tilde{h}^{new}(z) = \tilde{h}(z) - \tilde{g}(z)s(z^{-2}). \tag{4.52}$$

As a result, we have lifted the low-pass subband with the help of the high-pass subband. This is called the *primal lifting*.

4.4.4.2 Dual Lifting By *dual lifting* we mean lifting the high-pass subband with the help the low-pass subband. If (h, g) is complementary, then any other new FIR filter h^{new} complementary to g is of the form

$$h^{new}(z) = h(z) + g(z)t(z^2) \tag{4.53}$$

where $t(z^2)$ is a Laurent polynomial. Following the similar deduction as presented in the primal lifting section, the dual lifting creates a new high-pass filter

$$\tilde{g}^{new}(z) = \tilde{g}(z) - \tilde{h}(z)t(z^{-2}). \tag{4.54}$$

4.4.4.3 Lifting Factorization   In this section, we show how a complementary filter pair for wavelet transformation can be factorized into lifting steps.

We can compute the *greatest common divisor* (*gcd*) of $\tilde{h}_e(z)$ and $\tilde{h}_o(z)$ by applying the Euclidean algorithm as shown in Section 4.4.2. If K is the gcd of $\tilde{h}_e(z)$ and $\tilde{h}_o(z)$, we can express $\tilde{h}_e(z)$ and $\tilde{h}_o(z)$ as follows:

$$
\begin{bmatrix} \tilde{h}_e(z) \\ \tilde{h}_o(z) \end{bmatrix} = \prod_{k=1}^{n} \begin{bmatrix} q_i(z) & 1 \\ 1 & 0 \end{bmatrix} \begin{bmatrix} K \\ 0 \end{bmatrix}. \tag{4.55}
$$

According to the theory of lifting discussed in Section 4.4.4, if $(\tilde{h}, \tilde{g})$ is a complementary filter pair, then we can always find another complementary filter $\tilde{g}^{new}$ so that the polyphase matrix can be represented as

$$
\tilde{P}^{new}(z) = \begin{bmatrix} \tilde{h}_e(z) & \tilde{g}_e^{new} \\ \tilde{h}_o(z) & \tilde{g}_o^{new} \end{bmatrix} = \prod_{k=1}^{n} \begin{bmatrix} q_i(z) & 1 \\ 1 & 0 \end{bmatrix} \begin{bmatrix} K & 0 \\ 0 & 1/K \end{bmatrix}. \tag{4.56}
$$

We can again rewrite Eq. 4.56 as

$$
\tilde{P}^{new}(z) = \prod_{k=1}^{n/2} \begin{bmatrix} q_{2i-1}(z) & 1 \\ 1 & 0 \end{bmatrix} \begin{bmatrix} q_{2i}(z) & 1 \\ 1 & 0 \end{bmatrix} \begin{bmatrix} K & 0 \\ 0 & 1/K \end{bmatrix}. \tag{4.57}
$$

It should be noted that

$$
\begin{bmatrix} q_{2i-1}(z) & 1 \\ 1 & 0 \end{bmatrix} = \begin{bmatrix} 1 & q_{2i-1}(z) \\ 0 & 1 \end{bmatrix} \begin{bmatrix} 0 & 1 \\ 1 & 0 \end{bmatrix} \tag{4.58}
$$

and

$$
\begin{bmatrix} q_{2i}(z) & 1 \\ 1 & 0 \end{bmatrix} = \begin{bmatrix} 0 & 1 \\ 1 & 0 \end{bmatrix} \begin{bmatrix} 1 & 0 \\ q_{2i}(z) & 1 \end{bmatrix}. \tag{4.59}
$$

Applying the rules in Eqs. 4.58 and 4.59 into Eq. 4.57, we can rewrite it as

$$
\tilde{P}^{new}(z) = \prod_{k=1}^{n/2} \begin{bmatrix} 1 & q_{2i-1}(z) \\ 0 & 1 \end{bmatrix} \begin{bmatrix} 1 & 0 \\ q_{2i}(z) & 0 \end{bmatrix} \begin{bmatrix} K & 0 \\ 0 & 1/K \end{bmatrix}. \tag{4.60}
$$

We also know from the lifting formulation that we can always construct filter $\tilde{g}$ by lifting $\tilde{g}^{new}$ as

$$
\tilde{P}(z) = \tilde{P}^{new}(z) \begin{bmatrix} 1 & \tilde{s}(z) \\ 0 & 1 \end{bmatrix}. \tag{4.61}
$$

By combining all of the above formulations, we can conclude that given a complementary filter pair $(\tilde{h}, \tilde{g})$, there always exist Laurent polynomials $\tilde{s}_i(z)$ and $\tilde{t}_i(z)$ for $1 \le i \le n$ and we can factorize the polyphase matrix $\tilde{P}(z)$ into a finite sequence of alternating upper and lower triangular matrices as follows,

$$\tilde{P}(z) = \left\{ \prod_{i=1}^{m} \begin{bmatrix} 1 & \tilde{s}_i(z) \\ 0 & 1 \end{bmatrix} \begin{bmatrix} 1 & 0 \\ \tilde{t}_i(z) & 1 \end{bmatrix} \right\} \begin{bmatrix} K & 0 \\ 0 & 1/K \end{bmatrix} \qquad (4.62)$$

where K is a constant and acts as a scaling factor (so is $\frac{1}{K}$). In practice, $\tilde{s}_i(z)$ and $\tilde{t}_i(z)$ are usually of second- or lower-order polynomials, which correspond to usually one- to three-tap FIR filters. Computing the upper triangular matrix is known as *primal lifting*, and this is emphasized in the literature as lifting the low-pass subband with the help of the high-pass subband. Similarly, computation of the lower triangular matrix is called *dual lifting*, which is lifting of the high-pass subband with the help of the low-pass subband [13, 14]. Often these two basic lifting steps are called *update* and *predict* as well. The above factorization can also be formulated in the following way:

$$\tilde{P}(z) = \left\{ \prod_{i=1}^{m} \begin{bmatrix} 1 & 0 \\ \tilde{t}_i(z) & 1 \end{bmatrix} \begin{bmatrix} 1 & \tilde{s}_i(z) \\ 0 & 1 \end{bmatrix} \right\} \begin{bmatrix} K & 0 \\ 0 & 1/K \end{bmatrix}. \qquad (4.63)$$

4.4.4.4 *Lifting Algorithm*   Hence the lifting-based forward wavelet transform essentially means first applying the *lazy* wavelet transform on the input stream (split into even and odd samples), then alternately executing *primal* and *dual* lifting steps, and finally *scaling* the two output streams by $\frac{1}{K}$ and K respectively to produce low-pass and high-pass subbands, as shown in Figure 4.7(a). The inverse DWT using lifting can be derived by traversing the above steps in the reverse direction, first scaling the low-pass and high-pass subband inputs by K and $1/K$ respectively, and then applying the dual and primal lifting steps after reversing the signs of the coefficients in $\tilde{t}(z)$ and $\tilde{s}(z)$, and finally the inverse lazy transform by upscaling the output before merging them into a single reconstructed stream as shown in Figure 4.7(b).

Due to the linearity of the lifting scheme, if the input data are in integer format, it is possible to maintain data in integer format throughout the transform by introducing a rounding function in the filtering operation. Due to this property, the transform is reversible (i.e., lossless) and is called *integer wavelet transform* (IWT) [15, 16, 17]. It should be noted that filter coefficients need not be integers for IWT. However, if a scaling step is present in the factorization, IWT cannot be achieved. It has been proposed in [17] to split the scaling step into additional lifting steps to achieve IWT.

4.4.4.5 *Example*   Consider the Le Gall (5,3) spline filter [15] that has been used in the JPEG2000 standard, with $\tilde{h} = (-\frac{1}{8}, \frac{1}{4}, \frac{3}{4}, \frac{1}{4}, -\frac{1}{8})$ and $\tilde{g} = (-\frac{1}{2}, 1, -\frac{1}{2})$. Hence,

$$\tilde{h}(z) = -\tfrac{1}{8}z^{-2} + \tfrac{1}{4}z^{-1} + \tfrac{3}{4}z^{0} + \tfrac{1}{4}z - \tfrac{1}{8}z^{2},$$
$$\tilde{g}(z) = -\tfrac{1}{2}z^{-2} + z^{-1} - \tfrac{1}{2}z^{0}.$$

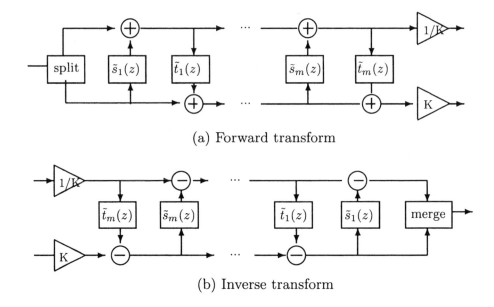

(a) Forward transform

(b) Inverse transform

Fig. 4.7 Lifting-based forward and inverse DWT.

From the above equations, we can easily derive that

$$\tilde{h}_e(z^2) = -\tfrac{1}{8}z^{-2} + \tfrac{3}{4} - \tfrac{1}{8}z^2, \quad \tilde{h}_o(z^2) = \tfrac{1}{4} + \tfrac{1}{4}z^2,$$
$$\tilde{g}_e(z^2) = -\tfrac{1}{2}z^{-2} - \tfrac{1}{2}, \qquad \tilde{g}_o(z^2) = 1.$$

As a result, the polyphase matrix of this filter bank is

$$\tilde{P}(z) = \begin{bmatrix} \tilde{h}_e(z) & \tilde{h}_o(z) \\ \tilde{g}_e(z) & \tilde{g}_o(z) \end{bmatrix} = \begin{bmatrix} -\tfrac{1}{8}z^{-1} + \tfrac{3}{4} - \tfrac{1}{8}z & \tfrac{1}{4} + \tfrac{1}{4}z \\ -\tfrac{1}{2}z^{-1} - \tfrac{1}{2} & 1 \end{bmatrix}.$$

Also based on conditions of perfect reconstructions of the complementary filters as described in Eq. 4.31, we can derive the corresponding synthesis filters as follows:

$$h(z) = -z^{-1}\tilde{g}(-z^{-1}) = \tfrac{1}{2}z^{-1} + 1 + \tfrac{1}{2}z,$$
$$g(z) = z^{-1}\tilde{h}(-z^{-1}) = -\tfrac{1}{8}z^{-3} - \tfrac{1}{4}z^{-2} + \tfrac{3}{4}z^{-1} - \tfrac{1}{4} - \tfrac{1}{8}z$$

and hence $h = (\tfrac{1}{2}, 1, \tfrac{1}{2})$ and $g = (-\tfrac{1}{8}, -\tfrac{1}{4}, \tfrac{3}{4}, -\tfrac{1}{4}, -\tfrac{1}{8})$.
    Now based on the lifting scheme for factorization of the polyphase matrix, the possible factorization of $\tilde{P}(z)$ that leads to a band matrix multiplication is

$$\tilde{P}(z) = \begin{bmatrix} 1 & \tfrac{1}{4}(1+z) \\ 0 & 1 \end{bmatrix} \begin{bmatrix} 1 & 0 \\ -\tfrac{1}{2}(1+z^{-1}) & 1 \end{bmatrix}.$$

If the samples are numbered starting from 0, we consider the even terms of the output stream as the samples of low-pass subband and similarly the odd terms as the samples of high-pass subband. Accordingly, we can interpret the above matrices in the time domain as $y_{2i+1} = -\frac{1}{2}(x_{2i} + x_{2i+2}) + x_{2i+1}$ and $y_{2i} = \frac{1}{4}(y_{2i+1} + y_{2i+3}) + x_{2i}$ where $0 \leq i \leq \frac{N}{2}$ for an input stream x of length N and y's are the transformed signal values. Note that the odd samples are calculated from even samples and even samples are calculated from the updated odd samples. The corresponding matrices M_1 and M_2 are shown below, where $a = -\frac{1}{2}$ and $b = \frac{1}{4}$. The transform of the signal X is $Y = X M_1 M_2$ while the inverse is $X = Y M_2 M_1$:

$$
M_1 =
\begin{bmatrix}
1 & a & 0 & . & . & . & . & . & . \\
0 & 1 & 0 & 0 & . & . & . & . & . \\
0 & a & 1 & a & 0 & . & . & . & . \\
. & 0 & 0 & 1 & 0 & 0 & . & . & . \\
. & . & 0 & a & 1 & a & 0 & . & . \\
. & . & . & 0 & 0 & 1 & 0 & 0 & . \\
. & . & . & . & 0 & a & 1 & a & 0 \\
. & . & . & . & 0 & 0 & 1 & 0 \\
0 & . & . & . & . & 0 & a & 1
\end{bmatrix}
, \quad
M_2 =
\begin{bmatrix}
1 & 0 & 0 & . & . & . & . & . \\
0 & 1 & b & 0 & . & . & . & . \\
0 & 0 & 1 & 0 & 0 & . & . & . \\
. & 0 & b & 1 & b & 0 & . & . \\
. & . & 0 & 0 & 1 & 0 & 0 & . \\
. & . & . & 0 & b & 1 & b & 0 & . \\
. & . & . & . & 0 & 0 & 1 & 0 & 0 \\
. & . & . & . & . & 0 & b & 1 & 0 \\
0 & . & . & . & . & 0 & 0 & 1
\end{bmatrix}
$$

The other wavelet filter bank that has been proposed in JPEG2000 Part 1 is the (9, 7) filter. The most efficient factorization of the polyphase matrix for (9, 7) filter is as follows [14];

$$
\tilde{P}(z) =
\begin{bmatrix} 1 & a(1 + z^{-1}) \\ 0 & 1 \end{bmatrix}
\begin{bmatrix} 1 & 0 \\ b(1 + z) & 1 \end{bmatrix}
\begin{bmatrix} 1 & c(1 + z^{-1}) \\ 0 & 1 \end{bmatrix}
\begin{bmatrix} 1 & 0 \\ d(1 + z) & 1 \end{bmatrix}
\begin{bmatrix} K & 0 \\ 0 & \frac{1}{K} \end{bmatrix}
$$

where a=−1.586134342, b=−0.0529801185, c=0.882911076, d=−0.443506852, K=1.149604398. In terms of banded matrix operation, the transform can be represented as $Y = X M_1 M_2 M_3 M_4$, while the inverse transform is represented as $X = Y M_4 M_3 M_2 M_1$. The matrices M_1, M_2, M_3, and M_4 are as follows:

$$
M_1 =
\begin{bmatrix}
1 & a & 0 & . & . & . & . & . \\
0 & 1 & 0 & 0 & . & . & . & . \\
0 & a & 1 & a & 0 & . & . & . \\
. & 0 & 0 & 1 & 0 & 0 & . & . \\
. & . & 0 & a & 1 & a & 0 & . \\
. & . & . & 0 & 0 & 1 & 0 & 0 & . \\
. & . & . & . & 0 & a & 1 & a & 0 \\
. & . & . & . & 0 & 0 & 1 & 0 \\
0 & . & . & . & . & 0 & a & 1
\end{bmatrix}
, \quad
M_2 =
\begin{bmatrix}
1 & 0 & 0 & . & . & . & . & . \\
0 & 1 & b & 0 & . & . & . & . \\
0 & 0 & 1 & 0 & 0 & . & . & . \\
. & 0 & b & 1 & b & 0 & . & . \\
. & . & 0 & 0 & 1 & 0 & 0 & . \\
. & . & . & 0 & b & 1 & b & 0 & . \\
. & . & . & . & 0 & 0 & 1 & 0 & 0 \\
. & . & . & . & . & 0 & b & 1 & 0 \\
0 & . & . & . & . & 0 & 0 & 1
\end{bmatrix}
$$

$$
M_3 =
\begin{bmatrix}
1 & c & 0 & . & . & . & . & . \\
0 & 1 & 0 & 0 & . & . & . & . \\
0 & c & 1 & c & 0 & . & . & . \\
. & 0 & 0 & 1 & 0 & 0 & . & . \\
. & . & 0 & c & 1 & c & 0 & . \\
. & . & . & 0 & 0 & 1 & 0 & 0 & . \\
. & . & . & . & 0 & c & 1 & c & 0 \\
. & . & . & . & 0 & 0 & 1 & 0 \\
0 & . & . & . & . & 0 & c & 1
\end{bmatrix}
, \quad
M_4 =
\begin{bmatrix}
1 & 0 & 0 & . & . & . & . & . \\
0 & 1 & d & 0 & . & . & . & . \\
0 & 0 & 1 & 0 & 0 & . & . & . \\
. & 0 & d & 1 & d & 0 & . & . \\
. & . & 0 & 0 & 1 & 0 & 0 & . \\
. & . & . & 0 & d & 1 & d & 0 & . \\
. & . & . & . & 0 & 0 & 1 & 0 & 0 \\
. & . & . & . & . & 0 & d & 1 & 0 \\
0 & . & . & . & . & 0 & 0 & 1
\end{bmatrix}
$$

Most of the practical wavelet filters are decomposed either into 2 or 4 matrices (primal and dual). For example, each of the filter banks C(13, 7), S(13, 7), (2,6), (2, 10) can be decomposed into 2 matrices and (6, 10) can be decomposed in 4 matrices, as has been described in detail in [18].

4.4.5   Data Dependency Diagram for Lifting Computation

Computation of the lifting-based discrete wavelet transform can be explained via a data dependency diagram as shown by a block diagram in Figure 4.8. For the DWT requiring four lifting factors, such as the (9, 7) filter, the computation is done in four stages as shown in Figure 4.8. For the DWT filters requiring only two lifting factors, such as the (5, 3) filter, the intermediate two stages can simply be bypassed.

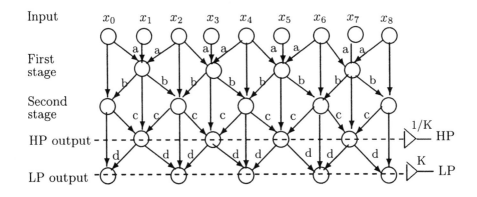

Fig. 4.8 Data dependency diagram with four lifting factors.

The results produced in the first stage of the data dependency diagram can be stored immediately in the registers containing the odd samples of the input data because these odd samples are not used in later stages of computation. Similarly the results produced in the second stage can be stored back to the registers allocated to the even samples of input data. Continuing in the same way, the high-pass (low-pass) output samples are stored into the registers where the odd (even) samples of the input data were originally stored at the beginning of the computation. As a result no extra memory is required at any stage. This property of lifting is popularly called "in-place" computation in the literature.

4.5   WHY DO WE CARE ABOUT LIFTING?

The idea of lifting-based implementation of discrete wavelet transform is a relatively recent development and it is still an active area of research in mathematics and signal processing. The lifting-based DWT has many advantages over the convolution-based approach. Some of them are as follows.

- *Computational efficiency*: Usually the Lifting-based DWT requires less computation (up to 50%) compared to the convolution-based approach. However, the savings depend on the length of the filters.

- *Memory savings*: During the lifting implementation, no extra memory buffer is required because of the in-place computation feature of lifting. This is particularly suitable for hardware implementation with limited available on-chip memory.

- *Integer-to-integer transform*: The lifting-based approach offers integer-to-integer transformation suitable for lossless image compression.

- *No boundary extension*: In lossless transformation mode, we can avoid the boundary extension (discussed in Section 6.6.1.3 of Chapter 6) of the input data because the original input can be exactly reconstructed by integer-to-integer lifting transformation.

- *Parallel processing*: From Figure 4.8, it is obvious that multiple MAC (*multiply* and *accumulate*) processors can produce the output samples in each stage in parallel. The computation of each MAC processor is of the form $a(x_i + x_{i+2}) + x_{i+1}$. Only sequential part is the order of the lifting operations.

4.6   SUMMARY

In this chapter we discussed the theoretical foundation of the discrete wavelet transform (DWT) both for convolution and lifting-based approaches. We discussed the multiresolution analysis feature of the wavelet transform, which makes it suitable for its application in image compression. We have discussed the pyramid algorithm for implementation of the DWT using the multiresolution approach. We have also discussed how the DWT is extended to two-dimensional signals as well. The multiresolution analysis-based discrete wavelet transform is the foundation of the new JPEG2000 standard. Lifting-based implementation of discrete wavelet transform is new and became very popular for a number of efficient features in it. We described the underlying theory behind the lifting algorithm for DWT and showed how it is implemented via banded matrix multiplication. We gave examples of the lifting factorization for the two default wavelet filter kernels (9, 7) and (5, 3) in the

JPEG2000 standard. We discussed the advantages of lifting-based DWT over the traditional convolution-based approach.

REFERENCES

1. K. Weierstrass, *Mathematische Werke,* Vol. II. Mayer & Muller, Berlin, 1895.

2. N. Ricker, "The Form and Nature of Seismic Waves and the Structure of Seismograms," *Geophysics,* Vol. 5, No. 4, pp. 348–366, October 1940.

3. J. Morlet, G. Arens, E. Fourgeau, and D. Giard, "Wave Propagation and Sampling Theory," *Geophysics,* Vol. 47, No. 2, pp. 203–236, February 1982.

4. A. Grossman and J. Morlet, "Decompositions of Hardy Functions into Square Integrable Wavelets of Constant Shape," *SIAM Journal of Mathematical Analysis,* Vol. 15, No. 4, pp. 723–736, July 1984.

5. A. Grossman and J. Morlet, "Decompositions of Functions into Wavelets of Constant Shape, and Related Transforms," in L. Streit, ed., *Mathematics and Physics: Lectures on Recent Results,* World Scientific, Singapore, 1985.

6. S. Mallat, "A Theory for Multiresolution Signal Decomposition: The Wavelet Representation," *IEEE Trans. on Pattern Analysis and Machine Intelligence,* Vol. 11, No. 7, pp. 674–693, July 1989.

7. Y. Meyers, *Wavelet: Algorithms and Applications.* SIAM, Philadelphia, 1993 (Translated by Robert D. Ryan).

8. JPEG2000 Final Committee Draft (FCD), "JPEG2000 Committee Drafts," http://www.jpeg.org/CDs15444.htm.

9. I. Daubechies, "The Wavelet Transform, Time-Frequency Localization and Signal Analysis," *IEEE Trans. on Inform. Theory,* Vol. 36, No. 5, pp. 961–1005, September 1990.

10. I. Daubechies, *Ten Lectures on Wavelets.* SIAM, CBMS series, Philadelphia, 1992.

11. R. M. Rao and A. S. Bopardikar, *Wavelet Transforms: Introduction to Theory and Applications.* Addison-Wesley, MA, 1998.

12. M. Antonini, M. Barlaud, P. Mathieu, and I. Daubechies, "Image Coding Using Wavelet Transform," *IEEE Trans. on Image Processing,* Vol. 1, No. 2, pp. 205–220, April 1992.

13. W. Sweldens, "The Lifting Scheme: A Custom-Design Construction of Biorthogonal Wavelets," *Applied and Computational Harmonic Analysis*, Vol. 3, No. 15, pp. 186–200, 1996.

14. I. Daubechies and W. Sweldens, "Factoring Wavelet Transforms into Lifting Schemes," *The J. of Fourier Analysis and Applications*, Vol. 4, pp. 247–269, 1998.

15. D. L. Gall and A. Tabatabai, "Subband Coding of Digital Images Using Symmetric Short Kernel Filters and Arithmetic Coding Techniques," *Proc. of IEEE Intl. Conf. Acoustics, Speech, and Signal Processing*, Vol. 2, pp. 761–764, New York, April 1988.

16. A. R. Calderbank, I. Daubechies, W. Sweldens, and B.-L. Yeo, "Wavelet Transforms that Map Integers to Integers," *Applied and Computational Harmonic Analysis*, Vol. 5, pp. 332–369, July, 1998.

17. M. D. Adams and F. Kossentini, "Reversible Integer-to-Integer Wavelet Transforms for Image Compression: Performance Evaluation and Analysis," *IEEE Trans. on Image Processing*, Vol. 9, pp. 1010–1024, June 2000.

18. K. Andra, C. Chakrabarti, and T. Acharya, "A VLSI Architecture for Lifting-Based Forward and Inverse Wavelet Transform," *IEEE Trans. of Signal Processing*, Vol. 50, No. 4, pp. 966–977, April 2002.

5

VLSI Architectures for Discrete Wavelet Transforms

5.1 INTRODUCTION

Discrete wavelet transform (DWT) is an efficient digital signal processing (DSP) tool and has been very successfully used for development of image and video compression algorithms [1, 2, 3, 4]. DWT has been found to be a versatile tool for many other image processing applications such as edge detection, object isolation, object detection [5, 6], denoising, speckle removal [7, 8], image editing [9], image fusion [10], etc. Because of these wide-spread application of DWT, development of VLSI algorithms and architectures for efficient hardware implementation of discrete wavelet transform has been an active area of research and development in the VLSI signal processing community for the last few years. The JPEG2000 standard for still image compression has been developed based on the salient features of discrete wavelet transforms [4]. Discrete wavelet transform is usually computed on a whole image (or very large tiles of images) as opposed to small-size blocks by traditional block-based transformation techniques such as *discrete cosine transform* (DCT). As a result, discrete wavelet transform is a computationally intensive process and hence very slow when computed by a general-purpose computing system, even for moderate-size images compared to the traditional block-based transformation techniques. Obviously, the memory requirement for its implementation is also very high. To make it suitable for real-time image processing applications, it is essential to develop special-purpose architectures and custom VLSI chips for computation of DWT by exploiting the underlying data parallelism to yield high throughput and hence high data rate. We discussed the principles and formulation of discrete wavelet transforms in greater detail in Chapter 4. In this chapter, we only concentrate on some VLSI architectures and algorithms reported in the literature for implementation of discrete wavelet transform.

The discrete wavelet transform (DWT) essentially decomposes an arbitrary discrete signal $\mathbf{x}=\{x_0, x_1,\ldots, x_{N-1}\}$ into two subbands—a low-pass subband $\mathbf{a}=\{a_0, a_1,\ldots, a_{\frac{N}{2}-1}\}$ and a high-pass subband $\mathbf{c}=\{c_0, c_1,\ldots, c_{\frac{N}{2}-1}\}$. The arithmetic computation of this transformation can be represented as

$$a_n = \sum_k h_{2n-k}x_k , \qquad c_n = \sum_k g_{2n-k}x_k \qquad (5.1)$$

where h_i and g_i are the low-pass and high-pass filter coefficients respectively. As mathematically shown in Eq. 5.1, the straightforward and traditional implementation of DWT is to apply two finite impulse response filters (FIR) in parallel—one a high-pass filter (g) and the other a low-pass filter (h). These two filtered outputs are then subsampled to produce two subbands $\mathbf{a}$ and $\mathbf{c}$ as shown in Figure 5.1. This is called the convolution-based approach. The signal reconstruction process is just the opposite where the subands are first upsampled and then filtered by a corresponding low-pass filter $(\tilde{h})$ and a high-pass filter $(\tilde{g})$ to generate x_L and x_H respectively. These two outputs (x_L and x_H) are then added to reconstruct the signal (x'), as shown in Figure 5.1.

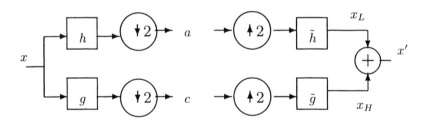

Fig. 5.1 Decomposition and reconstruction of signals in DWT.

The other computationally efficient approach for DWT is to apply the lifting-based approach [11, 12, 13, 14]. The main feature of the lifting-based discrete wavelet transform is to break up the high-pass and the low-pass wavelet filters into a sequence of smaller filters that in turn can be converted into a sequence of upper and lower triangular matrices. These upper and lower triangular matrices represent the lifting factors. We described principles behind lifting-based DWT formulation and its implementation in greater detail in Chapter 4. Many VLSI architectures for implementation of DWT using the convolution-based approach have been proposed in the literature [15, 16, 17, 18, 19, 20, 21, 22, 23, 24]. On the other hand, fewer architectures for implementation of the lifting-based DWT have been reported in the literature [25, 26, 27, 28, 29, 30, 31, 32, 33, 34, 35, 36, 37, 38].

In this chapter, we briefly present a VLSI architecture for implementation of DWT using the traditional convolution approach. Because of the inherent advantages of the lifting-based approach over the traditional convolution approach for implementation of DWT and its suitability for JPEG2000, we emphasize more the lifting architectures for DWT computation and review different types of architectures reported in the literature recently.

5.2   A VLSI ARCHITECTURE FOR THE CONVOLUTION APPROACH

In this section, we describe a semi-systolic architecture for implementation of the convolution-based discrete wavelet transform proposed by Acharya and Chen [23]. Although the basic principle of the architecture can be applied to implement any symmetric filter, we use the $(9, 7)$ wavelet filter here as an example. The $(9, 7)$ filter has been recommended for implementation of DWT in the JPEG2000 standard for its lossy mode of image compression. This $(9, 7)$ filter has 9 low-pass filter coefficients $h = \{h_{-4}, h_{-3}, h_{-2}, h_{-1}, h_0, h_1, h_2, h_3, h_4\}$ and 7 high-pass filter coefficients $g = \{g_{-2}, g_{-1}, g_0, g_1, g_2, g_3, g_4\}$. Output samples of the low-pass subband are as follows:

$$
\begin{aligned}
a_0 &= h_0 x_0 + h_{-1} x_1 + h_{-2} x_2 + h_{-3} x_3 + h_{-4} x_4 \\
a_1 &= h_2 x_0 + h_1 x_1 + h_0 x_2 + h_{-1} x_3 + h_{-2} x_4 + h_{-3} x_5 + h_{-4} x_6 \\
a_2 &= h_4 x_0 + h_3 x_1 + h_2 x_2 + h_1 x_3 + h_0 x_4 + h_{-1} x_5 + h_{-2} x_6 + \\
     & \quad h_{-3} x_7 + h_{-4} x_8 \\
     & \qquad\qquad \vdots \\
a_{\frac{N}{2}-2} &= h_4 x_{N-8} + h_3 x_{N-7} + h_2 x_{N-6} + h_1 x_{N-5} + h_0 x_{N-4} + \\
     & \quad h_{-1} x_{N-3} + h_{-2} x_{N-2} + h_{-3} x_{N-1} \\
a_{\frac{N}{2}-1} &= h_4 x_{N-6} + h_3 x_{N-5} + h_2 x_{N-4} + h_1 x_{N-3} + h_0 x_{N-2} + \\
     & \quad h_{-1} x_{N-1}.
\end{aligned}
$$

$$(5.2)$$

Since the low-pass filter coefficients are symmetric (i.e., $h_{-i} = h_i$), the above equations can be rearranged in a regular fashion as shown below, which is suitable for mapping them in a systolic-like (semi-systolic) architecture:

$$
\begin{aligned}
a_0 &= h_0(0 + x_0) + h_1(0 + x_1) + h_2(0 + x_2) + h_3(0 + x_3) + h_4(0 + x_4) \\
a_1 &= h_0(0 + x_2) + h_1(x_1 + x_3) + h_2(x_0 + x_4) + h_3(0 + x_5) + h_4(0 + x_6) \\
a_2 &= h_0(0 + x_4) + h_1(x_3 + x_5) + h_2(x_2 + x_6) + h_3(x_1 + x_7) + h_4(x_0 + x_8) \\
    & \qquad\qquad \vdots \\
a_{\frac{N}{2}-2} &= h_0(x_{N-4} + 0) + h_{-1}(x_{N-5} + x_{N-3}) + h_{-2}(x_{N-6} + x_{N-2}) + \\
    & \quad h_3(x_{N-7} + x_{N-1}) + h_4(x_{N-8} + 0) \\
a_{\frac{N}{2}-1} &= h_0(x_{N-2} + 0) + h_1(x_{N-3} + x_{N-1}) + h_2(x_{N-4} + 0) + h_3(x_{N-5} + 0) + \\
    & \quad h_4(x_{N-6} + 0).
\end{aligned}
$$

$$(5.3)$$

Similarly, the high-pass subband samples c_n, for $n = 0, 1, \cdots, \frac{N}{2} - 1$ are expressed as

$$
\begin{aligned}
c_0 &= g_0 x_0 + g_{-1} x_1 + g_{-2} x_2 \\
c_1 &= g_2 x_0 + g_1 x_1 + g_0 x_2 + g_{-1} x_3 + g_{-2} x_4 \\
c_2 &= g_4 x_0 + g_3 x_1 + g_2 x_2 + g_1 x_3 + g_0 x_4 + g_{-1} x_5 + g_{-2} x_6 \\
&\qquad\qquad \vdots \\
c_{\frac{N}{2}-2} &= g_4 x_{N-8} + g_3 x_{N-7} + g_2 x_{N-6} + g_1 x_{N-5} + g_0 x_{N-4} + g_{-1} x_{N-3} + \\
&\qquad g_{-2} x_{N-2} \\
c_{\frac{N}{2}-1} &= g_4 x_{N-6} + g_3 x_{N-5} + g_2 x_{N-4} + g_1 x_{N-3} + g_0 x_{N-2} + g_{-1} x_{N-1}.
\end{aligned}
$$

$$(5.4)$$

The (9, 7) filters are perfect reconstruction filters and follow the principles of perfect reconstruction as described in Chapter 4. According to the condition for perfect reconstruction, the high-pass filter coefficients in the (9, 7) biorthogonal spline filter are related with the synthesis (inverse) filters as $g_i = (-1)^i \tilde{h}_{1-i}$ and $\tilde{h}_{-i} = \tilde{h}_i$, where $\tilde{h} = \{\tilde{h}_{-3}, \tilde{h}_{-2}, \tilde{h}_{-1}, \tilde{h}_0, \tilde{h}_{-1}, \tilde{h}_{-2}, \tilde{h}_{-3}\}$ are the 7 low-pass filter coefficients used for reconstruction of the signal during the synthesis (inverse DWT) process. Accordingly, we can exploit the symmetry among the filter coefficients as follows:

$$
\begin{aligned}
g_{-2} &= \tilde{h}_3 = g_4, \\
g_{-1} &= \tilde{h}_2 = g_3, \\
g_0 &= \tilde{h}_1 = g_2, \\
g_1 &= \tilde{h}_0.
\end{aligned}
$$

As a result, we can rearrange the c_i terms in a regular fashion as shown below:

$$
\begin{aligned}
c_0 &= g_1(0+0) + g_2(0+x_0) + g_3(0+x_1) + g_4(0+x_2) \\
c_1 &= g_1(0+x_1) + g_2(x_0+x_2) + g_3(0+x_3) + g_4(0+x_4) \\
c_2 &= g_1(0+x_3) + g_2(x_2+x_4) + g_3(x_1+x_5) + g_4(x_0+x_6) \\
&\qquad\qquad \vdots \\
c_{\frac{N}{2}-2} &= g_1(0+x_{N-5}) + g_2(x_{N-6}+x_{N-4}) + g_3(x_{N-7}+x_{N-3}) + \\
&\qquad g_4(x_{N-8}+x_{N-2}) \\
c_{\frac{N}{2}-1} &= g_1(0+x_{N-3}) + g_2(x_{N-4}+x_{N-2}) + g_3(x_{N-5}+x_{N-1}) + \\
&\qquad g_4(x_{N-6}+0).
\end{aligned}
$$

$$(5.5)$$

5.2.1 Mapping the DWT in a Semi-Systolic Architecture

The regularity in the expressions for each a_i and c_i, as presented in Eqs. 5.3 and 5.5, is very much suitable for mapping them into a systolic-like (semi-systolic) algorithm for implementation of a VLSI architecture as proposed by Acharya and Chen [23]. The architecture to compute the a_i's and c_i's is shown in Figure 5.2(a).

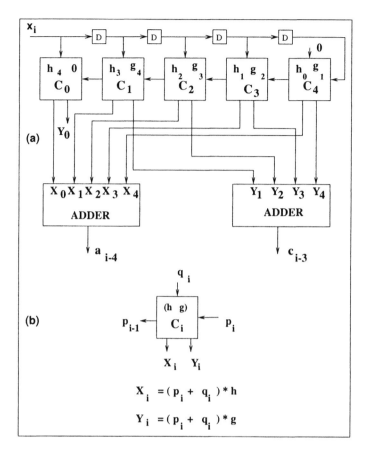

Fig. 5.2 (a) A semi-systolic architecture for computing one-dimensional DWT; (b) the basic processing element.

Functionality of each basic cell or the processing element C_i in the systolic array is shown in Figure 5.2(b). Each C_i has two inputs p_i and q_i and three outputs p_{i-1}, X_i and Y_i. There are two registers in each C_i which contain a low-pass filter coefficient h and a high-pass filter coefficient g during the forward DWT mode as shown in Figure 5.2(b). For example, filter coefficients h_2 and g_3 are stored in the two registers in the processing element C_2. Similarly, the content of the registers in the processing elements C_0, C_1, C_3, and C_4 are $(h_4, 0)$, (h_3, g_4), (h_1, g_2) and (h_0, g_1) respectively. Each processing element essentially adds the two inputs p_i and q_i. The sum $p_i + q_i$ is then multiplied by the corresponding low-pass filter coefficient h and the high-pass filter coefficient g to produce the two output samples X_i and Y_i respectively. The input p_i is simply passed through to output p_{i-1}. As a result, the output p_{i-1} from a processing element C_i becomes an input to the adjacent processing element C_{i-1}. Interconnection of the processing elements $C_0, \cdots, C_4$ is shown in Figure 5.2(a), where each $\mathbf{D}$ represents a delay element. Finally, $X_0, \cdots, X_4$ are added to produce an output sample a_i and $Y_1, \cdots, Y_4$ are added to produce an output c_i. The first three clock cycles are required to initially fill up the systolic array. The outputs c_i and a_i are obtained alternately at the trailing edges of the even and odd clock cycles (e.g., $c_0, c_1, c_2, \cdots$ are obtained at clock cycles $4, 6, 8, \cdots$ and $a_0, a_1, a_2, \cdots$ are obtained at clock cycles $5, 7, 9, \cdots$ respectively). As a result, one output is produced in every clock cycle and hence the architecture achieves 100% utilization.

Table 5.1 Output X_i from Processing Element C_i of the DWT Architecture in Figure 5.2 for the First 8 Clock Cycles

Clock Cycle	X_0	X_1	X_2	X_3	X_4
1	$h_4 x_0$	0	0	0	0
2	$h_4 x_1$	$h_3 x_0$	0	0	0
3	$h_4 x_2$	$h_3 x_1$	$h_2 x_0$	0	0
4	$h_4 x_3$	$h_3 x_2$	$h_2 x_1$	$h_1 x_0$	0
5	$h_4 x_4$	$h_3 x_3$	$h_2 x_2$	$h_1 x_1$	$h_0 x_0$
6	$h_4 x_5$	$h_3 x_4$	$h_2 x_3$	$h_1(x_2 + x_0)$	$h_0 x_1$
7	$h_4 x_6$	$h_3 x_5$	$h_2(x_4 + x_0)$	$h_1(x_3 + x_1)$	$h_0 x_2$
8	$h_4 x_7$	$h_3(x_6 + x_0)$	$h_2(x_5 + x_1)$	$h_1(x_4 + x_2)$	$h_0 x_3$

Table 5.2 Output Y_i from Processing Element C_i of the DWT Architecture in Figure 5.2 for the First 8 Clock Cycles

Clock Cycle	Y_0	Y_1	Y_2	Y_3	Y_4
1	0	0	0	0	0
2	0	$g_4 x_0$	0	0	0
3	0	$g_4 x_1$	$g_3 x_0$	0	0
4	0	$g_4 x_2$	$g_3 x_1$	$g_2 x_0$	0
5	0	$g_4 x_3$	$g_3 x_2$	$g_2 x_1$	$g_1 x_0$
6	0	$g_4 x_4$	$g_3 x_3$	$g_2(x_2 + x_0)$	$g_1 x_1$
7	0	$g_4 x_5$	$g_3(x_4 + x_0)$	$g_2(x_3 + x_1)$	$g_1 x_2$
8	0	$g_4(x_6 + x_0)$	$g_3(x_5 + x_1)$	$g_2(x_4 + x_2)$	$g_1 x_3$

In Tables 5.1 and 5.2, we show the outputs X_i and Y_i respectively from each processing element C_i for the first 8 clock cycles.

5.2.2 Mapping the Inverse DWT in a Semi-Systolic Architecture

During the inverse process, reconstruction of the original signal $\mathbf{x} = \{x_0, x_1, \ldots, x_{N-1}\}$ from the low-frequency subband $\mathbf{a} = \{a_0, a_1, \ldots, a_{\frac{N}{2}-1}\}$ and the high-frequency subband $\mathbf{c}=\{c_0, c_1, \ldots, c_{\frac{N}{2}-1}\}$ by the inverse discrete wavelet transform (IDWT) is expressed as

$$x_i = \sum_n [\tilde{h}_{2n-i}a_n + \tilde{g}_{2n-i}c_n] = \sum_n \tilde{h}_{2n-i}a_n + \sum_n \tilde{g}_{2n-i}c_n,$$

where $\tilde{g}_n = (-1)^n h_{1-n}$ and $g_n = (-1)^n \tilde{h}_{1-n}$ has been imposed to have exact reconstruction of the original signal $\mathbf{x} = \{x_0, x_1, \ldots, x_{N-1}\}$, that is, the filter coefficients $\tilde{g}$ and $\tilde{h}$ during the reconstruction process (IDWT) are not exactly the same as the filter coefficients g and h in the decomposition process (DWT). We can break the reconstruction of the original signal $\mathbf{x}$ into two steps. For example, we can express the ith sample x_i of $\mathbf{x}$ as $x_i = x_i^{(1)} + x_i^{(2)}$, where

$$x_i^{(1)} = \sum_n \tilde{h}_{2n-i}a_n, \qquad x_i^{(2)} = \sum_n \tilde{g}_{2n-i}c_n.$$

Again, the even and odd terms of both $x_i^{(1)}$ and $x_i^{(2)}$ can be separated and represented in a regular structure. For example, we can easily express the even terms $x_{2j}^{(1)}$ and $x_{2j}^{(2)}$, for $j = 0, 1, \cdots, \frac{N}{2} - 1$ using the coefficients $\tilde{g}$ and $\tilde{h}$ as

$$
\begin{aligned}
x_0^{(1)} &= \tilde{h}_0 a_0 + \tilde{h}_2 a_1, & x_0^{(2)} &= \tilde{g}_0 c_0 + \tilde{g}_2 c_1 + \tilde{g}_4 c_2, \\
x_2^{(1)} &= \tilde{h}_{-2} a_0 + \tilde{h}_0 a_1 + \tilde{h}_2 a_2, & x_2^{(2)} &= \tilde{g}_{-2} c_0 + \tilde{g}_0 c_1 + \tilde{g}_2 c_2 + \tilde{g}_4 c_3, \\
x_4^{(1)} &= \tilde{h}_{-2} a_1 + \tilde{h}_0 a_2 + \tilde{h}_2 a_3, & x_4^{(2)} &= \tilde{g}_{-2} c_1 + \tilde{g}_0 c_2 + \tilde{g}_2 c_3 + \tilde{g}_4 c_4,
\end{aligned}
$$

$$\vdots \qquad\qquad\qquad \vdots$$

$$
\begin{aligned}
x_{N-4}^{(1)} &= \tilde{h}_{-2} a_{\frac{N}{2}-3} + \tilde{h}_0 a_{\frac{N}{2}-2} + \tilde{h}_2 a_{\frac{N}{2}-1}, & x_{N-4}^{(2)} &= \tilde{g}_{-2} c_{\frac{N}{2}-3} + \tilde{g}_0 c_{\frac{N}{2}-2} + \tilde{g}_2 c_{\frac{N}{2}-1}, \\
x_{N-2}^{(1)} &= \tilde{h}_{-2} a_{\frac{N}{2}-2} + \tilde{h}_0 a_{\frac{N}{2}-1}, & x_{N-2}^{(2)} &= \tilde{g}_{-2} c_{\frac{N}{2}-2} + \tilde{g}_0 c_{\frac{N}{2}-1}.
\end{aligned}
$$

Since, $\tilde{g}_n = (-1)^n h_{1-n}$ and $\tilde{h}_n = \tilde{h}_{-n}$, we can exploit the symmetry between the filter coefficients as follows:

$$
\begin{aligned}
\tilde{g}_{-3} &= h_4 = \tilde{g}_5, \\
\tilde{g}_{-2} &= h_3 = \tilde{g}_4, \\
\tilde{g}_{-1} &= h_2 = \tilde{g}_3, \\
\tilde{g}_0 &= h_1 = \tilde{g}_2, \\
\tilde{h}_2 &= \tilde{h}_{-2}
\end{aligned}
$$

and rearrange the $x_{2j}^{(1)}$ and $x_{2j}^{(2)}$ terms by utilizing the above symmetric relationships as follows:

$$
\begin{aligned}
x_0^{(1)} &= \tilde{h}_0(0 + a_0) + \tilde{h}_2(0 + a_1), & x_0^{(2)} &= \tilde{g}_2(c_0 + c_1) + \tilde{g}_4(0 + c_2), \\
x_2^{(1)} &= \tilde{h}_0(0 + a_1) + \tilde{h}_2(a_0 + a_2), & x_2^{(2)} &= \tilde{g}_2(c_1 + c_2) + \tilde{g}_4(c_0 + c_3), \\
x_4^{(1)} &= \tilde{h}_0(0 + a_2) + \tilde{h}_2(a_1 + a_3), & x_4^{(2)} &= \tilde{g}_2(c_2 + c_3) + \tilde{g}_4(c_1 + c_4),
\end{aligned}
$$

$$\vdots \qquad\qquad\qquad \vdots$$

$$
\begin{aligned}
x_{N-4}^{(1)} &= \tilde{h}_0 a_{\frac{N}{2}-2} + \tilde{h}_2(a_{\frac{N}{2}-3} + a_{\frac{N}{2}-1}), & x_{N-4}^{(2)} &= \tilde{g}_2(c_{\frac{N}{2}-2} + c_{\frac{N}{2}-1}) + \tilde{g}_4 c_{\frac{N}{2}-3}, \\
x_{N-2}^{(1)} &= \tilde{h}_0(0 + a_{\frac{N}{2}-1}) + \tilde{h}_2(0 + a_{\frac{N}{2}-2}), & x_{N-2}^{(2)} &= \tilde{g}_4(0 + c_{\frac{N}{2}-2}) + \tilde{g}_2(0 + c_{\frac{N}{2}-1}).
\end{aligned}
$$

Implementation of this regular structure of computation for each expression $x_{2j}^{(1)}$ and $x_{2j}^{(2)}$ needs two processing elements as shown in the broken boxes I and II in Figure 5.3(a). The processing element C_4 is not used for computation of the even terms. The ADDER circuitry adds the outputs from the processing elements of the subarrays I and II to produce the final output samples $x_0, x_2, \cdots$, etc. Similarly, the odd samples $x_{2j+1}^{(1)}$ and $x_{2j+1}^{(2)}$ can be represented in a regular fashion as, for example,

$$x_1^{(1)} = \tilde{h}_1(a_0 + a_1) + \tilde{h}_3(0 + a_2), \quad x_1^{(2)} = \tilde{g}_1(0 + c_1) + \tilde{g}_3(c_0 + c_2) + \tilde{g}_5(0 + c_3),$$
$$x_3^{(1)} = \tilde{h}_1(a_1 + a_2) + \tilde{h}_3(a_0 + a_3), \quad x_3^{(2)} = \tilde{g}_1(0 + c_2) + \tilde{g}_3(c_1 + c_3) + \tilde{g}_5(c_0 + c_4),$$
$$x_5^{(1)} = \tilde{h}_1(a_2 + a_3) + \tilde{h}_3(a_1 + a_4), \quad x_5^{(2)} = \tilde{g}_1(0 + c_3) + \tilde{g}_3(c_2 + c_4) + \tilde{g}_5(c_1 + c_5).$$

Analyzing the above expressions, it is clear that computation of the $x_{2j+1}^{(1)}$ term needs two processing elements and each $x_{2j+1}^{(2)}$ term needs three processing elements as shown in Figure 5.3(b).

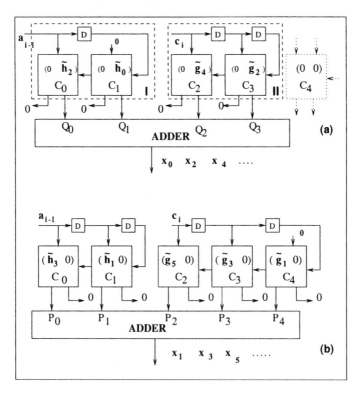

Fig. 5.3 Semi-systolic architectures for computing IDWT.

The logic of operations of the circuits in Figure 5.3(a) and Figure 5.3(b) is similar to the logic of operation of the DWT circuitry that we described in Figure 5.2. Also, the circuits in Figure 5.3(a) and Figure 5.3(b) can be merged into a single semi-systolic array by incorporating four multiplexers and another extra control signal I_2 as shown in Figure 5.4.

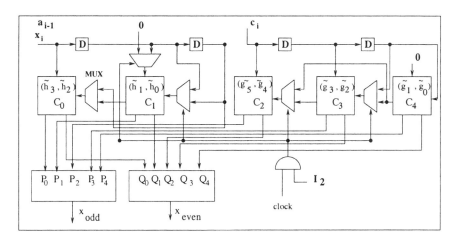

Fig. 5.4 The combined architecture of IDWT.

Table 5.3 Output P_i from Processing Element C_i of the IDWT Architecture in Figure 5.4 for the First 8 Clock Cycles

clock cycle	P_0	P_1	P_2	P_3	P_4
1(L)	0	0	$\tilde{g}_5 c_0$	0	0
(H)	0	0	$\tilde{g}_5 c_0$	0	0
2(L)	$\tilde{h}_3 a_0$	0	$\tilde{g}_5 c_1$	$\tilde{g}_3 c_0$	0
(H)	$\tilde{h}_3 a_0$	0	$\tilde{g}_5 c_1$	$\tilde{g}_3 c_0$	0
3(L)	$\tilde{h}_3 a_1$	$\tilde{h}_1 a_0$	$\tilde{g}_5 c_2$	$\tilde{g}_3 c_1$	$\tilde{g}_1 c_0$
(H)	$\tilde{h}_3 a_1$	$\tilde{h}_1 a_0$	$\tilde{g}_5 c_2$	$\tilde{g}_3(c_1 + c_0)$	$\tilde{g}_1 c_0$
4(L)	$\tilde{h}_3 a_2$	$\tilde{h}_1(a_1 + a_0)$	$\tilde{g}_5 c_3$	$\tilde{g}_3(c_2 + c_0)$	$\tilde{g}_1 c_1$
(H)	$\tilde{h}_3(a_2 + a_0)$	$\tilde{h}_1 a_1$	$\tilde{g}_5(c_3 + c_0)$	$\tilde{g}_3(c_2 + c_1)$	$\tilde{g}_1 c_1$
5(L)	$\tilde{h}_3(a_3 + a_0)$	$\tilde{h}_1(a_2 + a_1)$	$\tilde{g}_5(c_4 + c_0)$	$\tilde{g}_3(c_3 + c_1)$	$\tilde{g}_1 c_2$
(H)	$\tilde{h}_3(a_3 + a_1)$	$\tilde{h}_1 a_2$	$\tilde{g}_5(c_4 + c_1)$	$\tilde{g}_3(c_3 + c_2)$	$\tilde{g}_1 c_2$
6(L)	$\tilde{h}_3(a_4 + a_1)$	$\tilde{h}_1(a_3 + a_2)$	$\tilde{g}_5(c_5 + c_1)$	$\tilde{g}_3(c_4 + c_2)$	$\tilde{g}_1 c_3$
(H)	$\tilde{h}_3(a_4 + a_2)$	$\tilde{h}_1 a_3$	$\tilde{g}_5(c_5 + c_2)$	$\tilde{g}_3(c_4 + c_3)$	$\tilde{g}_1 c_3$
7(L)	$\tilde{h}_3(a_5 + a_2)$	$\tilde{h}_1(a_4 + a_3)$	$\tilde{g}_5(c_6 + c_2)$	$\tilde{g}_3(c_5 + c_3)$	$\tilde{g}_1 c_4$
(H)	$\tilde{h}_3(a_5 + a_3)$	$\tilde{h}_1 a_4$	$\tilde{g}_5(c_6 + c_3)$	$\tilde{g}_3(c_5 + c_4)$	$\tilde{g}_1 c_4$
8(L)	$\tilde{h}_3(a_6 + a_3)$	$\tilde{h}_1(a_5 + a_4)$	$\tilde{g}_5(c_7 + c_3)$	$\tilde{g}_3(c_6 + c_4)$	$\tilde{g}_1 c_5$
(H)	$\tilde{h}_3(a_6 + a_4)$	$\tilde{h}_1 a_5$	$\tilde{g}_5(c_7 + c_4)$	$\tilde{g}_3(c_6 + c_5)$	$\tilde{g}_1 c_5$

In IDWT mode, the internal registers in the processing elements C_0, C_1, C_2, C_3, and C_4 contain the pair of filter coefficients $(\tilde{h}_2, \tilde{h}_3)$, $(\tilde{h}_0, \tilde{h}_1)$, $(\tilde{g}_4, \tilde{g}_5)$, $(\tilde{g}_2, \tilde{g}_3)$, and $(0, \tilde{g}_1)$ respectively. During IDWT mode, the control signal I_2 is set to 1 and, depending on the clock phase, the inputs are selected by the multiplexers as shown in Figure 5.4. The output samples Q_0, Q_1, Q_2, Q_3, Q_4 from the processing elements C_0, C_1, C_2, C_3, C_4 are added to produce the even samples $x_0, x_2, \cdots$ of the reconstructed signal $\mathbf{x}=\{x_0, x_1, \cdots, x_{N-1}\}$ and P_0, P_1, P_2, P_3, P_4 are added to produce the odd output samples $x_1, x_3, \cdots$ of the reconstructed signal $\mathbf{x}$. Output samples P_i and Q_I of the processing elements for the first eight clock cycles in IDWT mode are shown in Tables 5.3 and 5.4 respectively. (H) or (L) in parentheses in the entries in the "Clock Cycle" column of Tables 5.3 and 5.4 indicate high or low.

Table 5.4   Output Q_i from Processing Element C_i of the IDWT Architecture in Figure 5.4 for the First 8 Clock Cycles

clock cycle	Q_0	Q_1	Q_2	Q_3	Q_4
1(L)	0	0	$\tilde{g}_4 c_0$	0	0
(H)	0	0	$\tilde{g}_4 c_0$	0	0
2(L)	$\tilde{h}_2 a_0$	0	$\tilde{g}_4 c_1$	$\tilde{g}_2 c_0$	0
(H)	$\tilde{h}_2 a_0$	0	$\tilde{g}_4 c_1$	$\tilde{g}_2 c_0$	0
3(L)	$\tilde{h}_2 a_1$	$\tilde{h}_0 a_0$	$\tilde{g}_4 c_2$	$\tilde{g}_2 c_1$	0
(H)	$\tilde{h}_2 a_1$	$\tilde{h}_0 a_0$	$\tilde{g}_4 c_2$	$\tilde{g}_2 (c_1 + c_0)$	0
4(L)	$\tilde{h}_2 a_2$	$\tilde{h}_1 (a_1 + a_0)$	$\tilde{g}_4 c_3$	$\tilde{g}_2 (c_2 + c_0)$	0
(H)	$\tilde{h}_2 (a_2 + a_0)$	$\tilde{h}_0 a_1$	$\tilde{g}_4 (c_3 + c_0)$	$\tilde{g}_2 (c_2 + c_1)$	0
5(L)	$\tilde{h}_2 (a_3 + a_0)$	$\tilde{h}_0 (a_2 + a_1)$	$\tilde{g}_4 (c_4 + c_0)$	$\tilde{g}_2 (c_3 + c_1)$	0
(H)	$\tilde{h}_2 (a_3 + a_1)$	$\tilde{h}_0 a_2$	$\tilde{g}_4 (c_4 + c_1)$	$\tilde{g}_2 (c_3 + c_2)$	0
6(L)	$\tilde{h}_2 (a_4 + a_1)$	$\tilde{h}_0 (a_3 + a_2)$	$\tilde{g}_4 (c_5 + c_1)$	$\tilde{g}_2 (c_4 + c_2)$	0
(H)	$\tilde{h}_2 (a_4 + a_2)$	$\tilde{h}_0 a_3$	$\tilde{g}_4 (c_5 + c_2)$	$\tilde{g}_2 (c_4 + c_3)$	0
7(L)	$\tilde{h}_2 (a_5 + a_2)$	$\tilde{h}_0 (a_4 + a_3)$	$\tilde{g}_4 (c_6 + c_2)$	$\tilde{g}_2 (c_5 + c_3)$	0
(H)	$\tilde{h}_2 (a_5 + a_3)$	$\tilde{h}_0 a_4$	$\tilde{g}_4 (c_6 + c_3)$	$\tilde{g}_2 (c_5 + c_4)$	0
8(L)	$\tilde{h}_2 (a_6 + a_3)$	$\tilde{h}_0 (a_5 + a_4)$	$\tilde{g}_4 (c_7 + c_3)$	$\tilde{g}_2 (c_6 + c_4)$	0
(H)	$\tilde{h}_2 (a_6 + a_4)$	$\tilde{h}_0 a_5$	$\tilde{g}_4 (c_7 + c_4)$	$\tilde{g}_2 (c_6 + c_5)$	0

5.2.3   Unified Architecture for DWT and Inverse DWT

As we discussed in the previous section, it is clear that the functional logics of the DWT and IDWT mode of operations differ in the way the input data are supplied to the processing elements. From Figures 5.2, 5.3, and 5.4, we find that five processing elements are enough for computation of both DWT and IDWT. Although interconnection of the processing elements for the DWT and IDWT mode of operations is not similar, it is possible to integrate these two functions into a single architecture by adding some multiplexers and using the control signals I_1 and I_2 as shown in Figure 5.5(a).

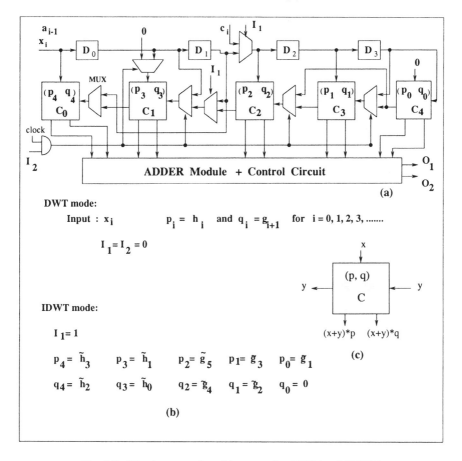

DWT mode:

    Input : x_i $p_i = h_i$ and $q_i = g_{i+1}$ for   i = 0, 1, 2, 3, ...

        $I_1 = I_2 = 0$

IDWT mode:

    $I_1 = 1$

   $p_4 = \tilde{h}_3$ $p_3 = \tilde{h}_1$ $p_2 = \tilde{g}_5$ $p_1 = \tilde{g}_3$ $p_0 = \tilde{g}_1$

   $q_4 = \tilde{h}_2$ $q_3 = \tilde{h}_0$ $q_2 = \tilde{g}_4$ $q_1 = \tilde{g}_2$ $q_0 = 0$

       (b)

Fig. 5.5   The integrated architecture for DWT and IDWT.

In DWT mode, we set $I_1 = I_2 = 0$ and hence $\mathbf{x} = \{x_0, x_1, \ldots, x_N - 1\}$ is the external input to all the processing elements. The output terminal O_1 produces the low-pass subband samples $\mathbf{a} = \{a_0, a_1, \ldots, a_{\frac{N}{2}-1}\}$ and O_2 produces the high-pass subband samples $\mathbf{c} = \{c_0, c_1, \ldots, c_{\frac{N}{2}-1}\}$ respectively. In IDWT mode, we set $I_1 = I_2 = 1$. As a result, the first two processing elements C_0 and C_1 receive external input $\mathbf{a} = \{a_0, a_1, \ldots, a_{\frac{N}{2}-1}\}$ and the other three processing elements C_2, C_3 and C_4 receive the external input $\mathbf{c} = \{c_0, c_1, \ldots, c_{\frac{N}{2}-1}\}$ selected by the multiplexor between delay elements D_1 and D_2. The input samples in i^{th} clock cycle are a_{i-1} and c_i and the corresponding output samples are x_{2i} (the even samples) and x_{2i+1} (the odd samples) respectively. The odd sample output is obtained via the O_1 terminal when the clock is low and the even sample output is obtained via O_2 when the clock is high. This is possible due to the following reason. When $I_1=1$ and $I_2=0$, the architecture performs similarly to the logic in Figure 5.3(b) and the odd samples x_{2j+1} of the reconstructed signal $\mathbf{x}$ are computed. When $I_1 = I_2=1$, the architecture performs similarly to the logic in Figure 5.3(a) and the even samples x_{2j} of the reconstructed signal are computed.

The convolution-based implementation of discrete wavelet transform has been studied extensively in the literature. There are many hardware architectures for VLSI implementation of the convolution-based DWT reported in the literature in last two decades [15, 16, 17, 18, 19, 20, 21, 22, 23, 24]. Development of VLSI architectures for lifting-based DWT is relatively a new area of study in both academia and industry. We describe some of the recent such architectures reported in the literature in the following sections.

5.3   VLSI ARCHITECTURES FOR LIFTING-BASED DWT

We have presented the underlying principles and formulation of the lifting-based discrete wavelet transform in Chapter 4. In this section, we present how the lifting operations can be mapped into hardware architectures and their possible VLSI implementations.

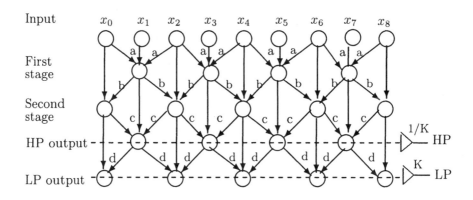

Fig. 5.6   Data dependency diagram of lifting-based DWT with four lifting factors.

The data dependency of the lifting scheme can be explained via a data-flow graph as shown by a block diagram in Figure 5.6. For the DWT filters which can be decomposed into four lifting factors (i.e., four lifting steps), the computation is done in four stages. These four stages are depicted in Figure 5.6. The values of a, b, c, d, and K depend on the selection of the DWT filters. Once the DWT filters are chosen, however, they are constant throughout the processing. The intermediate results generated in the first two stages for the first two lifting steps are stored temporarily and these intermediate results are subsequently processed to produce the high-pass (HP) outputs in the third stage followed by the low-pass (LP) outputs in the final stage. The popular $(9, 7)$ filter is an example of a DWT filter that requires four lifting steps with $a = -1.586134342$, $b = -0.05298011854$, $c = 0.8829110762$, $d = -0.4435068522$, and $K = 1.149604398$. For the DWT filters requiring only two factors such as the $(5, 3)$ filter proposed in JPEG2000 standard, the intermediate two stages can be simply bypassed.

Several architectures have been proposed in the literature for implementation of the lifting steps in VLSI. These architectures range from highly parallel architectures to programmable DSP-based architectures to folded architectures. We present systematic derivations of some of these architectures in the following sections.

5.3.1 Mapping the Data Dependency Diagram in Pipeline Architectures

A direct mapping of the data-flow diagram of the lifting steps into a pipelined architecture initially was proposed by Liu, Shiau, and Jou [28]. Block diagram of this pipeline architecture is shown in Figure 5.7. Several variations and enhancements of this architecture were proposed later for improved performance and better hardware efficiency.

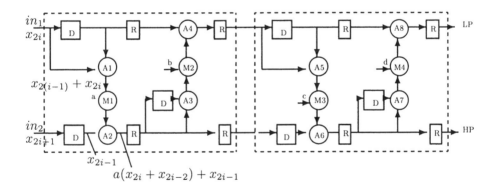

Fig. 5.7 Data dependency diagram mapped into a hardware architecture

The architecture shown in Figure 5.7 is designed with 8 adders (A1–A8), 4 multipliers (M1–M4), 6 delay elements (D), and 8 pipeline registers (R). There are two input lines in the architecture, one with all the even samples (x_{2i}) and the other with all the odd samples (x_{2i+1}). There are four pipeline stages in the architecture. In the first pipeline stage, the output of adder A1 is $x_{2i} + x_{2i-2}$ and the output of A2 is $a(x_{2i} + x_{2i-2}) + x_{2i-1}$, which represents the first intermediate results in the data dependency diagram for lifting as shown in Figure 5.6. In a similar fashion, the outputs of A4 in the second pipeline stage represent the second intermediate results. Continuing in this fashion, A6 in the third pipeline stage produces the high-pass output samples, whereas A8 produces the low-pass output samples. The cost of hardware of this architecture is very high because of requiring 4 multipliers and 8 adders. Moreover, for the lifting schemes requiring only two lifting steps, such as the (5, 3) filters, the last two pipeline stages need to be bypassed, causing hardware utilization to be only 50% or less. Also for a single read port memory, the odd and even samples are read serially in alternate clock cycles and buffered. This slows down the overall pipelined architecture by 50% as well.

A similar pipeline architecture for VLSI implementation of (9, 7) wavelet filters was proposed by Jou, Shiau, and Liu in [29] based on a pipeline scheduling technique adopted by converting the behavioral description of the lifting into the corresponding data flow graph (DFG). The resulting datapath is similar to Figure 5.7.

To minimize the hardware inefficiencies described in the above pipeline architecture, several architectural enhancements and design methodologies have been proposed in the literature. We describe some of them in the following sections.

5.3.2   Enhanced Pipeline Architecture by Folding

Hardware utilization of the pipeline architecture described in Figure 5.7 is 50% or less for the wavelet filters with only two lifting factors (e.g., (5, 3) filter). The utilization of the pipeline architecture can be further improved by carefully folding the last two pipeline stages into the first two pipeline stages, as shown in Figure 5.8.

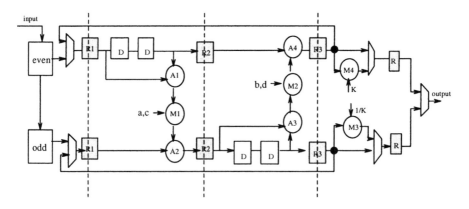

Fig. 5.8   A reconfigurable folded architecture [30].

Since the datapath architecture of the last two pipeline stages of the architecture in Figure 5.7 and their data dependency behavior is exactly identical to the first two stages, the last two pipeline stages can be folded into the first two. This can be accomplished by appropriately scheduling the necessary data for operation in the architecture. This folding architecture was proposed by Lian, Chen, Chen, and Chen in [30]. The architecture has two pipeline stages, with three pipeline registers, R1, R2, and R3. For the wavelet filters requiring computation of four lifting factors, such as the (9, 7) filter, intermediate data (R3) after first two lifting steps (phase 1) are folded back to R1 as shown in Figure 5.8 for computation of the last two lifting steps (phase 2). The architecture can be reconfigured so that computation of the two phases can be interleaved by selecting proper data by the multiplexers. As a result, we need two delay registers (D) in each lifting step in order to properly schedule the data for each phase. Based on the phase of interleaved computation, the coefficient for multiplier M1 is chosen as either a or c and similarly b or d for multiplier M2. As a result, the hardware utilization is always 100%. For wavelet filters requiring only two lifting steps, such as (5, 3) type wavelet filters, the folding is not required.

5.3.3   Flipping Architecture

While conventional lifting-based architectures require fewer arithmetic operations compared to the convolution-based approach for DWT, they sometimes have long critical paths. For instance, the critical path of the lifting-based architecture for the (9, 7) filter is $4T_m + 8T_a$ while that of the convolution implementation is $T_m + 2T_a$. One way of improving this is by pipelining, as has been demonstrated in [28, 29, 30]. However, this results in the number of registers increasing significantly. For instance, to pipeline the lifting-based (9, 7) filter such that the critical path is $t_m + T_a$, six additional registers are required.

Recently Huang, Tseng, and Chen [36] proposed a very efficient way of solving the timing accumulation problem. The basic idea is to remove the multiplications along the critical path by scaling the remaining paths by the inverse of the multiplier coefficients. Figures 5.9(a)–(c) describes how scaling at each level can reduce the multiplications in the critical path. Figure 5.9(d) further splits the three input addition nodes into two 2-input adders. The critical path is now $T_m + 5T_a$. Note that the flipping transformation changes the round-off noise considerably. Techniques to address precision and noise problems have also been addressed in [36].

5.3.4   A Register Allocation Scheme for Lifting

Chang, Lee, Peng, and Lee [31] proposed a programmable architecture to map the data dependency diagram of lifting-based DWT using four 3-input MAC (*multiply-adder calculator*), nine registers, and a register allocation scheme. The algorithm consists of two phases as shown in Figure 5.10. We explain

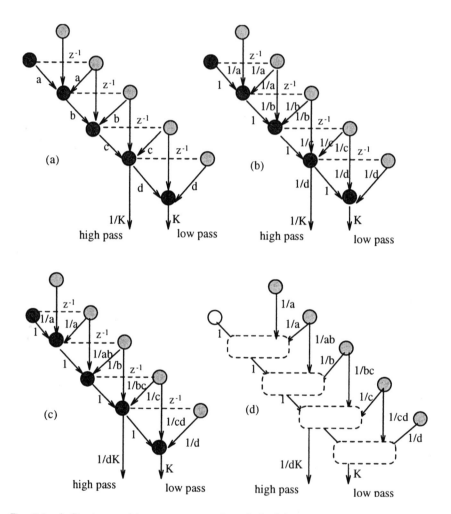

Fig. 5.9 A flipping architecture proposed in [36]; (a) original architecture, (b)-(c) scaling the coefficients to reduce the number of multiplications, (d) splitting the three-input addition nodes to two-input adders.

below the data-flow principle of the architecture in terms of the register allocation of the nodes in the data dependency diagram as proposed in [31].

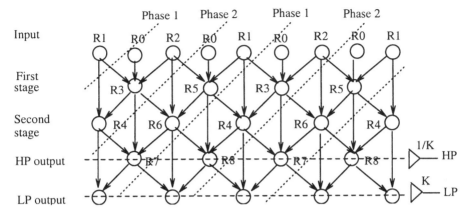

Fig. 5.10 Data-flow and register allocation of the data dependency diagram of lifting.

From the data-flow in Figure 5.10, it is obvious that the architecture has two phases (Phase 1 and Phase 2). These two phases operate in alternate fashion. The sequential computation and register allocation in phase 1 of the data dependency diagram shown in Figure 5.10 are in the following order:

$$R0 \leftarrow x_{2i-1}; \quad R2 \leftarrow x_{2i};$$
$$R3 \leftarrow R0 + a(R1 + R2);$$
$$R4 \leftarrow R1 + b(R5 + R3);$$
$$R8 \leftarrow R5 + c(R6 + R4);$$
$$Output_{LP} \leftarrow R6 + d(R7 + R8); \quad Output_{HP} \leftarrow R8.$$

Similarly, the sequential computation and register allocation in phase 2 of the data dependency diagram of lifting are as follows:

$$R0 \leftarrow x_{2i+1}; \quad R1 \leftarrow x_{2i+2};$$
$$R5 \leftarrow R0 + a(R2 + R1);$$
$$R6 \leftarrow R2 + b(R3 + R5);$$
$$R7 \leftarrow R3 + c(R4 + R6);$$
$$Output_{LP} \leftarrow R4 + d(R8 + R7); \quad Output_{HP} \leftarrow R7.$$

As explained above, two samples are input in each phase and two samples (LP and HP) are output at the end of every phase until the end of input data. The output samples are also stored into a temporary buffer for usage in the vertical filtering for the two-dimensional implementation of lifting-based discrete wavelet transform.

5.3.5   A Recursive Architecture for Lifting

According to the multiresolution decomposition principle of DWT, in every stage the low-pass subband is further decomposed recursively by applying the same analysis filters. The total number of the output samples to be processed for an L-level of DWT is

$$N + \frac{N}{2} + \frac{N}{4} + \cdots + \frac{N}{2^{L-1}} < 2N,$$

where N is the number of samples in the input signal.

Most of the traditional DWT architectures compute the second level of decomposition upon completion of the first level of decomposition and so on. Hence the ith level of decomposition is performed after completion of the $(i-1)^{\text{th}}$ level at stage i in recursion. However, the number of samples to be processed in each level is always half of the size in the previous level. As a result, it is possible to process multiple levels of decomposition simultaneously. This is the basic principle of *recursive architecture* for DWT computation, which was first proposed for a convolution-based DWT in [18]. Later the same principle was applied to develop recursive architecture for lifting-based DWT by Liao, Cockburn, and Mandal [34, 35]. Here computations in higher levels of decomposition are initiated as soon as enough intermediate data in low-frequency subband are available for computation. The architecture for a three-level of decomposition of an input signal using Daubaches-4 DWT proposed by Liao et al. is shown in Figure 5.11. However, the same principle can be extended to other wavelet filters as well.

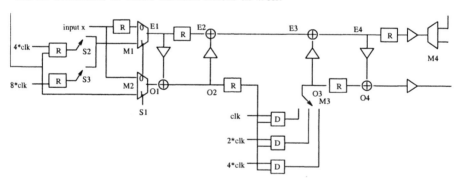

Fig. 5.11   Recursive architecture for lifting.

The basic circuit elements used in this architecture for arithmetic computation are delay elements, multipliers and multiply-accumulators (MAC). The MAC is designed using a multiplier, an adder, and two shifters. The multiplexers M1 and M2 select the even and odd samples of the input data as needed by the lifting scheme. The S1, S2, and S3 are the control signals for data flow of the architecture. For the first level of computation the select signal (S1) of each multiplexer is set to 0, and it is set to 1 during the second or third level of computation. The switches S2 and S3 select the input data for the second and third level of computation. The multiplexer M3 selects the delayed samples for each level of decomposition based on the clocked signals shown in Figure 5.11. The total time required by this recursive architecture to compute an L-level DWT is

$$T = N + T_d + 2(1 + 2 + \cdots + 2^{L-1}) = N + T_d + 2^L - 2,$$

where T_d is the circuit delay from input to output.

5.3.6 A DSP-Type Architecture for Lifting

A filter independent DSP-type parallel architecture has been proposed by Martina, Masera, Piccinini, and Zamboni in [37]. The architecture consists of $N_t = \max_i\{k_{s_i}, k_{t_i}\}$ number of MAC (multiply-accumulate) units, where k_{s_i} and k_{t_i} are length of the primal and dual lifting filters s_i and t_i respectively in step i of lifting factorization. The architecture is shown in Figure 5.12.

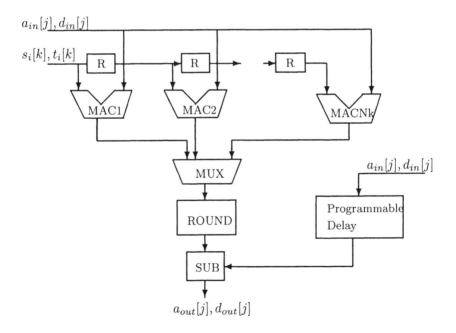

Fig. 5.12 Parallel MAC architecture for lifting.

The architecture essentially computes the following two streams in each lifting step.

$$a_{out}[j] = a_{in}[j] - \lfloor \sum_k d_{in}[j - k].s_i[k] + \tfrac{1}{2} \rfloor,$$
$$d_{out}[j] = d_{in}[j] - \lfloor \sum_k a_{out}[j - k].t_i[k] + \tfrac{1}{2} \rfloor,$$

where a_{in} and d_{in} are two input substreams formed by the even and odd samples of the original input signal stream x. It is obvious that streams a_{in} and b_{in} are not processed together in this architecture; while one is processed the other has to be delayed enough to guarantee a consistent subtraction at the end of the lifting step. The above architecture is designed to compute n_t simultaneous partial convolution products selected by the multiplexer (MUX), where n_t is the length of filter tap for the lifting step being currently executed in the architecture. After n_t clock cycles, the first filtered sample is available for rounding operation at the output of the first MAC_1 and subsequent samples are obtained in consecutive clock cycles from the subsequent MAC units (MAC_2, ..., MAC_{n_t}). The "programmable delay" is a buffer that guarantees the subtraction consistency to execute corresponding $a_{out}[j]$ and $d_{out}[j]$ samples at the output. The ROUND unit in Figure 5.12 computes the floor function shown in the lifting equations and the SUB unit processes the corresponding subtraction operations. The input sample streams (a two-dimensional image) are stored into a RAM in four sub-sampled blocks in order to properly address the row-wise and column-wise processing of the image for 2-D lifting DWT implementation. A detailed memory addressing scheme and their access patterns have been discussed in great detail in [37].

5.3.7   A Generalized and Highly Programmable Architecture for Lifting

The architecture proposed by Andra, Chakrabarti, and Acharya [25, 26, 27] is an example of a highly programmable architecture that can support a large set of wavelet filters. These include filters (5,3), (9,7), C(13,7), S(13,7), (2,6), (2,10), and (6,10). In this architecture, each stage of the data dependency diagram in Figure 5.6 is assigned to a processor. For wavelet filters requiring only two lifting stages (as in the (5, 3) wavelet filter), this maps to a two processor architecture. For wavelet filters with four lifting stages (such as the (9, 7) wavelet filter), this maps to a four-processor architecture. Figure 5.13 describes the assignment of computation to processors P1 and P2 for the (5, 3) wavelet filter.

The processor architecture consists of adders, multipliers, and shifters that are interconnected in a manner that would support the computational structure of the specific filter. Figure 5.14 describes the processor architectures for computation of the lifting steps. All the lifting steps for DWT and IDWT are essentially of the form $y_i = \alpha(x_{i-1} + x_{i+1}) + x_i$, where α is a constant multiplication factor. For the (5, 3) filter, the multiplication factors in both the lifting stages are multiplies of 2 and hence it can be executed by simple shift operations. As a result, the processor for computation of (5, 3) filter consists of two adders and a shifter, whereas the processor for computation of (9, 7) filter consists of two adders and a multiplier.

Figure 5.15 describes part of the schedule for the (5, 3) wavelet filter to transform a row (or in one dimension). The schedules are generated by mapping the dependency graph onto the resource-constrained architecture. It is

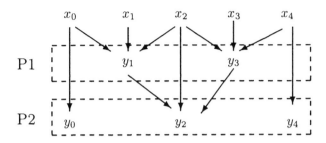

Fig. 5.13 Processor assignment for the (5, 3) wavelet filter.

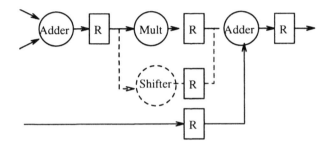

Fig. 5.14 Processor architecture for the (5, 3) and (9, 7) filters.

assumed that the delays of each adder, shifter, and the multiplier are 1, 1, and 4 time units respectively. For example, **Adder1** of P1 adds the elements (x_0, x_2) in the second cycle and stores the sum in register **RA1**. The shifter reads this sum in the next cycle (third cycle), carries out the required number of shifts (one right shift as $a = -0.5$) and stores the data in register **RS**. The second adder (**Adder2**) reads the value in **RS** and subtracts the element x_1 to generate y_1 in the next cycle. To process $N = 9$ data, the P1 processor takes four cycles. Adder 1 in P2 processor starts computation in the sixth cycle. The gaps in the schedules for P1 and P2 are required to store the zeroth element of each row.

5.3.8 A Generalized Two-Dimensional Architecture

Generally, two-dimensional wavelet filters are separable functions. A straightforward approach for two-dimensional implementation is to first apply the one-dimensional DWT row-wise (to produce L and H subbands) and then column-wise to produce four subbands LL, LH, HL, and HH in each level of decomposition as shown in Figure 4.3(a) in Chapter 4. Obviously, the processor utilization is a concern in direct implementation of this approach because it requires all the rows in the image be processed before the column-wise pro-

Cycle	Processor 1			Processor 2		
	Adder1	Shifter	Adder2	Adder1	Shifter	Adder2
1	–	–	–	–	–	–
2	$x_0 + x_2$	–	–	–	–	–
3	$x_2 + x_4$	RA1	–	–	–	–
4	$x_4 + x_6$	RA1	RS-x_1=y_1	–	–	–
5	$x_6 + x_8$	RA1	RS-x_3=y_3	–	–	–
6		RA1	RS-x_5=y_5	y_1, y_3	–	–
7		–	RS-x_7=y_7	y_3, y_5	RA1	y_0
8				y_5, y_7	RA1	RS+x_2
9					RA1	RS+x_4
10						RS+x_6

Fig. 5.15 Partial schedule for the (5, 3) filter implementation.

cessing can begin. As a result, it requires a size of memory buffer of the order of the image size and hence increase total computation delay. The alternative approach to reduce these inefficiencies is to begin the column-processing as soon as sufficient number of rows have been filtered. The column-wise processing is now performed on these available lines to produce wavelet coefficients row-wise. Similar approach can be adopted for implementation of two-dimensional lifting scheme as well.

The two-dimensional architecture proposed in [27] computes both the forward and inverse lifting-based DWT in the traditional row–column fashion. However, the scheduling of data is done in such a fashion that column-processing can start as soon as enough data is available after row-wise processing as explained earlier in order to minimize the computation delay. As shown in Figure 5.16, the architecture consists of a *row module*, a *column module*, and two memory modules (MEM1, MEM2). The row module consists of two processors RP1 and RP2 along with a register file REG1. The register file REG1 is used to store the intermediate data between two lifting steps computed by RP1 and RP2. Similarly, the column processor consists of two processors CP1 and CP2 along with a register file REG2. The register files REG1 and REG2 were used in between the processors mainly to locally store the intermediate results from the lifting steps in order to avoid access of memory for these intermediate data to store and read again. The register file REG2 is used to store the intermediate data between two lifting steps

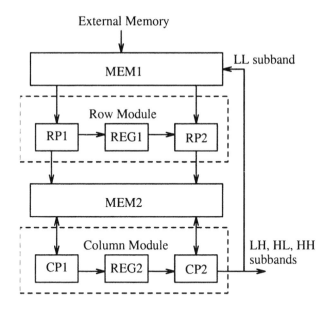

Fig. 5.16 Block diagram of the two-dimensional architecture.

computed by CP1 and CP2. Internal logic of all the four processors RP1, RP2, CP1, CP2 is the same as shown in Figure 5.14.

When the DWT requires two lifting steps (as in (5, 3) wavelet filters), processors RP1 and RP2 read the data from MEM1, perform the computation along the rows, and write the data into MEM2. We denote this mode of operation of the architecture as *2M architecture* mode. Processor CP1 reads the data from MEM2, performs the column-wise DWT along alternate *rows*, and writes the HH and LH subbands into MEM2 and an external memory (Ext.MEM). Processor CP2 reads the data from MEM2 and performs the column-wise DWT along the *rows* that CP1 did not work on and writes LL subband to MEM1 and HL subband to Ext.MEM. The data flow is shown in Figure 5.17(a).

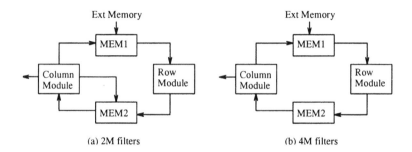

Fig. 5.17 Data flow for (a) 2M, (b) 4M architectures.

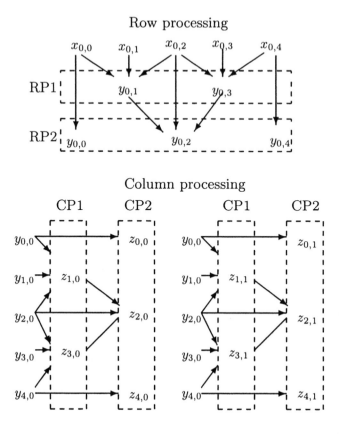

Fig. 5.18 Two-dimensional data-access patterns for the row and column modules for the (5,3) filter with $N=5$ in [27].

When the DWT requires four lifting steps (as in (9, 7) wavelet filters), we say the architecture is in *4M architecture* mode and it operates in two passes. In the first pass, the row-wise computation is performed. RP1 and RP2 read the data from MEM1, execute the first two lifting stages and write the result into MEM2. CP1 and CP2 execute the next two lifting stages, and write results to MEM2. In the second pass, the transform is computed along columns. At the end of the second pass, CP1 writes HH and LH subbands to Ext.MEM while CP2 writes LL subband to MEM1 and HL subband to Ext.MEM. The data flow is shown in Figure 5.17(b).

In the *2M Architecture* mode, the latency and memory requirements would be very large if the column transform is started after completion of the transformation of all the rows in the whole two-dimensional block. To overcome this, the column processors also need to compute row-wise. This is illustrated in Figure 5.18 for the (5, 3) filter with $N = 5$. The first processor RP1 computes the *high-pass* (odd) elements $y_{0,1}, y_{0,3}, ...$ along the rows, while the second processor RP2 calculates the *low-pass* (even) elements $y_{0,0}, y_{0,2}, y_{0,4}, ...$, also along the rows. Here an element $y_{i,j}$ denotes an element in i^{th} row and j^{th} column of the two-dimensional block. The processor CP1 calculates the *high-pass* and *low-pass* elements $z_{1,0}, z_{1,1}, ..., z_{3,0}, z_{3,1}, ...$ along the odd rows and CP2 calculates the *high-pass* and *low-pass* elements $z_{0,0}, z_{0,1}, ..., z_{2,0}, z_{2,1}, ..., z_{4,0}, z_{4,1}, ...$ along the even rows as shown in Figure 5.18. It should be noted that the processors CP1 and CP2 start their computations as soon as the required elements are generated by RP1 and RP2. Essentially, the processor RP1 calculates the *high-pass* values and RP2 calculates the *low-pass* values, along all the rows, whereas CP1 and CP2 calculate both *high-pass* and *low-pass* values along the odd rows and even rows respectively. In Table 5.5, we present a snapshot of the schedule of the data and their computation in the first 14 clock cycles for the RP1 and RP2 processors. Similarly, we present a part of the schedule of the data and their computation for the processors CP1 and CP2 in Tables 5.6 and 5.7 respectively.

In the *4M Architecture* mode, all four processors perform either a row transform or a column transform at any given instant. Specifically, the processors RP1 and CP1 compute the *high-pass* values along the *rows* in the first pass and along the *columns* in the second pass, whereas processors RP2 and CP2 compute the *low-pass* values.

Table 5.5 Partial Schedule of Processors RP1 and RP2 for the (5,3) Filter.

Cycle	RP1			RP2		
	Adder1	Shift	Adder2	Adder1	Shift	Adder2
1	-	-	-	-	-	-
2	$x_{0,0} + x_{0,2}$	-	-	-	-	-
3	$x_{0,2} + x_{0,4}$	RA1	-	-	-	-
4	$x_{0,4} + x_{0,6}$	RA1	RS-$x_{0,1} = y_{0,1}$	-	-	-
5	$x_{0,6} + x_{0,8}$	RA1	RS-$x_{0,3} = y_{0,3}$	-	-	-
6	-	RA1	RS-$x_{0,5} = y_{0,5}$	$y_{0,1} + y_{0,3}$	-	-
7	$x_{2,0} + x_{2,2}$	-	RS-$x_{0,7} = y_{0,7}$	$y_{0,3} + y_{0,5}$	RA1	$y_{0,0}$
8	$x_{2,2} + x_{2,4}$	RA1	-	$y_{0,5} + y_{0,7}$	RA1	RS+$x_{0,2} = y_{0,2}$
9	$x_{2,4} + x_{2,6}$	RA1	RS-$x_{2,1} = y_{2,1}$	-	RA1	RS+$x_{0,4} = y_{0,4}$
10	$x_{2,6} + x_{2,8}$	RA1	RS-$x_{2,3} = y_{2,3}$	-	-	RS+$x_{0,6} = y_{0,6}$
11	-	RA1	RS-$x_{2,5} = y_{2,5}$	$y_{2,1} + y_{2,3}$	-	$y_{0,8}$
12	$x_{1,0} + x_{1,2}$	-	RS-$x_{2,7} = y_{2,7}$	$y_{2,3} + y_{2,5}$	RA1	$y_{2,0}$
13	$x_{1,2} + x_{1,4}$	RA1	-	$y_{2,5} + y_{2,7}$	RA1	RS+$x_{2,2} = y_{2,2}$
14	$x_{1,4} + x_{1,6}$	RA1	RS-$x_{1,1} = y_{1,1}$	-	RA1	RS+$x_{2,4} = y_{2,4}$

The memory modules, MEM1 and MEM2, are both dual port with one read and one write port, and support two simultaneous accesses per cycle.

Table 5.6 Partial Schedule of Processor CP1 for the (5, 3) Filter.

Cycle	Adder1	Shift	Adder2
13	$y_{0,1} + y_{2,1}$	–	–
14	$y_{0,3} + y_{2,3}$	RA1	–
15	$y_{0,5} + y_{2,5}$	RA1	RS-$y_{1,1} = z_{1,1}$
16	$y_{0,7} + y_{2,7}$	RA1	RS-$y_{1,3} = z_{1,3}$
17	$y_{0,0} + y_{2,0}$	RA1	RS-$y_{1,5} = z_{1,5}$
18	$y_{0,2} + y_{2,2}$	RA1	RS-$y_{1,7} = z_{1,7}$
19	$y_{0,4} + y_{2,4}$	RA1	RS+$y_{1,0} = z_{1,0}$
20	$y_{0,6} + y_{2,6}$	RA1	RS+$y_{1,2} = z_{1,2}$
21	$y_{0,8} + y_{2,8}$	RA1	RS+$y_{1,4} = z_{1,4}$
22	$y_{2,1} + y_{4,1}$	RA1	RS+$y_{1,6} = z_{1,6}$
23	$y_{2,3} + y_{4,3}$	RA1	RS+$y_{1,8} = z_{1,8}$
24	–	RA1	RS-$y_{3,1} = z_{3,1}$

Table 5.7 Partial Schedule of Processor CP2 for the (5, 3) Filter.

Cycle	Adder1	Shift	Adder2
25	$z_{1,1} + z_{3,1}$	–	–
26	$z_{1,3} + z_{3,3}$	RA1	–
27	$z_{1,5} + z_{3,5}$	RA1	RS-$y_{2,1} = z_{2,1}$
28	$z_{1,7} + z_{3,7}$	RA1	RS-$y_{2,3} = z_{2,3}$
29	$z_{1,0} + z_{3,0}$	RA1	RS-$y_{2,5} = z_{2,5}$
30	$z_{1,2} + z_{3,2}$	RA1	RS-$y_{2,7} = z_{2,7}$
31	$z_{1,4} + z_{3,4}$	RA1	RS+$y_{2,0} = z_{2,0}$
32	$z_{1,6} + z_{3,6}$	RA1	RS+$y_{2,2} = z_{2,2}$
33	$z_{1,8} + z_{3,8}$	RA1	RS+$y_{2,4} = z_{2,4}$
34	$z_{3,1} + z_{5,1}$	RA1	RS+$y_{2,6} = z_{2,6}$
35	$z_{3,3} + z_{5,3}$	RA1	RS+$y_{2,8} = z_{2,8}$
36	–	RA1	RS-$y_{4,1} = z_{4,1}$

MEM1 consists of two banks and MEM2 consists of four banks. The multi-bank structure increases the memory bandwidth and helps support highly pipelined operation. Details of the memory organization and size, register file, and schedule for the overall architecture with specific details for each constituent filter have been included in [27].

Total time required to transform an $N \times N$ block using $(5, 3)$ wavelet filter using this architecture is $2\lfloor N/2 \rfloor + 3T_a + 2T_s + N + 5 + \lfloor N/2 \rfloor N$ clock cycles, where T_a is delay of an adder and T_s is delay of a shifter. Any other type of wavelet filters can be efficiently executed in this architecture as well. Details of these filters and their timing for execution in this architecture have been presented in [27].

5.4 SUMMARY

In this chapter, we presented VLSI algorithms and architectures for discrete wavelet transforms. We described the traditional convolution (filtering) approach for computation of discrete wavelet transform and described how a systolic architecture can be designed for wavelet filters by exploiting the symmetric relationship of the filter coefficients. Since the lifting-based wavelet transform is a development of the late 1990s and is new in the VLSI community, we emphasized more on the VLSI architectures for the lifting-based DWT computation in this chapter. Lifting-based DWT has many advantages over the traditional convolution-based approach. It requires less memory and computation for implementation compared to the convolution-based approach. We reviewed and presented the VLSI architectures that have been reported very recently for lifting-based DWT. We presented how the data-dependency diagram for the lifting computation can be mapped into pipelined architectures for suitable VLSI implementation, and proposed enhancement of the pipeline architectures by applying different schemes reported in the literature. We described in greater detail a highly folded VLSI architecture for computation of both one-dimensional and two-dimensional transformations.

REFERENCES

1. S. Mallat, "A Theory for Multiresolution Signal Decomposition: The Wavelet Representation," *IEEE Trans. Pattern Analysis And Machine Intelligence*, Vol. 11, No. 7, pp. 674–693, July 1989.

2. R. M. Rao and A. S. Bopardikar, *Wavelet Transforms: Introduction to Theory and Applications*. Addison-Wesley, MA, 1998.

3. M. Antonini, M. Barlaud, P. Mathieu, and I. Daubechies, "Image Coding Using Wavelet Transform," *IEEE Trans. on Image Processing*, Vol. 1, No. 2, pp. 205–220, April 1992.

4. JPEG 2000 Final Committee Draft (FCD), "JPEG 2000 Committee Drafts," http://www.jpeg.org/CDs15444.htm.

5. S. G. Mallat and W. L. Hwang, "Singularity detection and processing with wavelets," *IEEE Transactions on Information Theory*, Vol. 37, pp. 617–643, March 1992.

6. J. O. Chapa and M. R. Raghuveer, "Matched Wavelets — Their Construction, and Application to Object Detection". *IEEE International Conference on Acoustics, Speech and Signal Processing*, Atlanta, GA, April 1996.

7. D. L. Donoho, *De-noising via soft thresholding.* Technical report 409. Stanford, CA:Department of Statistics, Stanford University, November 1992.

8. H. Guo, J. E. Odegard, M. Lang, R. A. Gopinath, I. W. Selesnick, and C. S. Burrus, "Wavelet based Speckle Reduction with Applications to SAR based ATD/R," *Proceedings of 1st International Conference on Image Processing*, Vol. 1, pp. 75–79, Austin, TX, November 1994.

9. D. Berman, J. Bartell, and D. Salesin, "Multiresolution Painting and Compositing," *Proceedings of SIGGRAPH*, ACM, pp. 85–90, New York, 1994.

10. H. Li, B. S. Manjunath, and S. K. Mitra, "Multisensor Image Fusion using the Wavelet Transform," *Graphical Models and Image Processing*, Vol. 57, pp.235–245, May 1995.

11. W. Sweldens, "The Lifting Scheme: A Custom-Design Construction of Biorthogonal Wavelets," *Applied and Computational Harmonic Analysis*, Vol. 3, No. 15, pp. 186–200, 1996.

12. I. Daubechies and W. Sweldens, "Factoring Wavelet Transforms into Lifting Schemes," *The J. of Fourier Analysis and Applications*, Vol. 4, pp. 247–269, 1998.

13. A. R. Calderbank, I. Daubechies, W. Sweldens, and B.-L. Yeo, "Wavelet Transforms that Map Integers to Integers," *Applied and Computational Harmonic Analysis*, Vol. 5, pp. 332–369, July, 1998.

14. M. D. Adams and F. Kossentini, "Reversible Integer-to-Integer Wavelet Transforms for Image Compression: Performance Evaluation and Analysis," *IEEE Trans. on Image Processing*, Vol. 9, pp. 1010–1024, June 2000.

15. G. Knowles, "VLSI Architectures for the Discrete Wavelet Transform," *Electronics Letters*, Vol. 26, No. 15, pp. 1184–1185, July 1990.

16. A. S. Lewis and G. Knowles, "VLSI Architecture for 2-D Daubechies Wavelet Transform without Multipliers," *Electronics Letters*, Vol. 27, No. 2, pp. 171–173, January 1991.

17. K. Parhi and T. Nishitani, "VLSI Architectures for Discrete Wavelet Transforms," *IEEE Transactions on VLSI Systems*, Vol. 1, No. 2, pp. 191–202, 1993.

18. M. Vishwanath, "The Recursive Pyramid Algorithm for the Discrete Wavelet Transform," *IEEE Transactions on Signal Processing*, Vol. 42, pp. 673–676, March 1994.

19. M. Vishwanath, R.M. Owens, and M. J. Irwin, "VLSI Architecture for the Discrete Wavelet Transforms," *IEEE Transactions on Circuits and Systems II: Analog and Digital Signal Processing*, Vol. 42, No. 5, pp. 305–316, May 1995.

20. C. Chakrabarti and M. Vishwanath, "Efficient Realizations of the Discrete and Continuous Wavelet Transforms: From Single Chip Implementations to Mappings on SIMD Array Computers," *IEEE Transactions on Signal Processing*, Vol. 43, No. 3, pp. 759–771, March 1995.

21. C. Chakrabarti, M. Vishwanath, and R. M. Owens, "Architectures for Wavelet Transforms: A Survey," *Journal of VLSI Signal Processing*, Vol. 14, pp. 171–192, 1996.

22. T. Acharya, "A Reconfigurable Systolic Architecture for DWT Using VLSI," *Proceedings of the IEEE Global Telecommunications Conference* (GLOBECOM), Phoenix, November 1997.

23. T. Acharya and P. Chen, "VLSI Implementation of a DWT Architecture," *Proceedings of the IEEE International Symposium on Circuits and Systems* (ISCAS), Monterey, CA, May 31–June 3, 1998.

24. P. Chen, T. Acharya, H. Jafarkhani, "A Pipelined VLSI Architecture for Adaptive Image Compression," *International Journal of Robotics and Automation*, Vol. 14, No. 3, pp. 115–123, 1999.

25. T. Acharya and C. Chakrabarti, "A Survey on Lifting-based Discrete Wavelet Transform Architectures," Submitted to the *Journal of VLSI Signal Processing*, Kluwer Academic Publishers, 2004.

26. K. Andra, C. Chakrabarti and T. Acharya, "A VLSI Architecture for Lifting Based Wavelet Transform," *Proceedings of the IEEE Workshop on Signal Processing Systems*, Lafayette, LA, October 2000.

27. K. Andra, C. Chakraborti, and T. Acharya, "An Efficient Implementation of a Set of Lifting-based Wavelet Filters," *Proceedings of the IEEE Intl. Conference on Acoustics, Speech and Signal Processing (ICASSP 2001)*, Salt Lake City, UT, May 2001.

28. K. Andra, C. Chakrabarti, and T. Acharya, "A VLSI Architecture for Lifting-based Forward and Inverse Wavelet Transform," *IEEE Trans. on Signal Processing*, Vol. 50, No. 4, pp. 966–977, April 2002.

29. C. C. Liu, Y. H. Shiau, and J. M. Jou, "Design and Implementation of a Progressive Image Coding Chip Based on the Lifted Wavelet Transform," *Proc. 11ᵗʰ VLSI Design/CAD Symposium*, Taiwan, August 2000.

30. J. M. Jou, Y. H. Shiau, and C. C. Liu, "Efficient VLSI Architectures for the Biorthogonal Wavelet Transform by Filter Bank and Lifting Scheme," *IEEE International Symposium on Circuits and Systems*, Sydney, Australia, pp. 529–533, May 2001.

31. C. J. Lian, K. F. Chen, H. H. Chen, and L. G. Chen, "Lifting-based Discrete Wavelet Transform Architecture for JPEG 2000," *IEEE International Symposium on Circuits and Systems*, Sydney, Australia, pp. 445–448, May 2001.

32. W. H. Chang, Y. S. Lee, W. S. Peng, and C. Y. Lee, "A Line-based, Memory Efficient and Programmable Architecture for 2D DWT Using Lifting Scheme," *IEEE International Symposium on Circuits and Systems*, Sydney, Australia, pp. 330–333, May 2001.

33. W. Jiang and A. Ortega, "Lifting Factorization-based Discrete Wavelet Transform Architecture Design," *IEEE Trans. on Circuits and Systems for Video Technology*, Vol. 11, pp. 651–657, May 2001.

34. M. Ferretti and D. Rizzo, "A Parallel Architecture for the 2-D Discrete Wavelet Transform with Integer Lifting Scheme," *Journal of VLSI Signal Processing*, Vol. 28, pp. 165–185, July 2001.

35. H. Liao, B. F. Cockburn, and M. K. Mandal, "Novel Architectures for the Lifting-based Discrete Wavelet Transform," *Proceedings of the IEEE Canadian Conference on Electrical & Computer Engineering*, pp. 1020–1025, Winnipeg, Canada, May 2002.

36. H. Liao, M. K. Mandal, and B. F. Cockburn, "Novel Architectures for Lifting-based Discrete Wavelet Transform," *Electronics Letters*, Vol. 38, Issue 18, pp. 1010–1012, August 29, 2002.

37. C.T. Huang, P.C. Tseng, and L.G. Chen, "Flipping structure: An Efficient VLSI Architecture for Lifting-based Discrete Wavelet Transform," *IEEE Transactions on Signal Processing*, Vol. 54. No. 4, pp. 1080–1089, April 2004.

38. M. Martina, G. Masera, G. Piccinini, and M. Zamboni, "Novel JPEG 2000 Compliant DWT and IWT VLSI Implementations," *Journal of VLSI Signal Processing*, Vol. 34, pp. 137–153, 2003.

39. J. Reichel, M. Nadenau, and M. Kunt, "Row-based Wavelet Decomposition Using the Lifting Scheme," *Proceedings of the Workshop on Wavelet Transforms and Filter Banks*, Brandenburg an der Havel, Germany, March 5–7, 1999.

6

JPEG2000 Standard

6.1 INTRODUCTION

JPEG2000 is the new international standard for image compression [1, 2, 3] developed jointly by the *International Organization for Standardization* (ISO), and the *International Electrotechnical Commission* (IEC) and also recommended by *International Telecommunications Union* (ITU). The activity toward definition of the image compression standard originally started as early as 1982 and finally the JPEG (Joint Photographic Experts Group) was formed in 1987. However, JPEG for still image compression [4, 5] became an international standard in 1992. The JPEG standard described a family of image compression techniques rather than a single compression technique. It provides a "tool kit" of compression techniques from which an application can choose the elements needed to meet its requirements. The standard has four different modes of operations as described in Chapter 3. Each mode consists of a multiple number of options as well, totaling 44 different options or submodes. A particular option is a restricted form of the sequential Discrete Cosine Transform (DCT) based mode in JPEG called the *baseline* JPEG. Market studies show that more than 90% of users use this baseline JPEG and hence the rest of the standard was greatly underutilized. Although we call JPEG an image compression standard, the standards committee actually defines the syntax of the compressed bitstream in each mode and the underlying decoder to decompress the bitstream. It is the prerogative of the developers to develop the compression system. The compression system is said to be standard compliant if it follows the standard defined bitstream syntax in order to uniquely decode it by the standard decoder. From that perspective, JPEG (also JPEG2000) is actually a decoding standard.

Since the definition of the JPEG standard, the technology world and the marketplace have gone through a significant transformation because of the advent of Internet technology, its massive deployment and usage in every walk of life, and significant progress in multimedia and communications technologies and their applications. Although JPEG (actually baseline JPEG) has been very successful in the marketplace for more than a decade, it lacks many features desired by interactive multimedia applications, its usage in current communications (wired or wireless) environments, and Internet applications platforms. A fundamental shift in the image compression approach came after the Discrete Wavelet Transform (DWT) became popular [6, 7, 8, 9, 10]. Exploiting the interesting features in DWT, many scalable image compression algorithms were proposed in the literature [11, 12, 13, 14, 15, 16, 17]. To overcome the inefficiencies in the JPEG [4, 5] standard and serve emerging applications areas in this age of mobile and Internet communications, the new JPEG2000 standard has been developed based on the principles of DWT and currently more developments in this standard are still in progress in the ISO/IEC standard committee. It incorporated the latest advances in image compression to provide a unified optimized tool to accomplish both lossless and lossy compression and decompression using the same algorithm and the bitstream syntax. The systems architecture is not only optimized for compression efficiency at even very low bit-rates, it is also optimized for scalability and interoperability in networks and noisy mobile environments. The JPEG2000 standard will be effective in wide application areas such as Internet, digital photography, digital library, image archival, compound documents, image databases, color reprography (photocopying, printing, scanning, facsimile), graphics, medical imaging, multispectral imaging such as remotely sensed imagery, satellite imagery, mobile multimedia communication, 3G cellular telephony, client-server networking, e-commerce, etc.

As of writing this book, the JPEG2000 standard has 11 key parts (Part 7 has been abandoned) as described later. At this point, we are considering mainly Part 1 of the JPEG2000 standard [20] in this book. We summarize the features and purpose of other parts of the standard in Chapter 10.

The main drawback of the JPEG2000 standard compared to current JPEG is that the coding algorithm is much more complex and the computational needs are much higher. Moreover, bit-plane-wise computing may restrict good computational performance with a general-purpose computing platform. Analysis [1, 27] shows that the JPEG2000 compression is more than 30 times complex as compared with current JPEG. As a result, there is a tremendous need to develop high-performance architectures and special-purpose custom VLSI chips exploiting the underlying data parallelism to speed up the DWT and entropy encoding phase of JPEG2000 to make it suitable for real-time applications.

6.2   WHY JPEG2000?

The underlying philosophy behind development of the JPEG2000 standard was to compress an image once and decode the compressed bitstream in many ways to meet different applications requirements. The requirements guideline [18] of the JPEG2000 standard established some desired features to be supported by the standard in order to enable its usage in different applications areas as explained in the previous section.

Some of the salient features offered by the JPEG2000 standard that are effective in vast areas of applications are as follows:

- *Superior low bit-rate performance*: It offers superior performance in terms of visual quality and PSNR (peak signal-to-noise ratio) at very low bit-rates (below 0.25 bit/pixel) compared to the baseline JPEG. For equivalent visual quality JPEG2000 achieves more compression compared to JPEG. This has been demonstrated in Figure 3.6 in Chapter 3, and its color version is provided in the color figures page. This feature is very useful for transmission of compressed images through a low-bandwidth transmission channel.

- *Continuous tone and bi-level image compression*: The JPEG2000 standard is capable of compressing and decompressing both the continuous-tone (grayscale and color) and bi-level images. The JBIG2 standard was defined to compress the bi-level images and it uses the same MQ-coder that is used to entropy encode the wavelet coefficients of the grayscale or color image components.

- *Large dynamic range of the pixels*: The JPEG2000 standard-compliant systems can compress and decompress images with various dynamic ranges for each color component. Although the desired dynamic range for each component in the requirement document is 1 to 16 bits, the system is allowed to have a maximum of 38 bits precision based on the bitstream syntax. As a matter of fact, JPEG2000 is the only standard that can deal with pixels with more than 16 bits precision. This feature is particularly suitable both for software and hardware implementers to choose the precision requirement for targeted applications.

- *Large images and large numbers of image components*: The JPEG2000 standard allows the maximum size of an image to be $(2^{32}-1) \times (2^{32}-1)$ and the maximum number of components in an image to be 2^{14}. This feature is particularly suitable for satellite imagery and astronomical image processing involving multispectral images with a large number of components and size.

- *Lossless and lossy compression*: The single unified compression architecture can provide both the lossless and the lossy mode of image compression. Lossy and lossless decompression are also possible from a single compressed bitstream. The reversible color transform and the reversible wavelet transform (using integer wavelet filter coefficients) make the lossless compression possible by the same coding architecture. As a result, the same technology is applicable in varying applications areas ranging from medical imagery requiring lossless compression to digital transmission of images through communication networks.

- *Fixed size can be preassigned*: The JPEG2000 standard allows users to select a desired size of the compressed file. This is possible because of the bit-plane coding of the architecture and controlling the bit-rate through the rate control. The compression can continue bit-plane by bit-plane in all the code-blocks until the desired compressed size is achieved and the compression process can terminate. This is a very useful feature for restricted-buffer-size hardware implementation as in reprographic architectures such as printer, photocopier, scanner, etc. This is also a very useful feature to dynamically control the size of the compressed file in a limited-bandwidth communications networking environment.

- *Progressive transmission by pixel accuracy and resolution*: Using the JPEG2000 standard, it is possible to organize the code-stream in a progressive manner in terms of *pixel accuracy* (i.e., visual quality or SNR) of images that allows reconstruction of images with increasing pixel accuracy as more and more compressed bits are received and decoded. This is possible by progressively decoding most significant bit-plane to lower significant bit-planes until all the bit-planes are reconstructed. The code-stream can also be organized as progressive in resolution such that the higher-resolution images are generated as more compressed data are received and decoded. This is possible by decoding and inverse DWT of more and more higher level subbands that were generated by the multiresolution decomposition of the image by DWT, as shown in Figure 4.5 in Chapter 4, during the compression process. These features are very effective for real-time browsing of images on the Web, downloading or reconstructing the images in a system with limited memory buffer, transmission of images through limited-bandwidth channels, decoding the images depending on the available resolution of the rendering system, etc. More on the progression order will be discussed in Chapter 7.

- *Region of interest (ROI) coding*: The user may desire certain parts of an image that are of greater importance to be encoded with higher fidelity compared to the rest of the image. During decompression the quality of the image also can be adjusted depending on the degree of interest in each region of interest. For example, a medical practitioner may find a certain region (or number of regions) in the radiograph to be more informative than the other parts. It is then possible to archive the digital radiograph by compressing it such a way that the region of interest is compressed completely losslessly and introducing errors in other parts of the image in order to store it in a desired size of storage.

- *Random access and compressed domain processing*: By randomly extracting the code-blocks from the compressed bitstream, it is possible to manipulate certain areas (or regions of interest) of the image. Some of the examples of compressed-domain processing could be cropping, flipping, rotation, translation, scaling, feature extraction, etc. One might want to replace one object in the image with another, sometimes even with a synthetically generated image object. It is possible to extract the compressed code-blocks representing the object and replace them with compressed code-blocks of the desired object. This feature is very useful in many applications areas such as editing, studio, animation, graphics, etc.

- *Object-based functionality*: Because of random-access and compressed-domain processing capabilities in the JPEG2000 standard, we can apply different operations and manipulations in different objects in the compressed domain as explained in the previous item. The objects in an image can be defined in terms of a suitable group of code-blocks in the image. The information of the location of these code-blocks and corresponding bitstream are available in the header of the compressed file.

- *Robustness to bit-errors (error resiliency)*: Robustness to bit-errors is highly desirable for transmission of images over noisy communications channels. The JPEG2000 standard facilitates this by coding small size independent code-blocks and including resynchronization markers in the syntax of the compressed bitstream. There are also provisions to detect and correct errors within each code-block. This feature makes JPEG2000 applicable in emerging third-generation mobile telephony applications.

- *Sequential buildup capability*: The JPEG2000–compliant system can be designed to encode an image from top to bottom in a single sequential pass without the need to buffer an entire image, and hence is suitable for low-memory on-chip VLSI implementation. The line-based implementation of DWT and tiling of the images facilitates this feature.

- *Metadata*: The extended file syntax format allows inclusion of metadata information to describe the data (image) into the compressed bitstream. For example, the JPX file format, defined in JPEG2000 Part 2: Extensions, allows any legal ICC (International Color Consortium) profile to be embedded in the file.

- *Image security*: Although JPEG2000 does not dictate any particular image security mechanism, it is possible to introduce image security features into a JPEG2000–compliant compressed file by inserting water-marks, fingerprints, or intellectual property rights information, or apply the steganography approach into the desired object or blocks of the im-ages by accessing the corresponding compressed code-blocks and recom-pressing by introducing these image security features. In the JPEG2000 standards committee, definition of Part 8 (Secure JPEG2000) of the standard is an ongoing activity. Once finalized, Part 8 of the standard will guide the issues of image security and their implementation in a JPEG2000–compliant system.

In Figure 6.1, we have demonstrated the results of some of the capabilities of the JPEG2000 technology. The color version of Figure 6.1 is provided in the color figures page. The input image is a color image with three components (R, G, B) as shown in Figure 6.1(a). We applied three levels of DWT to decompose the image and generate the compressed bitstream with ROI encoding. The bitstream was generated by compressing the image losslessly. From the same bitstream, we decoded the image progressively until we reconstructed the original image as shown by the lossless arrow. While decoding in progressive manner, the reconstructed image is visually lossless at 5.2 bits per pixel or above as shown in Figure 6.1(b). In Figure 6.1(c), we show the random-access capability. We have accessed the compressed bits only for the code-blocks forming the subregion (or cropped version of the image) and decoded the result as shown in Figure 6.1(c). When we decode only one component (in this example we decoded G component), we get a grayscale image as shown in Figure 6.1(d). After decoding the bitstream progressively at two levels of resolution, we generate a 2:1 downscaled (horizontally and vertically) version of the image as shown in Figure 6.1(e). After decoding to 1.89 bits per pixel, we losslessly reconstructed the ROI portion of the image, but introducing artifacts in the rest of the image as shown in Figure 6.1(f). As a result, we can conclude that an image can be compressed once and the compressed bitstream can be decoded in many different ways to suit the desired requirement.

6.3   PARTS OF THE JPEG2000 STANDARD

As of writing this book, the standard has 11 parts (because Part 7 has been abandoned) with each part adding new features to the core standard in Part 1. The 11 parts and their features are as follows:

- Part 1—Core Coding System [20] is now published as an International Standard ISO/IEC 15444-1:2000, and this part specifies the basic feature set and code-stream syntax for JPEG2000.

- Part 2—Extensions [21] to Part 1. This part adds a lot more features to the core coding system. These extensions are described in greater detail in Chapter 10.

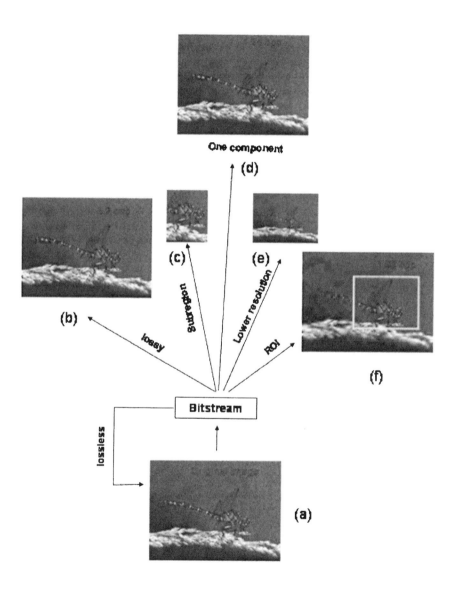

Fig. 6.1 Example of capabilities of JPEG2000 technology.

- Part 3—Motion JPEG2000 [22] specifies a file format (MJ2) that contains an image sequence encoded with the JPEG2000 core coding algorithm for motion video. It is aimed at applications where high-quality frame-based compression is desired.

- Part 4—Conformance Testing [23] is now published as an International Standard (ISO/IEC 15444-4:2002). It specifies compliance-testing procedures for encoding/decoding using Part 1 of JPEG2000.

- Part 5—Reference Software [24]. In this part, two software source packages (using Java and C programming languages) are provided for the purpose of testing and validation for JPEG2000 systems implemented by the developers.

- Part 6—Compound Image File Format [25] specifies another file format (JPM) for the purpose of storing compound images. The ITU-T T.44|ISO 16485 [26] multilayer Mixed Raster Content (MRC) model is used to represent a compound image in Part 6 of JPEG2000.

- *Part 7*—This part has been abandoned.

- Part 8—Secure JPEG2000 (JPSEC). This part deals with security aspects for JPEG2000 applications such as encryption, watermarking, etc.

- Part 9—Interactivity Tools, APIs and Protocols (JPIP). This part defines an interactive network protocol, and it specifies tools for efficient exchange of JPEG2000 images and related metadata.

- Part 10—3-D and Floating Point Data (JP3D). This part is developed with the concern of three-dimensional data such as 3-D medical image reconstruction, as an example.

- Part 11—Wireless (JPWL). This part is developed for wireless multimedia applications. The main concerns for JPWL are error protection, detection, and correction for JPEG2000 in an error-prone wireless environment.

- Part 12—ISO Base Media File Format has a common text with ISO/IEC 14496-12 for MPEG-4.

Parts 8 to 11 are still under development as of writing this book. However, since Part 12 has a common text with ISO/IEC 14496, it is published as ISO/IEC 15444-12:2004. We will have more discussion in Chapter 10 for parts beyond Part 1 of JPEG2000.

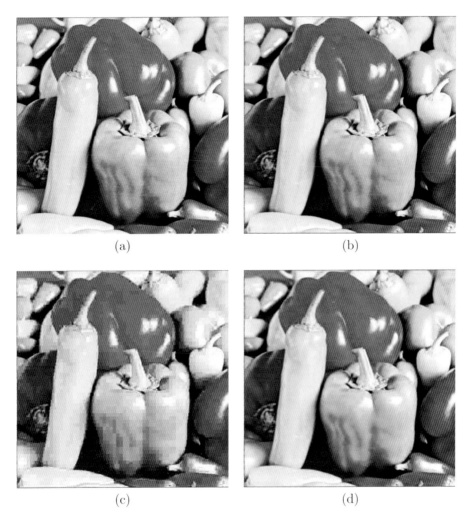

Fig. 3.6 (a) Original Pepper image, (b) compressed with baseline JPEG using quality factor 75 (1.57 bit/pixel), (c) compressed with baseline JPEG using quality factor 10 (0.24 bit/pixel), and (d) compressed with the new JPEG2000 standard using the same bit rate (0.24 bit/pixel).

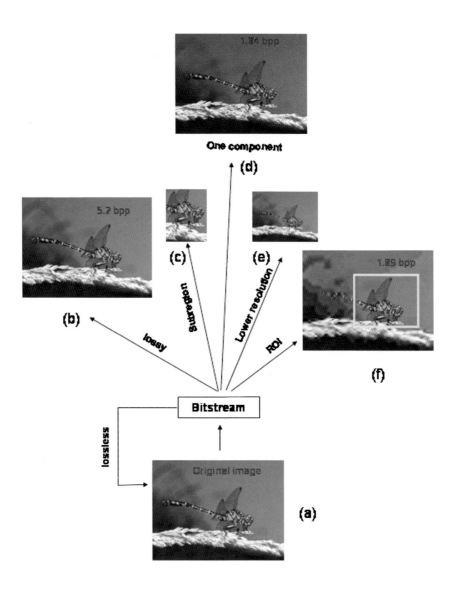

Fig. 6.1 Example of capabilities of JPEG2000 technology.

6.4   OVERVIEW OF THE JPEG2000 PART 1 ENCODING SYSTEM

Like other image and video compression standards (JPEG, MPEG-1, MPEG-2, MPEG-4), the JPEG2000 standard is also written from the decoder point of view. This means that the decoder is specified quite precisely from marker segments to bitstream syntax in the JPEG2000 standard document. The detail of the specification of the decoder is sufficient to dictate the functionalities of the encoder. However, it is very difficult for a beginner to understand the standard document. Once the encoder system is well understood, it becomes easier to comprehend the decoder system described in the standard document. In this section, we explain the encoder engine for the JPEG2000 Part 1 standard. The whole compression system is simply divided into three phases. We call them (1) image preprocessing, (2) compression, and (3) compressed bitstream formation. We explain the functionalities of these three phases in the following sections.

6.5   IMAGE PREPROCESSING

The image preprocessing phase consists of three optional major functions: first *tiling*, then *DC level shifting*, followed by the *multicomponent transformation*.

6.5.1   Tiling

The first preprocessing operation is *tiling*. In this step, the input source image is (optionally) partitioned into a number of rectangular nonoverlapping blocks if the image is very large. Each of these blocks is called a *tile*. All the tiles have exactly the same dimension except the tiles at the image boundary if the dimension of the image is not an integer multiple of the dimension of the tiles. The tile sizes can be arbitrary up to the size of the original image. For an image with multiple components, each tile also consists of these components. For a grayscale image, the tile has a single component. Since the tiles are compressed independently, visible artifacts may be created at the tile boundaries when it is heavily quantized for very-low-bit-rate compression as typical in any block transform coding. Smaller tiles create more boundary artifacts and also degrade the compression efficiency compared to the larger tiles. Obviously, no tiling offers the best visual quality. On the other hand, if the tile size is too large, it requires larger memory buffers for implementation either by software or hardware. For VLSI implementation, it requires large on-chip memory to buffer large tiles mainly for DWT computation. The tile size 256×256 or 512×512 is found to be a typical choice for VLSI implementation based on the cost, area, and power consideration. With the advances in memory technology with more compaction and reducing cost, the choice of tile size in the near future will be accordingly larger.

6.5.2   DC Level Shifting

Originally, the pixels in the image are stored in unsigned integers. For mathematical computation, it is essential to convert the samples into two's complement representation before any transformation or mathematical computation starts in the image. The purpose of DC level shifting (optional) is to ensure that the input image samples have a dynamic range that is approximately centered around the zero. The DC level shifting is performed on image samples that are represented by unsigned integers only. All samples $I_i(x, y)$ in the ith component of the image (or tile) are level shifted by subtracting the same quantity $2^{S_{siz}^i - 1}$ to produce the DC level shifted sample $I_i'(x, y)$ as follows,

$$I_i'(x, y) \leftarrow I_i(x, y) - 2^{S_{siz}^i - 1}$$

where S_{siz}^i is the precision of image samples signaled in the SIZ (image and tile size) marker segment in compressed bitstream. For images whose samples are represented by signed integers, such as CT (computed tomography) images, the dynamic range is already centered about zero, and no DC level shifting is required.

6.5.3   Multicomponent Transformations

The multicomponent transform is effective in reducing the correlations (if any) amongst the multiple components in a multicomponent image. This results in reduction in redundancy and increase in compression performance. Actually, the standard does not consider the components as color planes and in that sense the standard itself is colorblind. However, it defines an optional multicomponent transformation in the first three components only. These first three components can be interpreted as three color planes (R, G, B) for ease of understanding. That's why they are often called multicomponent color transformation as well. However, they do not necessarily represent Red-Green-Blue data of a color image. In general, each component can have different bit-depth (precision of each pixel in a component) and different dimension. However, the condition of application of multicomponent transform is that the first three components should have identical bit-depth and identical dimension as well.

The JPEG2000 Part 1 standard supports two different transformations: (1) reversible color transform (RCT), and (2) irreversible color transform (ICT). The RCT can be applied for both lossless and lossy compression of images. However, ICT is applied only in lossy compression.

6.5.3.1   Reversible Color Transformation   For lossless compression of an image, only the reversible color transform (RCT) is allowed because the pixels can be exactly reconstructed by the inverse RCT. Although it has been defined for lossless image compression, the standard allows it for lossy compression as well. In case of lossy compression, the errors are introduced by the transformation and/or quantization steps only, not by the RCT. The forward RCT and inverse RCT are given by:

Forward RCT:

$$Y_r = \lfloor \tfrac{R+2G+B}{4} \rfloor$$
$$U_r = B - G$$
$$V_r = R - G$$

(6.1)

Inverse RCT:

$$G = Y_r - \lfloor \tfrac{U_r+V_r}{4} \rfloor$$
$$R = V_r + G$$
$$B = U_r + G$$

(6.2)

6.5.3.2 Irreversible Color Transformation The irreversible color transformation (ICT) is applied for lossy compression only because of the error introduced due to forward and inverse transformation by using noninteger coefficients as the weighting parameters in the transformation matrix, as shown in Eqs. 6.3 and 6.4. The ICT is the same as the luminance–chrominance color transformation used in baseline JPEG. Y is the luminance component of the image representing intensity of the pixels (light) and Cb and Cr are the two chrominance components representing the color information in each pixel. In baseline JPEG, the chrominance components can be subsampled to reduce the amount of data to start with. However, in the JPEG2000 standard, this subsampling is not allowed. The forward ICT and inverse ICT are given by:

Forward ICT:

$$\begin{bmatrix} Y \\ Cb \\ Cr \end{bmatrix} = \begin{bmatrix} 0.299000 & 0.587000 & 0.114000 \\ -0.168736 & -0.331264 & 0.500000 \\ 0.500000 & -0.418688 & -0.081312 \end{bmatrix} \begin{bmatrix} R \\ G \\ B \end{bmatrix}$$

(6.3)

Inverse ICT:

$$\begin{bmatrix} R \\ G \\ B \end{bmatrix} = \begin{bmatrix} 1.0 & 0.0 & 1.402000 \\ 1.0 & -0.344136 & -0.714136 \\ 1.0 & 1.772000 & 0.0 \end{bmatrix} \times \begin{bmatrix} Y \\ Cb \\ Cr \end{bmatrix}$$

(6.4)

6.6 COMPRESSION

After the optional preprocessing phase, as described in the previous section, the compression phase actually generates the compressed code. The computational block diagram of the functionalities of the compression system is

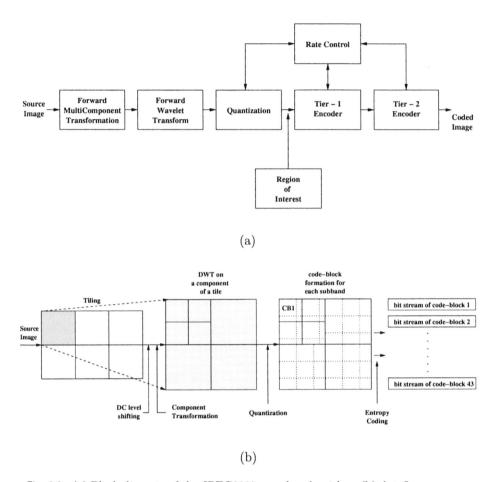

Fig. 6.2   (a) Block diagram of the JPEG2000 encoder algorithm; (b) dataflow.

shown in Figure 6.2(a). The data flow of the compression system is shown in Figure 6.2(b). As shown in Figure 6.2(b), each preprocessed component is independently compressed and transmitted as shown in Figure 6.2(a).

The compression phase is mainly divided into three sequential steps: (1) *Discrete Wavelet Transform* (DWT), (2) *Quantization*, and (3) *Entropy Encoding*. After preprocessing, each component is independently analyzed by a suitable discrete wavelet transform (DWT). The DWT essentially decomposes each component into a number of subbands in different resolution levels. Each subband is then independently quantized by a quantization parameter, in case of lossy compression. The quantized subbands are then divided into a number of smaller *code-blocks* of equal size, except for the code-blocks at the boundary of each subband. Typical size of the code-blocks is usually 32 × 32 or 64 × 64 for better memory handling and is very suitable for VLSI implementation with on-chip memory in the encoder architecture. The standard allows the limit of code-block sizes and the restrictions are discussed in Chapter 7. Each code-block is then entropy encoded independently to produce compressed bit-streams as shown in the dataflow diagram in Figure 6.2(b). We discuss the three major functions in the compression phase in the following sections.

6.6.1 Discrete Wavelet Transformation

The key difference between current JPEG [4] and JPEG2000 starts with the adoption of discrete wavelet transform (DWT) instead of the 8×8 block based discrete cosine transform (DCT). As we discussed earlier, the DWT essentially analyzes a tile (image) component to decompose it into a number of subbands at different levels of resolution. The two-dimensional DWT is performed by applying the one-dimensional DWT row-wise and then column-wise in each component as shown in Figure 4.4 in Chapter 4. In the first level of decomposition, four subbands LL1, HL1, LH1, and HH1 are created. The low-pass subband (LL1) represents a 2:1 subsampled in both vertical and horizonal directions, a low-resolution version of the original component. As explained in the theory of multiresolution analysis in Chapter 4, this is an approximation of the original image in subsampled form. The other subbands (HL1, LH1, HH1) represent a downsampled residual version (error because of coarser approximation) of the original image needed for the perfect recon-struction of the original image. The LL1 subband can again be analyzed to produce four subbands LL2, HL2, LH2, and HH2, and the higher level of decomposition can continue in a similar fashion. Typically, we don't get much compression benefit after five levels of decomposition in natural images. However, theoretically it can go even further. The maximum number of levels of decomposition allowed in Part 1 is 32. In Part 1 of the JPEG2000 stan-dard, only power of 2 dyadic decomposition in multiple levels of resolution is allowed.

   In Chapter 4 we discussed the theoretical background of the DWT and its implementation using both a convolution approach as well as a lifting-based approach. The standard supports both the convolution and the lifting-based approach for DWT. We also discussed issues of VLSI implementations of the DWT for both convolution and lifting-based approaches in Chapter 5. For details of DWT and their VLSI implementations, the reader is referred to Chapters 4 and 5 respectively. In the rest of this section, we present the two default wavelet filter pairs supported by Part 1 of the JPEG2000 standard.

6.6.1.1 Discrete Wavelet Transformation for Lossy Compression   For lossy com-pression, the default wavelet filter used in the JPEG2000 standard is the Daubechies (9, 7) *biorthogonal spline* filter. By (9, 7) we indicate that the analysis filter is formed by a 9-tap low-pass FIR filter and a 7-tap high-pass FIR filter. Both filters are symmetric. The analysis filter coefficients (for forward transformation) are as follows:

- 9-tap low-pass filter: $[h_{-4}, h_{-3}, h_{-2}, h_{-1}, h_0, h_1, h_2, h_3, h_4]$

$$
\begin{aligned}
h_4 = h_{-4} &= +0.026748757410810 \\
h_3 = h_{-3} &= -0.016864118442875 \\
h_2 = h_{-2} &= -0.078223266528988 \\
h_1 = h_{-1} &= +0.266864118442872 \\
h_0 &= +0.602949018236358
\end{aligned}
$$

- 7-tap high-pass filter: $[g_{-3}, g_{-2}, g_{-1}, g_0, g_1, g_2, g_3]$

$$
\begin{aligned}
g_3 = g_{-3} &= +0.0912717631142495 \\
g_2 = g_{-2} &= -0.057543526228500 \\
g_1 = g_{-1} &= -0.591271763114247 \\
g_0 &= +1.115087052456994
\end{aligned}
$$

For the synthesis filter pair used for inverse transformation, the low-pass FIR filter has seven filter coefficients and the high-pass FIR filter has nine coefficients. The corresponding synthesis filter coefficients are as follows:

- 7-tap low-pass filter: $[h'_{-3}, h'_{-2}, h'_{-1}, h'_0, h'_1, h'_2, h'_3]$

$$
\begin{aligned}
h'_3 = h'_{-3} &= -0.0912717631142495 \\
h'_2 = h'_{-2} &= -0.057543526228500 \\
h'_1 = h'_{-1} &= +0.591271763114247 \\
h'_0 &= +1.115087052456994
\end{aligned}
$$

- 9-tap high-pass filter: $[g'_{-4}, g'_{-3}, g'_{-2}, g'_{-1}, g'_0, g'_1, g'_2, g'_3, g'_4]$

$$
\begin{aligned}
g'_4 = g'_{-4} &= +0.026748757410810 \\
g'_3 = g'_{-3} &= +0.016864118442875 \\
g'_2 = g'_{-2} &= -0.078223266528988 \\
g'_1 = g'_{-1} &= -0.266864118442872 \\
g'_0 &= +0.602949018236358
\end{aligned}
$$

For lifting implementation, the (9, 7) wavelet filter pair can be factorized into a sequence of primal and dual lifting as explained in Chapter 4. The detailed explanation on the principles of lifting factorization of the wavelet filters has been presented in Section 4.4.4 in Chapter 4. The most efficient factorization of the polyphase matrix for the (9, 7) filter is as follows [10]:

$$
\tilde{P}(z) = \begin{bmatrix} 1 & a(1+z^{-1}) \\ 0 & 1 \end{bmatrix} \begin{bmatrix} 1 & 0 \\ b(1+z) & 1 \end{bmatrix} \begin{bmatrix} 1 & c(1+z^{-1}) \\ 0 & 1 \end{bmatrix} \begin{bmatrix} 1 & 0 \\ d(1+z) & 1 \end{bmatrix} \begin{bmatrix} K & 0 \\ 0 & \frac{1}{K} \end{bmatrix}
$$

where $a = -1.586134342$, $b = -0.05298011854$, $c = 0.8829110762$, $d = -0.4435068522$, $K = 1.149604398$.

6.6.1.2 Reversible Wavelet Transform for Lossless Compression   For lossless compression, the default wavelet filter used in the JPEG2000 standard is the Le Gall (5, 3) spline filter [28]. Although this is the default filter for lossless transformation, it can be applied in lossy compression as well. However, experimentally it has been observed that the (9, 7) filter produces better visual quality and compression efficiency in lossy mode than the (5, 3) filter. The analysis filter coefficients for the (5, 3) filter are as follows:

- 5-tap low-pass filter: $[h_{-2}, h_{-1}, h_0, h_1, h_2]$

$$\begin{aligned} h_2 = h_{-2} &= -1/8 \\ h_1 = h_{-1} &= 1/4 \\ h_0 &= 3/4 \end{aligned}$$

- 3-tap high-pass filter: $[g_{-1}, g_0, g_1]$

$$\begin{aligned} g_1 = g_{-1} &= -1/2 \\ g_0 &= 1 \end{aligned}$$

The corresponding synthesis filter coefficients are as follows:

- 3-tap low-pass filter: $[h'_{-1}, h'_0, h'_1]$

$$\begin{aligned} h'_1 = h'_{-1} &= 1/2 \\ h'_0 &= 1 \end{aligned}$$

- 5-tap high-pass filter: $[g'_{-2}, g'_{-1}, g'_0, g'_1, g'_2]$

$$\begin{aligned} g'_2 = g'_{-2} &= -1/8 \\ g'_1 = g'_{-1} &= -1/4 \\ g'_0 &= 3/4 \end{aligned}$$

The effective lifting factorization of the polyphase matrix for the (5, 3) filter has been derived in Section 4.4.4 in Chapter 4. This is shown below for the sake of completeness:

$$\tilde{P}(z) = \begin{bmatrix} 1 & \frac{1}{4}(1+z) \\ 0 & 1 \end{bmatrix} \begin{bmatrix} 1 & 0 \\ -\frac{1}{2}(1+z^{-1}) & 1 \end{bmatrix}.$$

6.6.1.3 Boundary Handling   Like a convolution, filtering is applied to the input samples by multiplying the filter coefficients with the input samples and accumulating the results. Since these filters are not causal, they cause discontinuities at the tile boundaries and create visible artifacts at the image boundaries as well. This introduces the dilemma of what to do at the boundaries. In order to reduce discontinuities in tile boundaries or reduce artifacts at image boundaries, the input samples should be first extended *periodically* at both sides of the input boundaries before applying the one-dimensional filtering both during row-wise and column-wise computation. By symmetrical/mirror extension of the data around the boundaries, one is able to deal with the noncausal nature of the filters and avoid edge effects. The number of additional samples needed to extend the boundaries of the input data is dependent on filter length. The general idea of period extension of the finite-length signal boundaries is explained by the following two examples.

Example 1: Consider the finite-length input signal $A\,B\,C\,D\,E\,F\,G\,H$. For an FIR filter of odd length, the signal can be extended periodically as

$$\cdots F\,G\,\underline{H\,G\,F\,E\,D\,C\,B}\,\overline{A\,B\,C\,D\,E\,F\,G\,H}\,\underline{G\,F\,E\,D\,C\,B}\,A\,B\,C\,\cdots$$

The two underlined sequences demonstrate the symmetry of extension with respect to the first sample (A) and the last sample (H) of the input signal as axis, and hence the boundary samples (A and H) are not included in the extension. The overlined sequence is the original input signal. This is called "whole-sample" symmetric (WSS) extension. The (9, 7) and (5, 3) filter kernels in Part 1 of the standard are odd-length filters and the boundary handling is done using the whole-sample symmetric extension.

Example 2: For an FIR filter of even length, the signal can be extended periodically as

$$\cdots F\,G\,H\,\underline{H\,G\,F\,E\,D\,C\,B\,A}\,\overline{A\,B\,C\,D\,E\,F\,G\,H}\,\underline{H\,G\,F\,E\,D\,C\,B\,A}\,A\,B\,C\,\cdots$$

The two underlined sequences demonstrate the *mirror* symmetry of the input signal at both of the boundaries and the overlined sequence is the original input signal. This is called "half-sample" symmetric (HSS) extension, in which the boundary samples (A and H) are also included in the extension because of the mirror symmetry. The even-length filters are allowed in the Part 2 extension of the standard and the boundary handling is accomplished by the half-sample symmetric extension.

6.6.2 Quantization

After the DWT, all the subbands are quantized in lossy compression mode in order to reduce the precision of the subbands to aid in achieving compression. Quantization of DWT subbands is one of the main sources of information loss in the encoder. Coarser quantization results in more compression and hence in reducing the reconstruction fidelity of the image because of greater loss of information. Quantization is not performed in case of lossless encoding. In Part 1 of the standard, the quantization is performed by uniform scalar quantization with dead-zone about the origin. In dead-zone scalar quantizer with step-size $\triangle_b$, the width of the dead-zone (i.e., the central quantization bin around the origin) is $2\triangle_b$ as shown in Figure 6.3. The standard supports separate quantization step sizes for each subband. The quantization step size ($\triangle_b$) for a subband (b) is calculated based on the dynamic range of the subband values. The formula of uniform scalar quantization with a dead-zone is

$$q_b(i,j) = sign(y_b(i,j)) \left\lfloor \frac{|y_b(i,j)|}{\triangle_b} \right\rfloor, \tag{6.5}$$

where $y_b(i,j)$ is a DWT coefficient in subband b and $\triangle_b$ is the quantization step size for the subband b. All the resulting qunantized DWT coefficients $q_b(i,j)$ are signed integers.

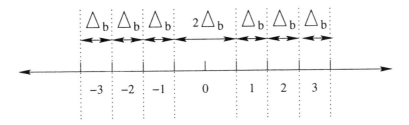

Fig. 6.3   Dead-zone quantization about the origin.

All the computations up to the quantization step are carried out in two's complement form. After the quantization, the quantized DWT coefficients are converted into sign-magnitude represented prior to entropy coding because of the inherent characteristics of the entropy encoding process, which will be described in greater detail in Chapter 7.

6.6.3   Region of Interest Coding

The *region of interest* (ROI) coding is a unique feature of the JPEG2000 standard. It allows different regions of an image to be coded with different fidelity criteria. These regions can have arbitrary shapes and be disjoint to each other. In Figure 6.4, we show an example of ROI coding. We compressed the ROI portion of the Zebra image losslessly and introduced losses in the non-ROI (background) part of the image. The reconstructed image after decompression is shown in Figure 6.4(a). We indicate the ROI by a circle around the head of the Zebra in Figure 6.4(a). In Figure 6.4(b), we pictorially show the difference between the original image and the reconstructed image after ROI coding and decoding. The values of difference of the original and the reconstructed pixels in the ROI region (i.e., inside the circle) are all zeros (black) and they are nonzero (white) in the non-ROI parts of the image. This shows the capability of the JPEG2000 standard in how we can compress different regions of an image with different degrees of fidelity.

(a)   (b)

Fig. 6.4 (a) Reconstructed image with circular shape ROI. (b) Difference between original image and reconstructed image.

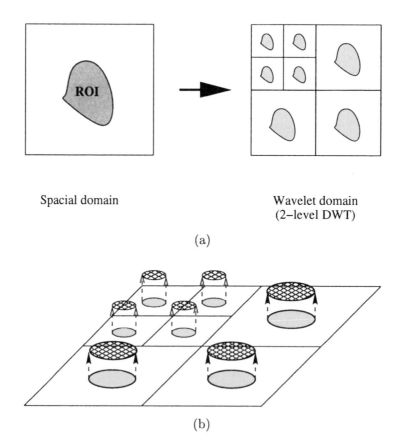

Fig. 6.5 (a) ROI mask. (b) Scaling of ROI coefficients.

The ROI method defined in the JPEG2000 Part 1 standard is called the MAXSHIFT method [29]. The MAXSHIFT method is an extension of the scaling-based ROI coding method [30]. During ROI coding, a binary mask is generated in the wavelet domain for distinction of the ROI from the background as shown in Figure 6.5(a). In the scaling-based ROI coding, the bits associated with the wavelet coefficients corresponding to an ROI (as indicated by the ROI mask) are scaled (shifted) to higher bit-planes than the bits associated with the non-ROI portion of the image. This is shown by a block diagram in Figure 6.5(b). During the encoding process, the most significant ROI bit-planes are encoded and transmitted progressively before encoding the bit-planes associated with the non-ROI background region. As a result, during the decoding process, the most significant bit-planes of ROI can be decoded before the background region progressively in order to produce high fidelity in the ROI portions of the image compared to its background. In this method, the encoding can stop at any point and still the ROI portion of the reconstructed image will have higher quality than the non-ROI portion. In scaling-based ROI, the scaling parameter and the shape information needs to be transmitted along with the compressed bitstream. This is used in the Part 2 extension of the standard.

In JPEG2000 Part 1, the MAXSHIFT technique is applied instead of the more general scaling-based technique. The MAXSHIFT allows arbitrary-shaped regions to be encoded without requiring to transmit the shape information along with the compressed bitstream. As a result, there is no need for shape coding or decoding in the MAXSHIFT technique. The basic principle of the MAXSHIFT method is to find the minimum value (V_{min}) in the ROI and the maximum value in the background (both in wavelet transformed domain) and then scale (shift) the wavelet coefficients in ROI in such a manner that the smallest coefficient in the ROI is always greater than the largest coefficient in the background. Then the bit-planes are encoded in the order of the most significant bit (MSB) plane first to the least significant bit (LSB) plane last. Figure 6.6 shows an example where the LSB plane of ROI is shifted above the MSB plane of the background region. During the decompression process, the wavelet coefficients that are larger than V_{min} are identified as the ROI coefficients without requiring any shape information or the binary mask that was used during the encoding process. The ROI coefficients are now shifted down relative to V_{min} in order to represent it with original bits of precision.

In JPEG2000, due to the sign-magnitude representation of the quantized wavelet coefficients required in the bit-plane coding, there is an implementation precision for number of bit-planes. Scaling the ROI coefficients up may cause an overflow problem when it goes beyond this implementation precision. Therefore, instead of shifting ROI up to higher bit-planes, the coefficients of background are downscaled by a specified value s, which is stored in the RGN (ReGioN of interest, discussed in Chapter 8) marker segment in the bitstream header. The decoder can deduce the shape information based on this shift

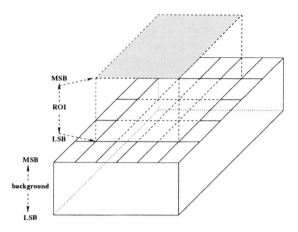

Fig. 6.6 MAXSHIFT.

value s and magnitude of the coefficients. By choosing an appropriate value of s, we can decide how many bit-planes to truncate in the background in order to achieve overall bit-rate without sacrificing the visual quality of the ROI.

6.6.4 Rate Control

Although the key encoding modules of JPEG2000 such as wavelet transformation, quantization, and entropy coding (bit-plane coding and binary arithmetic coding) are clearly specified, some implementation issues are left up to the prerogative of the individual developers. Rate control is one such open issue in JPEG2000 standard. Rate control is a process by which the bit-rates (sometimes called coding rates) are allocated in each code-block in each subband in order to achieve the overall target encoding bit-rate for the whole image while minimizing the distortion (errors) introduced in the reconstructed image due to quantization and truncation of codes to achieve the desired code rate [31]. It can also be treated in another way. Given the allowed distortion in the MSE (mean square energy) sense, the rate control can dictate the optimum encoding rate while achieving the maximum given MSE.

The JPEG2000 encoder generates a number of independent bitstreams by encoding the code-blocks. Accordingly a rate-distortion optimization algorithm generates the truncation points for these bitstreams in an optimal way in order to minimize the distortion according to a target bit rate. After the image is completely compressed, the rate-distortion optimization algorithm is applied once at the end using all the rate and rate-distortion slope information of each coding unit. This is the so-called postcompression rate-distortion (PCRD) algorithm [32].

There is another simple way to control bit-rate by choosing the quantization step size. The bigger the step size, the lower the rate will be. However, this method can apply only to lossy compression mode, and every time the step sizes change, the Tier-1 encoding (discussed in Chapter 7) needs to be recomputed. Since the Tier-1 coding is a very computationally intensive module in JPEG2000 standard, this approach of bit-rate control may not be suitable for some applications that are computationally constrained.

However, the bit-rate control is purely an encoder issue, and remains an open issue for the JPEG2000 standard. It is up to the prerogative of the developers how they want to accomplish the rate-distortion optimization in a computationally efficient way without incurring too much computation and/or hardware cost. Detailed discussion on this topic is beyond the scope of this book.

From the hardware implementation perspective, the rate-distortion algorithm requires a microcontroller to compute the breakpoints using a rate-distortion optimization technique and supply these breakpoints to the entropy encoding engine for formation of the compress bitstream.

6.6.5 Entropy Encoding

Physically the data are compressed by the entropy encoding of the quantized wavelet coefficients in each code-block in each subband. We have devoted a complete chapter (Chapter 7) to discussion of entropy encoding. Here we just summarize the entropy-encoding scheme at the top level for the sake of completeness of this chapter. The entropy coding and generation of compressed bitstream in JPEG2000 is divided into two coding steps: *Tier-1* and *Tier-2* coding.

6.6.5.1 Tier-1 Coding In Tier-1 coding, the code-blocks are encoded independently. If the precision of the elements in the code-block is p, then the code-block is decomposed into p bit-planes and they are encoded from the most significant bit-plane to the least significant bit-plane sequentially. Each bit-plane is first encoded by a *fractional bit-plane coding* (BPC) mechanism to generate intermediate data in the form of a *context* and a binary *decision* value for each bit position. In JPEG2000 the *embedded block coding with optimized truncation* (EBCOT) algorithm [32] has been adopted for the BPC. EBCOT encodes each bit-plane in three coding passes, with a part of a bit-plane being coded in each coding pass without any overlapping with the other two coding passes. That is the reason why the BPC is also called *fractional* bit-plane coding. The three coding passes in the order in which they are performed on each bit-plane are *significant propagation pass, magnitude refinement pass,* and *cleanup pass*. The algorithm is very complex and we have devoted a complete chapter on this with a number of examples to aid the reader in better understanding of the algorithm. The details of these coding passes and the EBCOT algorithm are dealt with in Chapter 7.

The binary decision values generated by the EBCOT are encoded using a variation of *binary arithmetic coding* (BAC) to generate compressed codes for each code-block. The variation of the binary arithmetic coder is a *context adaptive BAC* called the MQ-coder, which is the same coder used in the JBIG2 standard to compress bi-level images [33]. The *context* information generated by EBCOT is used to select the estimated probability value from a lookup table and this probability value is used by the MQ-coder to adjust the intervals and generate the compressed codes. JPEG2000 standard uses a predefined lookup table with 47 entries for only 19 possible different contexts for each bit type depending on the coding passes. This facilitates rapid probability adaptation in the MQ-coder and produces compact bitstreams.

The basic principles behind arithmetic coding and binary arithmetic coding are given in greater detail in Chapter 2. The working principles and detail flowchart (algorithm) for implementation of the MQ-coder are presented in Chapter 7.

6.7 TIER-2 CODING AND BITSTREAM FORMATION

After the compressed bits for each code-block are generated by Tier-1 coding, the Tier-2 coding engine efficiently represents the layer and block summary information for each code-block. A *layer* consists of consecutive bit-plane coding passes from each code-block in a tile, including all the subbands of all the components in the tile. The concept of layer and other constructs used in the JPEG2000 standard is discussed with examples in Chapter 7. The block summary information consists of length of compressed code words of the code-block, the most significant magnitude bit-plane at which any sample in the code-block is nonzero, as well as the truncation point between the bitstream layers, among others. The decoder receives this information in an encoded manner in the form of two tag trees. This encoding helps to represent this information in a very compact form without incurring too much overhead in the final compressed file. The encoding process is popularly known as *Tag Tree coding*. The details of this Tag Tree coding algorithm with examples and further details of the bitstream formation methodology are discussed in Chapter 7.

Details of the code-stream organization and the file format for JPEG2000 Part 1 are discussed in Chapter 8.

6.8 SUMMARY

In this chapter, we presented an overview of the JPEG2000 standard for image compression. We discussed different salient features of the new JPEG2000 standard and how they influence vast applications areas. We introduced different parts of the standard. The core coding system in JPEG2000 has been defined in Part 1 of the standard. We dealt in great length with the underlying principles and algorithms for the Part 1 core coding system for JPEG2000 standard. The whole compression system can be divided into three phases—image preprocessing, compression, and compressed bitstream formation. In this chapter, we first discussed the concepts behind the preprocessing functionalities, including tiling of the input image, DC level shifting, and multicomponent transformation, before the actual compression takes place. We discussed the implementation issues of the discrete wavelet transform supported by the JPEG2000 Part 1 standard including the symmetric extension at the boundary of the signals both for lossless and lossy compression. Theoretical foundation of the discrete wavelet transform and its implementation issues were elaborated on earlier in Chapter 4. In lossy compression mode, a dead-zone scalar quantization technique is applied on the wavelet coefficients. The concept of region of interest coding allows one to encode different regions of the input image with different fidelity. We discussed the region of interesting coding can be achieved in terms of simply scaling the wavelet coefficients, and demonstrated some examples. The entropy coding and the generation of compressed bitstream in JPEG2000 are divided into two coding steps: *Tier-1* and *Tier-2* coding. We introduced the Tier-1 coding step in entropy encoding based on a fractional bit-plane coding scheme (EBCOT) and an adaptive binary arithmetic coding (MQ-coder). The Tier-2 coding and the bitstream formation concept was introduced in this chapter. The details of the algorithms for both the Tier-1 coding and the Tier-2 coding are presented in greater detail in Chapter 7. In Chapter 8, we discuss the actual code-stream organization and file format for the JPEG2000 Part 1 standard. We introduce other parts of the standard in Chapter 10.

REFERENCES

1. A. N. Skodras, C. A. Christopoulos, and T. Ebrahimi, "JPEG2000: The Upcoming Still Image Compression Standard," *Proceedings of the 11th Portuguese Conference on Pattern Recognition*, Porto, Portugal, pp. 359–366, May 11–12, 2000.

2. A. Skodras, C. Christopoulos, and T. Ebrahimi, "The JPEG2000 Still Image Compression Standard," *IEEE Signal Processing Magazine*, pp. 36–58, September 2001.

3. D. S. Taubman and M. W. Marcellin. *JPEG2000: Image Compression Fundamentals, Standards and Practice*. Kluwer Academic Publishers, MA, 2002.

4. ISO/IEC 10918 (JPEG), "Information Technology—Digital Compression and Coding of Continuous-Tone Still Images."

5. W. B. Pennebaker and J. L. Mitchell, *JPEG Still Image Compression Standard.* Chapman & Hall, New York, 1993.

6. S. Mallat, "A Theory for Multiresolution Signal Decomposition: The Wavelet Representation," *IEEE Trans. on Pattern Analysis and Machine Intelligence*, Vol. 11, No. 7, pp. 674–693, July 1989.

7. I. Daubechies, "The Wavelet Transform, Time-Frequency Localization and Signal Analysis," *IEEE Trans. on Inform. Theory*, Vol. 36, No. 5, pp. 961–1005, September 1990.

8. Y. Meyers, *Wavelet: Algorithms and Applications.* SIAM, Philadelphia, 1993 (Translated by Robert D. Ryan).

9. W. Sweldens, "The Lifting Scheme: A Custom-Design Construction of Biorthogonal Wavelets," *Applied and Computational Harmonic Analysis*, Vol. 3, No. 15, pp. 186–200, 1996.

10. I. Daubechies and W. Sweldens, "Factoring Wavelet Transforms into Lifting Schemes," *Journal of Fourier Analysis and Applications*, Vol. 4, pp. 247–269, 1998.

11. R. A. DeVore, B. Jawerth, and B. J. Lucier, "Image Compression Through Wavelet Transform Coding," *IEEE Trans. on Information Theory*, Vol. 38, No. 2, pp. 719–746, March 1992.

12. M. Antonini, M. Barlaud, P. Mathieu, and I. Daubechies, "Image Coding Using Wavelet Transform," *IEEE Trans. on Image Processing*, Vol. 1, No. 2, pp. 205–220, April 1992.

13. A. S. Lewis and G. Knowles, "Image Compression Using the 2-D Wavelet Transform," *IEEE. Trans. on Image Processing*, Vol. 1, No. 2, pp. 244–250, April 1992.

14. J. M. Shapiro, "Embedded Image Coding Using Zerotrees of Wavelet Coefficients," *IEEE Trans. on Signal Processing*, Vol. 41, No. 12, pp. 3445–3462, December 1993.

15. A. Said and W. A. Peralman, "A New Fast and Efficient Image Codec Based on Set Partitioning in Hierarchical Trees," *IEEE Trans. on Circuits and Systems for Video Technology*, Vol. 6, No. 3, pp. 243–250, June 1996.

16. A. Said and W. A. Peralman, "An Image Multiresolution Representation for Lossless and Lossy Compression," *IEEE Trans. on Image Processing*, Vol. 5, pp. 1303–1310, September 1996.

17. P. Chen, T. Acharya, and H. Jafarkhani, "A Pipelined VLSI Architecture for Adaptive Image Compression," *International Journal of Robotics and Automation*, Vol. 14, No. 3, pp. 115–123, 1999.

18. *JPEG2000 Requirements and Profiles*, ISO/IEC JTC1/SC29/WG1 N1271, March 1999.

19. I. H. Witten, R. M. Neal, and J. G. Cleary, "Arithmetic Coding for Data Compression," *Communications of the ACM*, Vol. 30, No. 6, June 1987.

20. ISO/IEC 15444-1, "Information Technology—JPEG2000 Image Coding System—Part 1: Core Coding System," 2000.

21. ISO/IEC 15444-2, Final Committee Draft, "Information Technology— JPEG2000 Image Coding System—Part 2: Extensions," 2000.

22. ISO/IEC 15444-3, "Information Technology—JPEG2000 Image Coding System—Part 3: Motion JPEG2000," 2002.

23. ISO/IEC 15444-4, "Information Technology—JPEG2000 Image Coding System—Part 4: Conformance Testing," 2002.

24. ISO/IEC 15444-5, "Information Technology—JPEG2000 Image Coding System—Part 5: Reference Software," 2003.

25. ISO/IEC 15444-6, Final Committee Draft, "Information Technology— JPEG2000 Image Coding System—Part 6: Compound Image File Format," 2001.

26. ITU-T T.44|ISO/IEC 16485, "Information Technology—Mixed Raster Content (MRC)," 2000.

27. D. Santa-Cruz and T. Ebrahima, "An Analytical Study of JPEG2000 Functionalities," *Proceedings of International Conference on Image Processing*, September 10–13, 2000, Vancouver, Canada.

28. D. L. Gall and A. Tabatabai, "Subband Coding of Digital Images Using Symmetric Short Kernel Filters and Arithmetic Coding Techniques," *Proceedings of IEEE International Conference Acoustics, Speech, and Signal Processing*, Vol. 2, pp. 761–764, New York, April 1988.

29. D. Nister and C. Christopoulos, "Lossless Region of Interest with Embedded Wavelet Image Coding," *Signal Processing*, Vol. 78, No. 1, pp. 1–17, 1999.

30. E. Atsumi and N. Farvardin, " Loss/Lossless Region-of-Interest Image Coding Based on Set Partitioning in Hierarchical Tree," *IEEE International Conference Image Processing*, pp. 87–91, Chicago, October 1998.

31. A. Ortega and K. Ramchandran, "Rate-Distortion Methods for Image and Video Compression," *IEEE Signal Processing Magazine*, Vol. 15, No. 6, pp. 23–50, November 1998.

32. D. S. Taubman, "High Performance Scalable Image Compression with EBCOT," *IEEE Transaction Image Processing*, Vol. 9, No. 7, pp. 1158–1170, July 2000.

33. ISO/IEC 14492-1, "Lossy/Lossless Coding of Bi-level Images," 2000.

7

Coding Algorithms in JPEG2000

7.1 INTRODUCTION

As shown in Section 6.6, Figure 6.2(a), after the DWT and quantization, the encoding phase in JPEG2000 is divided into two steps—*Tier-1* coding and *Tier-2* coding. In Tier-1 coding, each code-block is entropy encoded independently. In Tier-2 coding, the information of the compressed codewords generated in the Tier-1 coding step are encoded using a Tag Tree coding mechanism, which will be discussed in great detail in this chapter.

Entropy coding in JPEG2000 [5] is combination of fractional bit-plane coding (BPC) [1] and binary arithmetic coding (BAC) [2] as opposed to the classical Huffman coding [3] and run-length coding in current JPEG [4]. Combination of BPC and BAC is known as Tier-1 coding in JPEG2000. In this chapter, we will explain this new paradigm of fractional bit-plane coding technique and implementation of the MQ-coder for binary arithmetic coding. We shall also discuss the Tag Tree coding mechanism used in Tier-2 coding with examples. Tag Tree is a particular type of quad-tree data structure, which provides the framework for efficiently representing information of the code-blocks and their compressed codewords, such as the number of leading-zero MSB (most significant bit) planes in a code-block, etc., in the Tier-2 coding engine in JPEG2000.

7.2 PARTITIONING DATA FOR CODING

During entropy encoding, each wavelet subband is further divided into a number of code-blocks. At this stage all the elements in all the subbands are represented in sign and magnitude representation of integers instead of two's complement. Dimension of the code-blocks is always a power of 2 with the minimum height and width being 4 and maximum height and width being 1024. Further restriction in dimension of a code-block is that if height of a code-block is 2^x and width of the code-block 2^y then $x + y$ is limited to be less than or equal to 12. Typical choice of code-block size is 64 × 64 or 32 × 32. It has been found experimentally that the compression performance degrades when the code-block size is chosen below 16 × 16. It should be noted that the profile-0 of JPEG2000 Part 1 amendments further restricts the code-block size to be either 32 × 32 or 64 × 64.

During the coding phase, each code-block is decomposed into a number of bit-planes. If the precision of the subband is P bits, then each code-block in the subband is decomposed into P number of bit-planes. *Bit-plane coding* (BPC) is applied on each bit-plane of the code-blocks to generate intermediate data in the form of a *context* and a *binary decision value*. The intermediate data is input to the *binary arithmetic coding* (BAC) step to generate the final compressed bitstream.

7.3 TIER-1 CODING IN JPEG2000

In JPEG2000, the **Embedded Block Coding with Optimized Truncation (EBCOT)** algorithm by David S. Taubman [1, 7] has been adapted to implement the BPC. This algorithm has been built to exploit the symmetries and redundancies within and across the bit-planes so as to minimize the statistics to be maintained and minimize the coded bitstream that BAC would generate. EBCOT encodes each bit-plane in three passes, with a part of the bit-plane being coded in each of these passes without any overlapping with the other two passes. That is the reason why this bit-plane coding is also called **fractional** bit-plane coding. The three passes in the order they are performed on each bit-plane are:

- **Significance Propagation Pass (SPP)**: Bit positions that have a magnitude of 1 for the first time (i.e., the most significant bit of the corresponding sample coefficients) are coded in this pass.

- **Magnitude Refinement Pass (MRP)**: Bit positions that have not been coded in SPP and that have had magnitude of 1 in previous bit-planes (i.e., the current bit is not the most significant bit of the corresponding sample coefficient) are coded in this pass.

- **Cleanup pass (CUP)**: Bit positions that have not been coded in either of the two earlier passes are coded in this pass. This pass also incorporates a form of run-length coding to help in coding a string of zeros.

7.3.1 Fractional Bit-Plane Coding

In order to make it easy for readers to understand this complex algorithm, we first provide the definition of terms used to describe the algorithm, followed by the explanation of four basic *coding operations* and three *coding passes*. Then we provide a simple example to illuminate the detailed process of the BPC coder.

7.3.1.1 Definition of Terms

- **Code-Block (y)**: A code-block is a two-dimensional array that consists of integers (wavelet coefficients with or without quantization). Each code-block has width and height that specify its size. Each integer of the code-block can be either positive, zero, or negative. Each of the elements of a code-block are associated with σ, σ', and η to indicate their coded states (see σ, σ', and η for detailed descriptions).

- **Sign Array (χ)**: χ is a two-dimensional array representing the signs of the elements of a code-block. It has the exact same dimensions as the code-block. Each element $\chi[m, n]$ represents the sign information of the corresponding element $y[m, n]$ in the code-block as follows.

$$\chi[m, n] = \begin{cases} 1 & \text{if } y[m, n] < 0 \\ 0 & \text{otherwise} \end{cases}$$

  When referenced to $\chi[m, n]$ during encoding or decoding, m or n may be out of range of a code-block, such as $m = -1$. This will happen when we are working on the boundary of the code-block. In those cases, $\chi[m, n]$ is always set to equal zero.

- **Magnitude Array (v)**: v is a two-dimensional array of unsigned integers. Dimension of this array is exactly the same as the dimension of the code-block. Each element of v represents the absolute value of the integer at the corresponding location in the code-block, that is, $v[m, n] = |y[m, n]|$, where $y[m, n]$ is the integer element at spatial location (m, n) in the code-block. The notation $v^P[m, n]$ is used to denote the Pth bit of $v[m, n]$.

- **Bit-Plane**: The magnitude array v can be conceptually viewed as a three-dimensional array, with the bit sequence of the integers in the third dimension. Each particular order of bits of every element of v

constitutes a single bit-plane. We can also view v as a one-dimensional array consisting of a number of bit-planes.

Example: Consider $(2, 0)$ denotes a 2×1 array v with only two elements. The two bit-planes for this array will be $(1, 0)$ and $(0, 0)$.

We say one bit-plane is more significant than the other if its bits are more significant than those of the other. Not all bit-planes of v are going to be coded because a bit sequence may have as many leading zeros as possible for a particular nonnegative value. We code only the most significant bit-plane containing at least one 1 and all the other subsequent less significant bit-planes, regardless of whether they have 1 or not. In other words, a bit-plane that entirely consists of 0 is ignored unless there is a higher significant bit-plane that contains at least one 1. We call those uncoded bit-planes "leading-zero bit-planes." A nonnegative integer P is frequently used to refer to a bit-plane to be coded. We use $v^P[m, n]$ to represent the bit at spatial location (m, n) of the bit-plane P of the code-block.

- **Scan Pattern:** Scan pattern defines the order of encoding or decoding the bit-planes of a code-block. The scan pattern of a code-block can be conceptually divided into sections (or stripes), each with four consecutive rows starting from the first row of a code-block. If the total number of rows of a code-block is not a multiple of 4, all the sections will have four consecutive rows except the very last section. The scan starts from the first section and down to the last section until all elements of a code-block are encoded or decoded. Each section is scanned from the first row of the first column. The next location to be scanned will be the next row on the same column. After a column in the section is completely coded, start scanning at the first row of the next column in the same section. Continue the coding process until all columns in a section are coded. This same process is then applied to the next adjacent section until all of them are coded. An example of scan pattern for a 5×10 code-block is shown in Figure 7.1. Figure 7.1(a) shows the regular mode of the scan pattern. The JPEG2000 Part 1 also specified another scanning mode, **vertical causal** mode. In vertical causal mode, every section (sometimes referred to as stripe), that is, 4 rows by N columns, will be considered as a standalone module. In other words, under the vertical causal mode, all the information of neighbors from the same code-block but different sections will not be used in the current section. Figure 7.1(b) shows the vertical causal mode for the same example shown in Figure 7.1(a).

- **State Variables σ, σ' and η:** Three two-dimensional "binary" arrays, σ, σ', and η, are created to indicate the coding states of each element in the code-block during the coding process. These arrays have the exact the same dimension as the code-block. Initially, each of the elements of

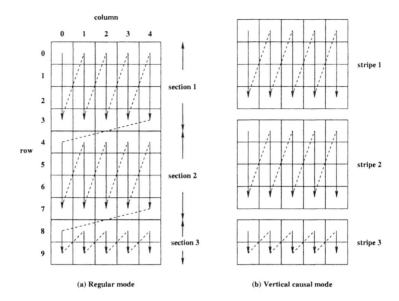

Fig. 7.1 Scan pattern with a 5 × 10 code-block: (a) regular mode; (b) vertical causal mode.

these arrays are set to 0 (i.e., $\sigma[m,n] = 0$, $\sigma'[m,n] = 0$, and $\eta[m,n] = 0$, for all m and n). Once the coding process starts, the values of the two variables $\sigma[m,n]$ and $\sigma'[m,n]$ may change to 1 depending on certain conditions, but are never changed back to 0 until the entire code-block is encoded. On the other hand, the values of $\eta[m,n]$ are reset to 0 right after completion of coding of each bit-plane. Interpretations of these three variables are as follows:

- When $\sigma[m,n] = 1$, it indicates that the first nonzero bit of $v[m,n]$ at row m and column n has been coded; otherwise it is equal to 0. When referenced to $\sigma[m,n]$ during encoding or decoding, m or n may be out of range or have an invalid value, such as $m = -1$. In this case, $\sigma[m,n]$ is equal to 0.

- When $\sigma'[m,n] = 1$, it indicates that a *magnitude refinement coding* operation (defined in the next section) has been applied to $v[m,n]$; otherwise, it is equal to zero.

- When $\eta[m,n] = 1$, it indicates that *zero coding* operation (defined in the next section) has been applied to $v^P[m,n]$ in the *significant propagation pass*; otherwise, it is equal to 0.

- **Preferred Neighborhood:** An element $y[m,n]$ in the code-block is said to be in a preferred neighborhood if at least one of its eight adjacent neighbors has σ value equal to 1.

- **Zero Coding Tables:** There are three zero coding tables for the purpose of *zero coding* operations as shown in Tables 7.1–7.3. The *context* information generated in zero coding operation is based on the values of the *significance* states (σ) of the eight neighbors of the element being encoded. In Figure 7.2, we show the eight neighbors of an element (say **X**) used in these tables to form the "context." For example, **X** is an element in the LL subband, and the two horizonal neighbors have significance state value of 1 (i.e., $\sum H = 2$). The context value 8 will be used as shown in Table 7.1.

$\mathbf{D_0}$	$\mathbf{V_0}$	$\mathbf{D_1}$
$\mathbf{H_0}$	$\mathbf{X}$	$\mathbf{H_1}$
$\mathbf{D_3}$	$\mathbf{V_1}$	$\mathbf{D_2}$

Fig. 7.2   Neighborhood for *zero coding* context generation.

Table 7.1   Zero Coding Context Table for Code-Blocks from LL and LH Subbands

LL and LH Subbands			Context Label
$\sum H$	$\sum V$	$\sum D$	**CX**
2	x	x	8
1	≥ 1	x	7
1	0	≥ 1	6
1	0	0	5
0	2	x	4
0	1	x	3
0	0	≥ 2	2
0	0	1	1
0	0	0	0

Note: "x" in the table denotes "do not care."

7.3.1.2 Coding Operations   There are four possible coding operations used in EBCOT to generate the values of **context** (CX) and **decision** (D) as intermediate data before the BAC. CX is a nonnegative integer while D is a binary value, 0 or 1. There are nineteen different context values (0–18) used in these four coding operations. The index of the current bit-plane is assumed to be P. Exactly when or where these operations are applied is subject to current coding pass, the location of the current element, and the status of the state variables.

- **Zero Coding (ZC):** For zero coding operation, the decision bit D is equal to $v^P[m,n]$ and CX is selected from one of the three "zero coding context tables" related to the relevant subband (LH, HL or HH) the code-block belongs to. There are nine entries in each context table.

Table 7.2   Zero Coding Context Table for Code-Blocks from HL Subbands

HL Subbands			Context Label
$\sum H$	$\sum V$	$\sum D$	CX
x	2	x	8
≥ 1	1	x	7
0	1	≥ 1	6
0	1	0	5
2	0	x	4
1	0	x	3
0	0	≥ 2	2
0	0	1	1
0	0	0	0

Table 7.3   Zero Coding Context Table for Code-Blocks from HH Subbands

HH Subbands		Context Label
$\sum (H+V)$	$\sum D$	CX
x	≥ 3	8
≥ 1	2	7
0	2	6
≥ 2	1	5
1	1	4
0	1	3
≥ 2	0	2
1	0	1
0	0	0

They are derived using the values of the significance states of the eight surrounding neighbors of the current coefficient bit, $v^P[m,n]$. As shown in the tables, each entry depends on how many and which neighbors of $v^P[m,n]$ are significant.

- **Sign Coding (SC):** The D and CX for the sign coding are determined by a horizontal reference value H and a vertical reference value V. Suppose that the current scan location is (m,n); the values of H and V are obtained by the following equations.

$$H = \min[1, \max(-1, \sigma[m, n-1] \times (1 - 2\chi[m, n-1]) + \sigma[m, n+1] \times (1 - 2\chi[m, n+1]))]$$

$$V = \min[1, \max(-1, \sigma[m-1, n] \times (1 - 2\chi[m-1, n]) + \sigma[m+1, n] \times (1 - 2\chi[m+1, n]))]$$

The reference values of H and V indicate three possible situations as follows:

1. **0** indicates that both neighbors are insignificant, or both neighbors are significant but have opposite signs.

2. **1** indicates that one or both neighbors are significant with positive sign.

3. **−1** indicates that one or both neighbors are significant with negative sign.

The neighbors mean the two adjacent horizontal locations of the current scan location for H and the two vertical locations of the current scan location for V. Significant at a location means the value of the state variable σ at that location is 1 while insignificant means the value of σ is 0.

As shown in Table 7.4, H and V are used together to determine the context (CX) and a binary value $\hat{\chi}$, which in terms is used to calculate the value of D as $D = \hat{\chi} \otimes \chi[m, n]$, where $\otimes$ represents an Exclusive-OR operation.

Table 7.4   Reference Table for Sign Coding

H	V	$\hat{\chi}$	CX
1	1	0	13
1	0	0	12
1	−1	0	11
0	1	0	10
0	0	0	9
0	−1	1	10
−1	1	1	11
−1	0	1	12
−1	−1	1	13

- **Magnitude Refinement Coding (MRC):** For magnitude refinement coding, D at position (m, n) in the Pth bit-plane is simply equal to the bit value $v^P[m, n]$. The value of CX is determined by $\sigma'[m, n]$ and the sum of its eight adjacent values of the state variable σ is as follows:

  - If $\sigma' = 1$ at the current position, which indicates that it is not the first magnitude refinement for this element, then CX $= 16$.
  - When $\sigma' = 0$ at the current position and the sum of the values of σ of its eight adjacent neighbors is also 0, then CX $= 14$.
  - When $\sigma' = 0$ at the current position and the sum of the values of σ of its eight adjacent neighbors is greater than 0, then CX $= 15$.

In Table 7.5, we summarized the logic for generation of the context values (CX) as described above.

Table 7.5   Reference Table for Magnitude Refinement Coding

$\sigma'[m,n]$	$\sigma[m-1,n]$ + $\sigma[m+1,n]$ + $\sigma[m-1,n-1]$ + $\sigma[m-1,n+1]$ + $\sigma[m+1,n-1]$ + $\sigma[m+1,n+1]$	CX
1	x	16
0	≥ 1	15
0	0	14

- **Run-Length Coding (RLC):** Unlike the other three coding operations, run-length coding may code from one to four consecutive bits in the current scan pattern stripe. Exactly how many bits are encoded depends on where the first 1 bit (if any) is located in the four consecutive bits. If all of them are 0's, then all four bits are coded. If one (or more) of these four bits is 1, then the first 1 in the scan pattern and any preceding 0's in between the current scan location are coded. For example, suppose that 0101 are four consecutive bits along the scan pattern of a bit-plane. If the current location is at the first 0 and we are going to apply run-length coding, then the first two bits, 01, are coded and the next location will be at the second 0.

A run-length coding operation may generate either one D or three D's, depending on whether the four consecutive bits are all 0's or not. The first D is equal to 0 if all four bits are equal to 0; otherwise it is equal to 1. For both cases, CX is equal to a unique run-length context value 17. In other words, a (CX, D) pair with values (17, 0) indicates four consecutive 0 bits, and a (CX, D) pair with values (17, 1) means there is at least one 1 bit in the current scan pattern stripe.

In the case that at least one of the four bits in the current scan pattern is 1, two more D's are used with a "UNIFORM" context value 18 to indicate the location of the first 1 bit in the 4-bit scan pattern. Since height of the scan pattern is four, a zero-based index with two bits is sufficient to indicate the location of the first 1 bit from the top. The first and the second D's with a UNIFORM context represent the most significant and the least significant bits of these two bits representing the distance.

Continuing with the example for coding 01, the values of the first and the second D's are 0 and 1, respectively. The corresponding (CX, D) pairs will be (18, 0) and (18, 1).

Table 7.6 shows the summary of all nineteen different contexts used in the four different coding operations, and their corresponding initial index values for the probability estimation lookup table used in BAC (discussed in next section).

Table 7.6 Nineteen Different Contexts and Their Initial Index for BAC Probability Estimation Lookup Table

Operation	Context CX	Initial Index I(CX)
Zero Coding	0	**4**
	1	0
	2	0
	3	0
	4	0
	5	0
	6	0
	7	0
	8	0
Sign Coding	9	0
	10	0
	11	0
	12	0
	13	0
Magnitude Refinement Coding	14	0
	15	0
	16	0
Run-Length Coding	17	**3**
UNIFORM	18	**46**

7.3.1.3 Coding Passes There are three coding passes—*significance propagation pass* (SPP), *magnitude refinement pass* (MRP), and *cleanup pass* (CUP). Three different coding passes are applied to each bit-plane of a code-block except the first bit-plane (the most significant bit-plane), which is applied only with the cleanup pass.[1] After each coding pass completes a run of scan pattern in the current bit-plane, the next coding pass restarts the scan pattern from the beginning. The first bit-plane is only encoded by the cleanup pass. The remaining bit-planes are coded in the order of significance propagation pass, magnitude refinement pass, and cleanup pass. They are described below.

- **Cleanup Pass (CUP):** CUP applies to every bit-plane of a code-block after completion of MRP, except the first bit-plane, which does not need the MRP.

  In each position (m, n) follow in the scan pattern, CUP first checks where $\sigma[m, n]$ and $\eta[m, n]$ are both 0's. If any one of them is not 0, then proceed to the next bit position in the bit-plane. If they are both 0's, then check

---

[1] Even if we do apply the SPP and MRP to the most significant bit-plane, due to the initial condition there will be no bits coded in those two passes.

whether to apply run-length coding (RLC) or zero coding (ZC), but not both. RLC is applied when all the following three conditions are true:

1. m is a multiple of four, including $m = 0$.

2. $\sigma = 0$ for the four consecutive locations on the same column, starting from current scan position.

3. $\sigma = 0$ for all the adjacent neighbors of the four consecutive bits in the column.

If any one of the above conditions is false, then zero coding (ZC) is applied to the current location. Depending on whether run-length coding or zero coding is applied in the current location, the number of bits coded may vary. The next bit to be coded is the bit after the last coded bit. Note that run-length coding should not be applied to the last section with fewer than four rows in a scan pattern because there would not be four consecutive bits available in the same column.

After completion of the run-length coding or zero coding, we need to check whether we need to apply *sign coding* (SC) before we move on to code the next bit. Suppose the last coded position is (i, j). If $v^P[i, j] = 1$, which indicates this bit is the most significant bit of the current sample, the cleanup pass applies sign coding and assigns σ value of the last coded location to be 1 (i.e., $\sigma[i, j] = 1$) right after run-length or zero coding is done. Otherwise, no sign coding is needed.

Continue coding the bits along the scan pattern until all of the bits of the bit-plane are coded. After completion of the cleanup pass for a bit-plane, reset $\eta[m, n] = 0$ for all m and n in the bit-plane before moving into the next bit-plane. Figure 7.3 shows the flowchart of the cleanup pass we just described.

- **Significance Propagation Pass (SPP):** This is the first pass applied to every bit-plane of a code-block, except the first bit-plane. Significance propagation pass first applies zero coding if the current scan position (m, n) is in a preferred neighborhood and $\sigma[m, n] = 0$. If zero coding cannot be applied, then proceed to the next bit position. If the zero coding is applied, $\eta[m, n]$ is set to 1. After zero coding is completed, we need to check whether sign coding is needed at the current bit position (m, n). If $v^P[m, n] = 1$, then sign coding is applied and we set $\sigma[m, n] = 1$.

Continue coding the bits along the scan pattern until all of the bits of the bit-plane are coded. Figure 7.4 shows the flowchart of the significance propagation pass.

- **Magnitude Refinement Pass (MRP):** This is the second pass applied to every bit-plane of a code-block, except the first bit-plane, which does not need magnitude refinement pass.

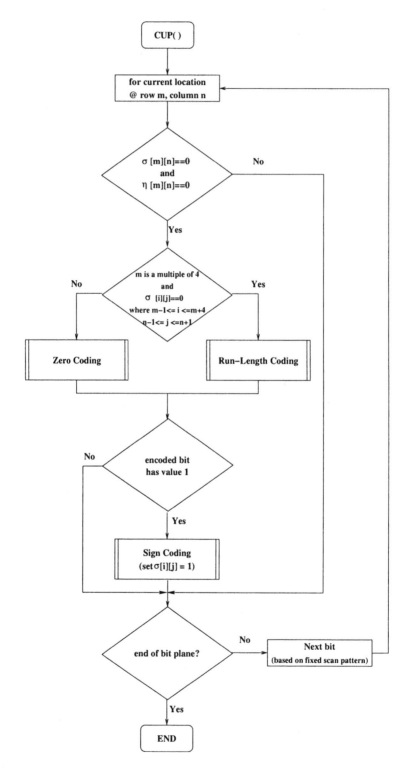

Fig. 7.3 Flowchart of cleanup pass.

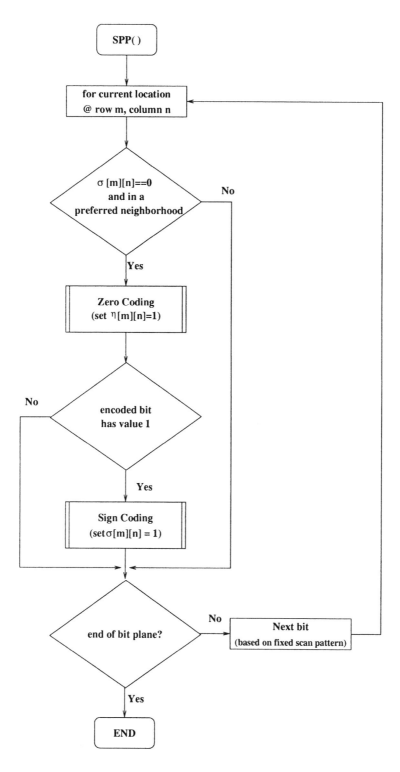

Fig. 7.4 Flowchart of significance propagation pass.

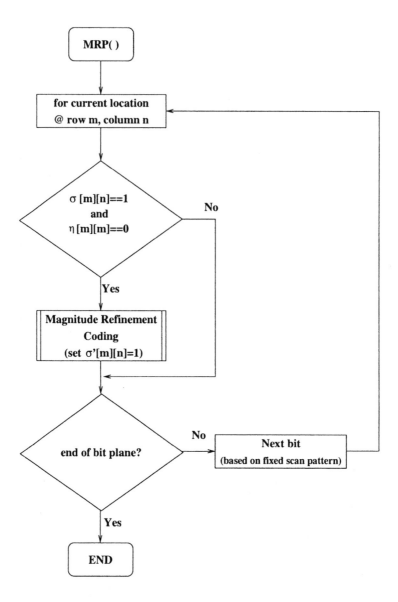

Fig. 7.5   Flowchart of magnitude refinement pass.

If the state variables $\sigma[m,n] = 1$ and $\eta[m,n] = 0$, then we apply magnitude refinement coding (MRC) to the current scan position (m,n) and set $\sigma'[m,n] = 1$. Continue coding the bits along the scan pattern until all of the bits of the bit-plane are coded. Figure 7.5 shows the flowchart of the magnitude refinement pass.

- **Selective binary arithmetic coding—bypass mode:**   Instead of applying the binary arithmetic coding (MQ-coder[2]) on symbols (the contexts and decision bits) generated during all three coding passes, the bypass mode allows bypassing MQ-coder for the SPP and MRP after the four most significant bit-planes are coded. In other words, only those symbols generated in the CUP will be coded with the MQ-coder, and raw decision bits and sign bits will be coded during the SPP and MRP, if the bypass mode is selected.

7.3.1.4 JPEG2000 Bit-Plane Coding: Encoder and Decoder Algorithms   As we discussed earlier, the quantized wavelet coefficients in each subband are converted into sign-magnitude represented before the entropy encoding starts. For each input code-block, we can first initialize the two-dimensional arrays v and χ, where the value of $v[m, n]$ is the magnitude and $\chi[m, n]$ is the sign information of the element at position (m, n) in the code-block. The number of bit-planes in the code-block to be encoded (P) is determined by searching the largest value in array v. Initially, all elements in two-dimensional arrays σ, σ', and η are set to 0's.

The first bit-plane to be coded is the most significant bit-plane. As mentioned at the definition of bit-plane, the leading-zero bit-planes consisting entirely of zeros are ignored. A more (higher) significant bit-plane is always coded before coding a less (lower) significant bit-plane. If $P = 0$, we don't need to do any coding and the output is empty. If $P \geq 1$, then we apply the cleanup pass only to the first bit-plane. For the remaining bit-planes, we first apply the significance propagation pass, then the magnitude refinement pass, and then the cleanup pass. Figure 7.6 shows the top-level flowchart of the fractional bit-plane coder.

The procedure of the decoder is essentially the same as for the encoder. For the sake of completeness, we also show the encoding and decoding procedures via the flowcharts as shown in Figures 7.7 and 7.8 respectively for $P \geq 1$.

7.3.2 Examples of BPC Encoder

In this section we present an example detailing all the operations step by step and the output generated by encoding a 4×4 code-block.

- Input of the encoder: An input 4×4 code-block is shown below:

3	0	0	5
-3	7	2	1
-4	-1	-2	3
0	6	0	2

---

[2]The MQ-coder will be discussed in the next section.

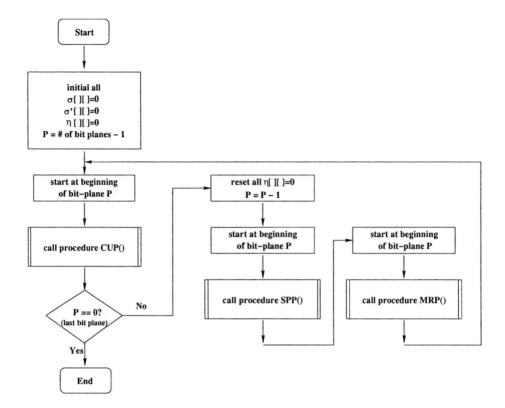

Fig. 7.6   Top-level flowchart of fractional bit-plane coder for $P > 0$.

- The magnitude array (v) is shown below:

3	0	0	5
3	7	2	1
4	1	2	3
0	6	0	2

- The sign array (χ) is shown below:

0	0	0	0
1	0	0	0
1	1	1	0
0	0	0	0

- The three bit-planes are shown below as bit-planes of the magnitude array v^2, v^1, and v^0 respectively:

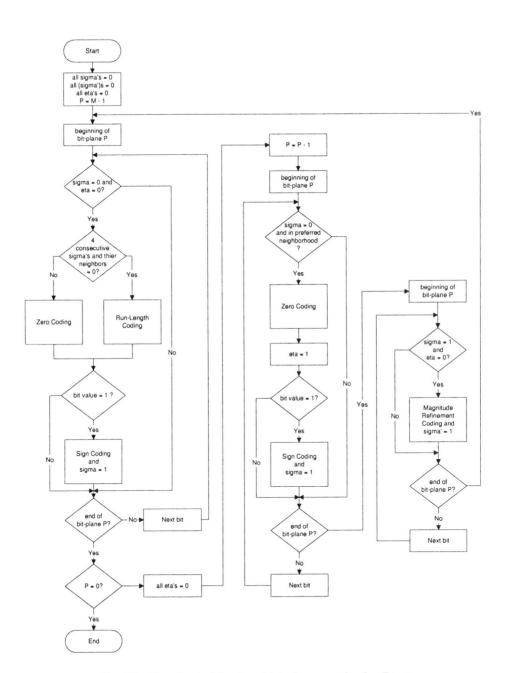

Fig. 7.7   Flowchart of fractional bit-plane encoder for $P > 0$.

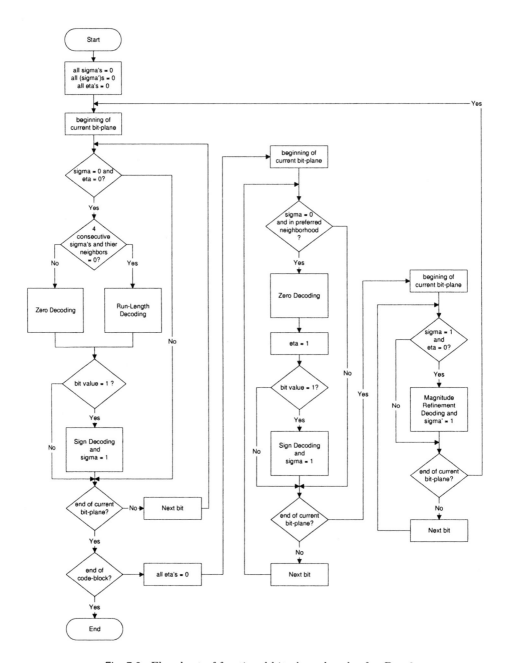

Fig. 7.8   Flowchart of fractional bit-plane decoder for $P > 0$.

$$v^2 \qquad\qquad v^1 \qquad\qquad v^0$$

0	0	0	1
0	1	0	0
1	0	0	0
0	1	0	0

1	0	0	0
1	1	1	0
0	0	1	1
0	1	0	1

1	0	0	1
1	1	0	1
0	1	0	1
0	0	0	0

- The coding sequence for the code-block and the output (CX, D) generated are shown here. We show the sequence of coding operations (ZC, RLC, SC, or MRC) at bit position (*row, column*) for the bit-plane P. The resulting CX and D are shown after each colon in each step. For example, the first operation in the sequence below indicates a run-length coding (RLC) applied in CUP at position (0, 0) in the first bit-plane. The output are CX = 17 and D = 1. The (CX, D) pair with (17, 1) indicates there is a 1 bit in the current four rows of scanned samples. Therefore, two pairs of (CX, D) are generated with values (18, 1) and (18, 0). The two decision bits indicate that the first 1 bit is at the zero-based location $(10)_2 = 2$ as shown in first column of v^2. A sign coding (SC) is followed after the RLC, and since all the state variables have initial value zeros, a context 9 and $\hat{\chi} = 0$ are selected from Table 7.4. The decision bit $D = \chi(0,0) \otimes \hat{\chi} = 1 \otimes 0 = 1$ is generated as shown in step 4 of CUP for bit-plane 2 below. After each pass, the temporal contents of the state variables σ, η, and σ' in the current bit-plane are also listed.

CUP for Bit-Plane 2

1. RLC for (0, 0): CX=17, D=1
2. RLC for (2, 0): 18, 1
3. RLC for (2, 0): 18, 0
4. SC for (2, 0) : 9, 1
5. ZC for (3, 0) : 3, 0
6. ZC for (0, 1) : 0, 0
7. ZC for (1, 1) : 1, 1
8. SC for (1, 1) : 9, 0
9. ZC for (2, 1) : 7, 0
10. ZC for (3, 1) : 1, 1
11. SC for (3, 1) : 9, 0
12. ZC for (0, 2) : 1, 0
13. ZC for (1, 2) : 5, 0
14. ZC for (2, 2) : 2, 0

15. ZC for $(3, 2)$: 5, 0

16. RLC for $(0, 3)$: 17, 1

17. RLC for $(0, 3)$: 18, 0

18. RLC for $(0, 3)$: 18, 0

19. SC for $(0, 3)$: 9, 0

20. ZC for $(1, 3)$: 3, 0

21. ZC for $(2, 3)$: 0, 0

22. ZC for $(3, 3)$: 0, 0

v^2					σ					η					σ'			
0	0	0	1		0	0	0	1		0	0	0	0		0	0	0	0
0	1	0	0		0	1	0	0		0	0	0	0		0	0	0	0
1	0	0	0		1	0	0	0		0	0	0	0		0	0	0	0
0	1	0	0		0	1	0	0		0	0	0	0		0	0	0	0

SPP for Bit-Plane 1

23. ZC for $(0, 0)$: CX=1, $D = 1$

24. SC for $(0, 0)$: 9, 0

25. ZC for $(1, 0)$: 7, 1

26. SC for $(1, 0)$: 12, 1

27. ZC for $(3, 0)$: 7, 0

28. ZC for $(0, 1)$: 7, 0

29. ZC for $(2, 1)$: 7, 0

30. ZC for $(0, 2)$: 6, 0

31. ZC for $(1, 2)$: 6, 1

32. SC for $(1, 2)$: 12, 0

33. ZC for $(2, 2)$: 3, 1

34. SC for $(2, 2)$: 10, 1

35. ZC for $(3, 2)$: 7, 0

36. ZC for $(1, 3)$: 7, 0

37. ZC for $(2, 3)$: 6, 1

38. SC for $(2, 3)$: 12, 1

39. ZC for $(3, 3)$: 3, 1

40. SC for $(3, 3)$: 10, 0

v^1

1	0	0	0
1	1	1	0
0	0	1	1
0	1	0	1

σ

1	0	0	1
1	1	1	0
1	0	1	1
0	1	0	1

η

1	1	1	0
1	0	1	1
0	1	1	1
1	0	1	1

σ'

0	0	0	0
0	0	0	0
0	0	0	0
0	0	0	0

MRP for Bit-Plane 1

41. MRC for $(2, 0)$: CX=15, $D=0$
42. MRC for $(1, 1)$: 15, 1
43. MRC for $(3, 1)$: 14, 1
44. MRC for $(0, 3)$: 14, 0

v^1

1	0	0	0
1	1	1	0
0	0	1	1
0	1	0	1

σ

1	0	0	1
1	1	1	0
1	0	1	1
0	1	0	1

η

1	1	1	0
1	0	1	1
0	1	1	1
1	0	1	1

σ'

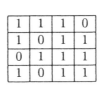

0	0	0	1
0	1	0	0
1	0	0	0
0	1	0	0

CUP for Bit-Plane 1

(Note: This pass does not generate any CX or D.)

v^1

1	0	0	0
1	1	1	0
0	0	1	1
0	1	0	1

σ

1	0	0	1
1	1	1	0
1	0	1	1
0	1	0	1

η

1	1	1	0
1	0	1	1
0	1	1	1
1	0	1	1

σ'

0	0	0	1
0	1	0	0
1	0	0	0
0	1	0	0

SPP for Bit-Plane 0

45. ZC for $(3, 0)$: CX=7, $D=0$
46. ZC for $(0, 1)$: 7, 0
47. ZC for $(2, 1)$: 8, 1
48. SC for $(2, 1)$: 11, 0
49. ZC for $(0, 2)$: 7, 0
50. ZC for $(3, 2)$: 8, 0

51. ZC for (1, 3) : 7, 1
52. SC for (1, 3) : 13, 0

v^0				σ				η				σ'			
1	0	0	1	1	0	0	1	0	1	1	0	0	0	0	1
1	1	0	1	1	1	1	1	0	0	0	1	0	1	0	0
0	1	0	1	1	1	1	1	0	1	0	0	1	0	0	0
0	0	0	0	0	1	0	1	1	0	1	0	0	1	0	0

MRP for Bit-Plane 0

53. MRC for (0, 0): CX=15, D= 1
54. MRC for (1, 0): 15, 1
55. MRC for (2, 0): 16, 0
56. MRC for (1, 1): 16, 1
57. MRC for (3, 1): 16, 0
58. MRC for (1, 2): 15, 0
59. MRC for (2, 2): 15, 0
60. MRC for (0, 3): 16, 1
61. MRC for (2, 3): 15, 1
62. MRC for (3, 3): 15, 0

v^0				σ				η				σ'			
1	0	0	1	1	0	0	1	0	1	1	0	1	0	0	1
1	1	0	1	1	1	1	1	0	0	0	1	1	1	1	0
0	1	0	1	1	1	1	1	0	1	0	0	1	0	1	1
0	0	0	0	0	1	0	1	1	0	1	0	0	1	0	1

CUP for Bit-Plane 0

(Note: This pass does not generate any CX or D.)

v^0				σ				η				σ'			
1	0	0	1	1	0	0	1	0	1	1	0	1	0	0	1
1	1	0	1	1	1	1	1	0	0	0	1	1	1	1	0
0	1	0	1	1	1	1	1	0	1	0	0	1	0	1	1
0	0	0	0	0	1	0	1	1	0	1	0	0	1	0	1

7.3.3 Binary Arithmetic Coding—MQ-Coder

As explained in the previous section, the fractional bit-plane coding (EBCOT) produces a sequence of symbols, pairs of context and decision (CX, D), in each coding pass. The context-based adaptive binary arithmetic MQ-coder that is used in JBIG2 [6] is adapted in JPEG2000 standard to encode these symbols. The probability values (Qe) and probability estimation/mapping process are provided by the standard as a lookup table with four fields (or four functions), which is defined in Table 7.7. We discussed the principles of arithmetic coding, binary arithmetic coding (BAC), and the implementation procedure of an adaptive version of BAC (the QM-coder, used in JPEG) in Chapter 2. In JPEG2000, the binary arithmetic coder is called the MQ-coder, which is a variation of the QM-coder. Here we present the implementation procedures of the MQ-coder based on the informative materials provided by the standard. Besides the probability table, the Qe-table (Table 7.7), we need two more lookup tables, I(CX) and MPS(CX). This is because there could be 19 different contexts generated by the bit-plane coder, and we need to keep track of the state and the index of the Qe-table for each context. The I(CX) is used to keep track of the index of the Qe-table and the initial values are provided by the standard (as shown in Table 7.6). The MPS(CX) specifies the sense (0 or 1) of the more probable symbol of context CX, and all MPS(CX) are initialized with value zero. Table 7.7 can be viewed as four lookup tables, Qe(I(CX)), NMPS(I(CX)), NLPS(I(CX)), and SWITCH(I(CX)) respectively. The I(CX) is the current index for the context CX. The Qe(I(CX)) provides the probability value, NMPS(I(CX))/NLPS(I(CX)) indicates the next index for a MPS/LPS renormalization, and SWITCH(I(CX)) is a flag used to indicate whether a change of the sense of MPS(CX) is needed. The same tables and initial values will be used in both encoder and decoder. We will see more details on how these variables are used in following implementation subsections.

7.3.3.1 Implementation of the MQ-Encoder Implementation of the MQ-encoder requires two 32-bit registers (**A** and **C**). We show the structures of registers **A** and **C** in Table 7.8. Register **A** is the interval register and contains the value of current interval as required in the MQ-encoder, while register **C** is the code register containing the partial codeword at any stage of encoding. Register **A** is initialized with the value 0x00008000, which indicates the beginning probability interval, and register **C** is initialized with 0x00000000, which means no codeword been generated yet.

The top-level flowchart for MQ-encoder is shown in Figure 7.9. Depending on the value of the decision bit (D) and the value of more probable symbol of context (MPS(CX)), either the "CodeMPS" or the "CodeLPS" procedure is executed. After all the symbols have been processed, a "FLUSH register" procedure is executed to stuff register **C** with as many 1 bits as possible before

Table 7.7 BAC Qe-value and Probability Estimation Lookup Table

Index	Qe	NMPS	NLPS	SWITCH
0	0x5601	1	1	1
1	0x3401	2	6	0
2	0x1801	3	9	0
3	0x0AC1	4	12	0
4	0x0521	5	29	0
5	0x0221	38	33	0
6	0x5601	7	6	1
7	0x5401	8	14	0
8	0x4801	9	14	0
9	0x3801	10	14	0
10	0x3001	11	17	0
11	0x2401	12	18	0
12	0x1C01	13	20	0
13	0x1601	29	21	0
14	0x5601	15	14	1
15	0x5401	16	14	0
16	0x5101	17	15	0
17	0x4801	18	16	0
18	0x3801	19	17	0
19	0x3401	20	18	0
20	0x3001	21	19	0
21	0x2801	22	19	0
22	0x2401	23	20	0
23	0x2201	24	21	0
24	0x1C01	25	22	0
25	0x1801	26	23	0
26	0x1601	27	24	0
27	0x1401	28	25	0
28	0x1201	29	26	0
29	0x1101	30	27	0
30	0x0AC1	31	28	0
31	0x09C1	32	29	0
32	0x08A1	33	30	0
33	0x0521	34	31	0
34	0x0441	35	32	0
35	0x02A1	36	33	0
36	0x0221	37	34	0
37	0x0141	38	35	0
38	0x0111	39	36	0
39	0x0085	40	37	0
40	0x0049	41	38	0
41	0x0025	42	39	0
42	0x0015	43	40	0
43	0x0009	44	41	0
44	0x0005	45	42	0
45	0x0001	45	43	0
46	0x5601	46	46	0

Table 7.8 BAC Encoder Register Structures

32-Bit Register	MSB	LSB
C (Code Register)	0000 cbbb bbbb b*sss* xxxx xxxx xxxx xxxx	
A (Current Interval Value)	0000 0000 0000 0000 **aaaa aaaa aaaa aaaa**	

Note:

- "a" represents fractional bits in the A register.
- "x" represents fractional bits in the C register.
- "s" represents space bits, which provides constraints on carryover.
- "b" represents bits for ByteOut.
- "c" represents the carry bit.

sending out the final bytes as compressed codewords. The pseudocodes of the underlying procedures of the MQ-coder algorithm are described as follows.

- **Initialization():** The "Initialization" procedure initializes the registers and variables for the MQ-encoder. The variable B is the byte pointed to by the compressed data buffer pointer BP. The BPST is the pointer that points to the position where the first byte is going to be placed. CT is a counter for counting the number of shifts applied on registers A and C.

```
Initialization()
{
    A = 0x00008000;
    C = 0x00000000;
    BP = BPST - 1;
    CT = 12;
    if ( B == 0xFF ) CT = 13;
    reset I(CX) and MPS(CX) with their initial values.
}
```

- **CodeMPS():** The "CodeMPS" procedure basically adds the probability value of the current context, qe = Qe(I(CX)), to the C register, and adjusts the interval A to A − qe (as explained in the description of QM-coder algorithm in Section 2.4.2 in Chapter 2). Depending on the new subinterval for the MPS, the MPS/LPS conditional exchange may occur, and both registers A and C are renormalized. The variable NMPS(I(CX)) chooses the next index for the current context CX.

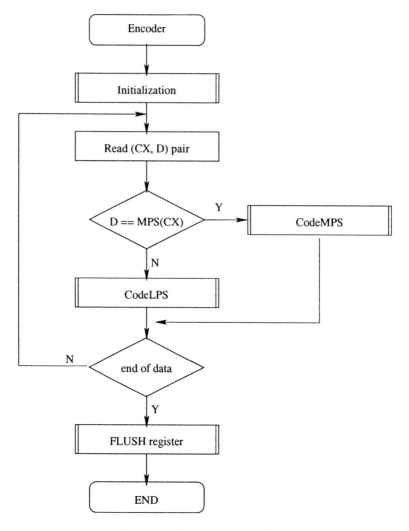

Fig. 7.9 BAC encoder flowchart.

```
CodeMPS()
{
    qe = Qe(I(CX));
    A = A - qe;              /* new subinterval for MPS */

    if ( A < 0x8000 ){
        if ( A < qe )   /* condition exchange */
            A = qe;
        else
            C = C + qe;
```

```
        /* choose next index for MPS */
        I(CX) = NMPS(I(CX));

        call RenormalizationENC();
    }
    else
        C = C + qe;
}
```

- **CodeLPS():** The "CodeLPS" procedure first adjusts the interval A to A − qe, where qe = Qe(I(CX)). If the value of the new subinterval for MPS is larger than qe, then A is adjusted to qe and register C remains unchanged; otherwise C is adjusted to C + qe. Depending on the index of the context (I(CX)), the sense of MPS for CX (i.e., MPS(CX)) may change if the SWITCH flag for the index I(CX) is 1 as shown in Table 7.7. The "renormalization" procedure is always applied in CodeLPS(). The variable NLPS(I(CX)) chooses the next index for the current context CX.

```
CodeLPS()
{
    qe = Qe(I(CX));
    A = A - qe;             /* new subinterval for MPS */

    if ( A >= qe )
        A = qe;             /* C is left unchanged */
    else                    /* conditional exchange */
        C = C + qe;

    if ( switch(I(CX)) == 1 )
        /* change the sense of MPS(CX) */
        MPS(CX) = 1 - MPS(CX);

    /* choose next index for LPS */
    I(CX) = NLPS(I(CX));
    call RenormalizationENC();
}
```

- **RenormalizationENC():** The RenormalizationENC() function is always applied after coding the LPS, and also whenever the interval value in register A becomes less than 0x8000 after coding MPS. The normalization process is executed to ensure that interval A is always above 0x8000 by repeatedly left-shifting both the A and C register 1 bit at a time until A is greater than or equal to 0x8000 (as discussed in the

QM-coder section in Chapter 2), and calls the "ByteOut()" procedure to output compressed data, if necessary.

```
RenormalizationENC()
{
    do
    {
        A = A << 1;       /* left shift 1 bit */
        C = C << 1;       /* left shift 1 bit */
        CT = CT -1;
        if ( CT == 0 ) call ByteOut();
    } while ( A < 0x8000 )
}
```

- **ByteOut():** The "ByteOut" procedure is the one a that actually outputs the compressed data one byte at a time. It contains necessary procedures (bit_Stuffing() or no_bit_Stuffing()) to limit carry propagation into completed bytes, and bit-stuffing after a 0xFF byte.

```
ByteOut()
{
    if ( B == 0xFF ) call bit_Stuffing();
    else{
        if ( C < 0x08000000 )    /* no carry bit */
            call no_bit_Stuffing();
        else {
            B = B + 1;  /* add carry bit to B */
            if ( B == 0xFF ){
                C = C & 0x07FFFFFF;
                call bit_Stuffing();
            }
            else
                call no_bit_Stuffing();
        }
    }
}
```

- **bit_Stuffing():** The carry bit **c** and the upper 7 ByteOut bits **bs** (as shown in Table 7.8) are moved into the byte B.

```
bit_Stuffing()
{
    BP = BP + 1;      /* output B                */
    B = C >> 20;      /* "cbbb bbbb" bits of C */
```

```
        C = C & 0x000FFFFF;
        CT = 7;
}
```

- **no_bit_Stuffing():** The 8 ByteOut bits **bs** (as shown in Table 7.8) are moved into the byte B.

```
no_bit_Stuffing()
{
    BP = BP + 1;    /* output B                    */
    B = C >> 19;    /* "bbb bbbb b" bits of C */
    C = C & 0x0007FFFF;
    CT = 8;
}
```

- **FLUSHregister():** After encoding all the symbols for each code-block generated by EBCOT, the "FLUSHregister" procedure is executed to stuff the register **C** with as many 1 bits as possible before it outputs the final bytes as compressed codewords.

```
FLUSHregister()
{
    TempC = C + A;
    C = C | 0x0000FFFF;
    if ( C >= TempC) C = C - 0x00008000;

    C = C << CT;
    call ByteOut();
    C = C << CT;
    call ByteOut();

    if ( B == 0xFF)
        discard B;
    else
        BP = BP + 1;    /* output B */
}
```

7.3.3.2 Implementation of MQ-Decoder MQ-decoder requires three 16-bit registers **Chigh, Clow,** and **A.** Structures of these three registers are defined Table 7.9. Registers **Chigh** and **Clow** together can be considered as one 32-bit register **C.** During decoding, the new data is inserted into the upper 8 bits (**b** bits as shown in Table 7.9) of the **Clow** register one byte at a time. Register **A** is initialized with value 0x8000, as in the encoder.

Table 7.9 BAC Decoder Register Structures

Register	MSB	LSB
Chigh	xxxx xxxx	xxxx xxxx
Clow	bbbb bbbb	0000 0000
A	aaaa aaaa	aaaa aaaa

The top-level flowchart for the MQ-decoder is shown in Figure 7.10. The pseudocode underlying procedures for implementation of the MQ-decoder algorithm is as follows.

- **InitializationDEC():** The first input compressed byte will be put into the lower 8 bits position of the register Chigh, and then a new byte is read in using ByteIn() procedure. In order to align the C register with the starting value of A, it is left-shifted 7 bits and the shift counter CT is adjusted accordingly.

```
InitializationDEC()
{
    /* BP is pointing to the first compressed byte */
    /* B is the byte pointed to by the pointer BP  */
    BP = BPST;
    C = B << 16;

    call ByteIn();

    C = C << 7;
    CT = CT - 7;
    A = 0x8000;
    reset I(CX) and MPS(CX) with their initial values.
}
```

- **ByteIn():** The "ByteIn" procedure reads one byte of the compressed bitstream every time it is called, and compensates for any stuff bits following the 0xFF byte that was inserted in the encoding process. If a 0xFF byte is found with the next byte bigger than 0x8F, 1 bits are fed to the decoder.

```
ByteIn()
{
```

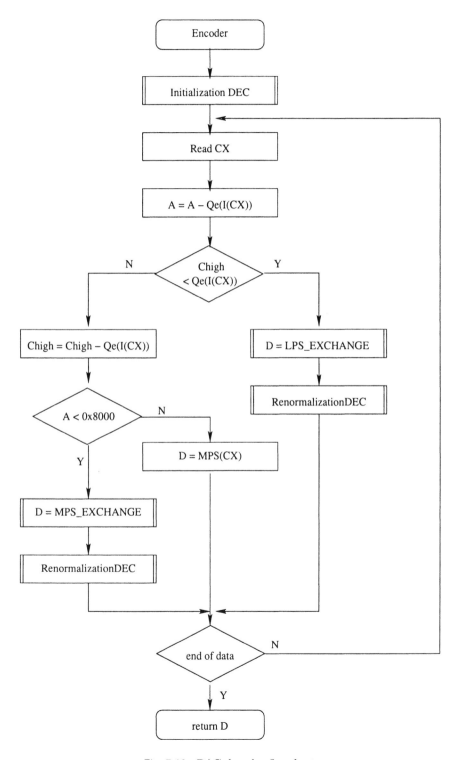

Fig. 7.10   BAC decoder flowchart.

```
    if ( B == 0xFF ){
        /* B1 is the byte pointed to by BP+1 */
        if ( B1 > 0x8F ){
            /* feed '1' bits to the decoder */
            C = C + 0xFF00;
            CT = 8;
        }
        else {
            BP = BP + 1;
            C = C + ( B << 9 );
            CT = 7;
        }
    }
    else {
        BP = BP + 1;
        C = C + ( B << 8 );
        CT = 8;
    }
}
```

- **LPS_EXCHANGE():** Based on the LPS subinterval value $Qe(I(CX))$ and the MPS subinterval value A, a conditional exchange may or may not occur. In either case, the new subinterval A will be updated with $Qe(I(CX))$. The decision bit D will be decoded according to the condition.

```
LPS_EXCHANGE()
{
    if ( A < Qe(I(CX)) ){ /* conditional exchange */
        A = Qe(I(CX));
        D = MPS(CX);
        I(CX) = NMPS(I(CX));
    }
    else {
        A = Qe(I(CX));
        D = 1 - MPS(CX);
        if ( SWITCH(I(CX)) == 1 ) MPS(CX) = 1 - MPS(CX);
        I(CX) = NLPS(I(CX));
    }

    return D;
}
```

- **MPS_EXCHANGE():** Similar to the LPS_EXCHANGE() procedure, a conditional exchange may occur depending on the values of A and

Qe(I(CX)). The decision bit D will be decoded according to the condition. However, the MPS subinterval value A will not be updated inside the MPS_EXCHANGE() procedure.

```
MPS_EXCHANGE()
{
    if ( A < Qe(I(CX)) ){ /* conditional exchange */
        D = 1 - MPS(CX);
        if ( SWITCH(I(CX)) == 1 ) MPS(CX) = 1 - MPS(CX);
        I(CX) = NLPS(I(CX));
    }
    else {
        D = MPS(CX);
        I(CX) = NMPS(I(CX));
    }

    return D;
}
```

- **RenormalizationDEC():** As shown in Figure 7.10, a decoder renormalization procedure is needed after calling either MPX_EXCHANGE() or LPS_EXCHANGE(). The counter CT keeps track of the number of compressed bits remaining in the Clow section of the C register. If CT is down to zero, a new compressed byte will be brought in using the ByteIn() procedure.

```
RenormalizationDEC()
{
    do
    {
        if ( CT == 0 ) call ByteIn();
        A = A << 1;
        C = C << 1;
        CT = CT - 1;
    } while ( A < 0x8000 )
}
```

7.4 TIER-2 CODING IN JPEG2000

In JPEG2000 standard [5], the Tier-2 coding engine is responsible for efficiently representing layer and block summary information for each code-block, including:

- The bitstream layers to which the code-block contributes the compressed codewords; this is also known as the "inclusion information."

- The length of these codewords.

- The most significant magnitude bit-plane at which any sample in the code-block is nonzero, also known as the zero bit-planes information.

- The truncation points between the bitstream layers, that is, the number of coding passes information.

This information is known to the encoder. The decoder receives this information in an encoded format, which combines two Tag Trees (one for the inclusion information and the other for the zero bit-planes information) in the encoding procedure.

Tag Tree is a particular type of quad-tree data structure, which provides the framework for efficiently representing information in the Tier-2 coding engine of JPEG2000. Size of the header included in the compressed file in the JPEG2000 standard is much larger than in the JPEG standard and contains lots of important information. The Tag Tree coding mechanism helps in representing the layer and block summary information for each code-block to be included in the header of the compressed file. In this section, we first discuss the basic Tag Tree compression technique. Then we discuss the bitstream formation methodology and how the Tag Trees are integrated in Tier-2 coding in detail.

7.4.1 Basic Tag Tree Coding

7.4.1.1 Basic Data Structure   A Tag Tree is a way to represent a two-dimensional array of nonnegative integers in a hierarchical way. Consider the two-dimensional array of integers of dimension 6×3 in Figure 7.11(a) as an example. Figures 7.11(b)–(d) are the reduced resolution levels of these two-dimensional arrays. The elements in an array at level n are formed by selecting the minimum of each 2×2 subarray (other than the boundary elements) from the two-dimensional array at level $n + 1$ as shown in Figure 7.11. For example, the elements in the array in level 2 (Figure 7.11(b)) are generated from the array in level 3 (Figure 7.11(a)) as follows.

$$q_2(0,0) = \min\{q_3(0,0), q_3(1,0), q_3(0,1), q_3(1,1)\} = 1,$$
$$q_2(1,0) = \min\{q_3(2,0), q_3(3,0), q_3(2,1), q_3(3,1)\} = 1,$$
$$q_2(2,0) = \min\{q_3(4,0), q_3(5,0), q_3(4,1), q_3(5,1)\} = 2,$$
$$q_2(0,1) = \min\{q_3(0,2), q_3(1,2)\} = 2,$$
$$q_2(1,1) = \min\{q_3(2,2), q_3(3,2)\} = 2,$$
$$q_2(2,1) = \min\{q_3(4,2), q_3(5,2)\} = 1.$$

Similarly, the elements in the array in level 1 (Figure 7.11(c)) are generated from the array in level 2 (Figure 7.11(b)) as follows.

$$q_1(0,0) = \min\{q_2(0,0), q_2(1,0), q_2(0,1), q_2(1,1)\} = 1,$$
$$q_1(1,0) = \min\{q_2(2,0), q_2(2,1)\} = 1$$

and

$$q_0(1,0) = \min\{q_1(0,0), q_1(1,0)\} = 1.$$

Figure 7.12 is a compact representation of Figure 7.11 into a quad-tree data structure. The leaf nodes contain elements from the original two-dimensional array (Figure 7.11(a)), and the internal nodes represent the elements of the reduced dimension arrays in different levels Figures 7.11(b)–(d)). The notation, $q_i(x,y)$, is the value at the node that is the $(x+1)^{\text{th}}$ from the left and $(y+1)^{\text{th}}$ from the top of the two-dimensional array, at the ith level. Level 0 is the lowest level; it contains only the root node. This quad-tree-like data structure is the basic data structure for Tag Tree coding.

7.4.1.2 Basic Coding Procedure   The coding procedure for a Tag Tree is very simple. Each node is encoded as d number of 0's followed by a 1, where d is the difference between the current node and its parent node. For the root node, the parent node is assumed to be a 0 value node. However, nodes at higher levels cannot be encoded until their parent nodes at lower levels are entirely encoded. The first row of the table in Figure 7.13 shows part of the bitstream generated for the example in Figure 7.11, and the second row in the table shows the corresponding encoded node(s). For example, the code for the number at $q_3(0,0)$ would be 01111. The first two bits (01) imply that the value of the root node at $q_0(0,0)$ is 1. The third bit (1) implies that the value at node $q_1(0,0)$ is also 1. The forth bit (1) implies that the value at node $q_2(0,0)$ is also 1. And the final bit (1) implies that the value at the target node $q_3(0,0)$ is also 1. To encode the next node $q_3(1,0)$, the code would be 001. Since all the parent nodes of $q_3(1,0)$ have already been encoded (while encoding $q_3(0,0)$ in the previous step), the first two bits (00) imply that the difference between the current node, $q_3(0,0)$, and its parent node, $q_2(0,0)$ is 2. This process continues for the entire two-dimensional array in raster scan order (left to right and top to bottom).

7.4.2   Bitstream Formation

Before we discuss how Tag Tree encoding can be used to encode the packet header information, we need to explain some terminology about bitstream formation and the progression order defined in JPEG2000.

7.4.2.1 Definition of Terms

Packet — compressed data representing a component, specific tile, layer, resolution level, and precinct.

Layer — The coded data (bitstream) of each code-block is distributed across one or more layers in the code-stream. Each layer consists of some number of consecutive bit-plane coding passes from each code-block in the tile, including all subbands of all components for that tile.

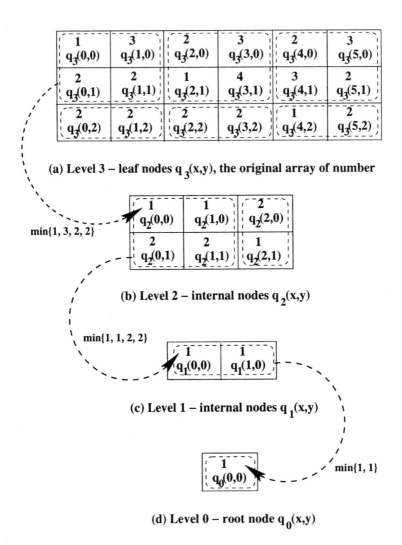

(a) Level 3 – leaf nodes $q_3(x,y)$, the original array of number

(b) Level 2 – internal nodes $q_2(x,y)$

(c) Level 1 – internal nodes $q_1(x,y)$

(d) Level 0 – root node $q_0(x,y)$

Fig. 7.11 Example of a *tag tree* data structure (example used in ITU-T Rec. T.8000, 2000 FCD V1.0).

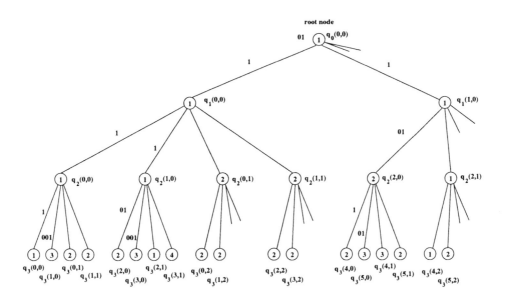

Fig. 7.12 Quad-tree structure for the example in Figure 7.11.

01111	001	101	001	1011	...
$(q_0(0,0), q_1(0,0), q_2(0,0))$ $q_3(0,0)$	$q_3(1,0)$	$(q_2(1,0))$ $q_3(2,0)$	$q_3(3,0)$	$(q_1(1,0), q_2(2,0))$ $q_3(4,0)$	...

Fig. 7.13 Bitstream generated for the same example in Figures 7.11 and 7.12.

Resolution — partition of DWT subbands in one tile.

There are $(N_L +1)$ resolutions for N_L levels DWT decomposition.

$r = 0$: $LL(N_L)$ subband only

$r = 1$: $HL(N_L)$, $LH(N_L)$, $HH(N_L)$

$\vdots$

r : $HL(N_L\text{-}r+1)$, $LH(N_L\text{-}r+1)$, $HH(N_L\text{-}r+1)$

$\vdots$

$r = N_L$:   HL1, LH1, HH1

Precinct — partition in each resolution (formed in DWT domain). Power of 2 in size (line up with code-block size boundary). Don't cause block (tile) artifacts. Figure 7.14 shows an example for a precinct from a two-level DWT with three resolutions.

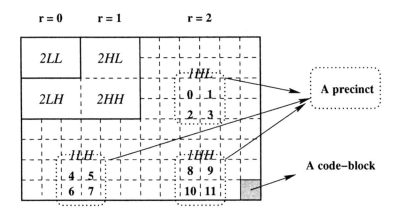

Fig. 7.14   A precinct from a two-level DWT with three resolutions.

Component — A color image may have several components from a specified color space. A component is a two-dimensional array of samples from an image.

7.4.2.2 Progression Order   The standard allows five different progression orders, which are specified in the coding style default (COD) markers unless otherwise overridden by the progression order default (POD) marker. The COD and POD markers will be discussed in the next chapter. Five different possible progression orders defined by the standard are listed below.

1. Layer—resolution—component—position progressive

2. Resolution—layer—component—position progressive

3. Resolution—position—component—layer progressive

4. Position—component—resolution—layer progressive

5. Component—position—resolution—layer progressive

The standard has the layer-resolution-component-position progressive order as the default order.

Figure 7.15(a) shows an example of a single-component image applied with two-level DWT decomposition and partitioned into 16 code-blocks. For the sake of discussion and simplicity, as shown in Figure 7.15(b), we assume all code-blocks (CB1–CB16) have four bit-planes (BP4 denotes the MSB plane); the letters *S*, *M*, and *C* stand for the bitstream generated during significance propagation pass, magnitude refinement pass, and cleanup pass, respectively. Conceptually, the bottom-nested dash-line boxes stand for progressive in terms of resolution where the bitstreams generated from the lowest-resolution code-block (CB1) were sent out first, followed by the bitstreams generated from resolution 1 (CB2, CB3, and CB4), and then the bitstreams generated from resolution 2 (CB5–CB16). The progressive in terms of quality can be done by first sending out all the bitstreams generated from all the code-blocks for the MSB plane (BP4), followed by the bitstreams generated from all the code-blocks for the next bit-plane (BP2), and so on (as shown in Figure 7.15(b) with nested solid-line boxes). On the other hand, in order to meet a certain bandwidth or target file size with the highest resolution, we can even send out the bitstreams that are corresponding to the shading area as shown in Figure 7.15(b).

7.4.3   Packet Header Information Coding

All the compressed bitstreams from a specific tile, layer, resolution, component, and precinct are stored in a contiguous segment called a **packet**. The packet header information appears in the bitstream immediately preceding the packet data, unless one of the PPM (main packed packet header marker) or PPT (tile-part packed packet header) marker segments has been used. Both the packet header information and packet data are constructed based on the order of contribution from the LL, HL, LH, and HH subbands. The packet header contains the following information:

- **Zero-length packet**, which is encoded using one bit; the value 0 denotes a zero-length packet, and the value 1 indicates a nonzero-length packet.

- **Inclusion information**, which is encoded with a separate Tag Tree. The value in this Tag Tree is the number of the layer (a zero-based index) in which the code-block is first included.

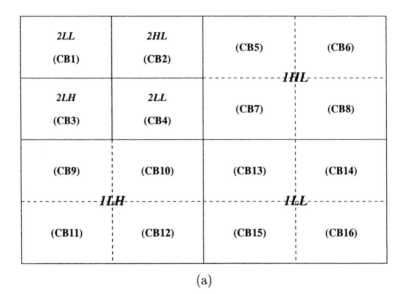

(a)

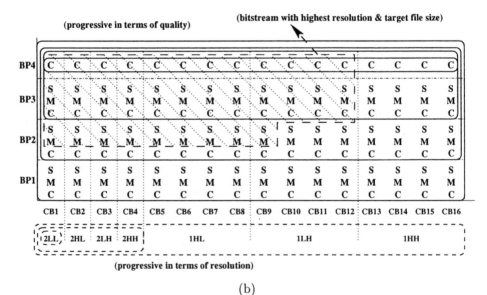

(b)

Fig. 7.15 (a) A two-level DWT with 16 code-blocks. (b) Bitstream formations. (Note: the letters *S*, *M*, and *C* in (b) stand for the bitstream generated during significance propagation pass, magnitude refinement pass, and cleanup pass, respectively.)

- Number of (leading) **zero bit-planes**, which is used to identify the actual number of bit-planes for coefficients from the code-block. A second Tag Tree is used to encode this information.

- Number of **coding passes** for each code-block in this packet. This number is encoded using the codewords shown in Table 7.10.

- **Length** (in bytes) of the bitstream from a given code-block, which is encoded either in a single-codeword segment or a multiple-codeword segment.[3]

The codewords (as shown in Table 7.10) for the number of coding passes for each code-block are variable-length codes. The number 37 through 164 has a 9-bit 1111 11111 as prefix followed by 7 bits as the offset from 37. The number 6 through 36 has a 4-bit 1111 as prefix followed by 5 bits as the offset from 6.

Table 7.10 Codewords for the Number of Coding Passes

# of Coding Passes	Codeword
1	0
2	10
3	1100
4	1101
5	1110
6–36	**1111** *0000 0*–**1111** *1111 0*
37–164	**1111 11111** *0000 000*–**1111 11111** *1111 111*

The single-codeword segment is used to encode the number of bytes contributed to a packet by a code-block. The number of bits needed to represent the length of bytes can be derived using

$$bits = LBlocks + \lfloor log_2(number\ of\ coding\ passes) \rfloor,$$

where $LBlocks$ is a code-block-wise state variable with initial value **three**. The value of $LBlocks$ can be increased if there are k 1's (i.e., '$\overbrace{11111....1}^{k}$') followed by a bit 0 (this is also known as the code-block length indicator); the value of $LBlocks$ is increased by k. If $k = 0$, then the bit 0 is used as a delimiter, which means no increase for the value of $LBlocks$. There is no restriction on number of bits used to represent the code length in the packet.

---

[3]This is the case when a termination occurs between coding passes that are included in the packet.

The Tier-2 coding procedure for a packet representing a specific layer, component, resolution, and precinct of the tile can be summarized as follows:

```
encode one bit for zero or nonzero length packet. ('1' indicates
a nonzero packet, and '0' means a zero-length packet.)

for each subbands (in the order of LL or HL, LH, and HH)

  for all code-blocks in this subband (in raster order)
    /* code-block included bits */
    if [code-block is not previously included]
      encode with a Tag Tree
    else
        encode one bit (bit '1' means included in this layer,
                        bit '0' otherwise)

    if [code-block included] /* i.e. # of coding passes > 0 */
    {
      if [this is the first instance of a code-block]
        encode zero-bit-plane information with a second Tag Tree

      encode # of coding passes using variable length codeword

      encode code-block length indicator (k '1's + '0')

      length of code-block contribution
    }
```

7.4.3.1 Examples In order to illuminate how Tier-2 coding works, we compressed a small single-component, 80 × 60 image with code-block size 32 × 32, two-level DWT, three resolutions, single layer, and no tile partition. There are a total of three packets, with index 0, 1 and 2. The size of the compressed file is 3,202 bytes. We also set an EPH (end-of-packet) marker, so we can clearly see the boundary of a packet header (from SOP to EPH) in the compressed bitstream.

```
FF 4F (SOC) @ 0

FF 51 (SIZ) @ 3
00 29 00 00 00 00 00 50   00 00 00 3C 00 00 00 00 00 00
00 00 00 00 00 00 50 00   00 00 3C 00 00 00 00 00 00 00
00 00 00 01 07 01 01
```

```
FF 5C (QCD) @ 45
00 11 42 57 86 48 03 48  03 48 45 4F D2 4F D2 4F
61

FF 52 (COD) @ 64
00 0C 06 02 00 00 01 03  03 00 00 00

FF 90 (SOT) @ 78
00 0A 00 00 00 00 0C 32  00 01

FF 93 (SOD) @ 90

FF 91 (SOP) @ 92, Packet sequence number = 0
00 04 00 00 C7 DF A6 E0

FF 92 (EPH) @ 102

. . . . . . . .


FF 91 (SOP) @ 415, Packet sequence number = 1

00 04 00 01 C7 D9 70 47  D9 76 C7 DB 66 00

FF 92 (EPH) @ 431

. . . . . . . .


FF 91 (SOP) @ 1098, Packet sequence number = 2

00 04 00 02 E3 F6 F4 A9  3E 7B 0E 3F 6F 4D 93 E7
B2 67 F0 E9 12 3E 7A 88

FF 92 (EPH) @ 1124

. . . . . . . .

FF D9 (EOC) @ 3200
```

The first packet header with sequence index number 0 contains information only for the LL2 subbands; it starts at byte 92 with start-of-packet marker (SOP) FF 91, and can be decoded as follows:

```
FF 91 ==> SOP marker (start at byte 92)
00 04 ==> 4 bytes length for marker segment, excluding the marker
00 00 ==> packet sequence number = 0
```

	C7		DF		A6		E0
(1)(1)(00	01)(11	1101	111)(1	10)(10	0110	11)0	0000
0 1	2	3		4		5	

LL2 with 1 × 1 code-block

Tag Tree 1 Inclusion	Tag Tree 2 Zero-Bit-Plane	# of Coding Pass	Length (bytes)
$\boxed{0}$	$\boxed{3}$	$\boxed{21}$	$\boxed{311}$

0: "1" means nonzero packet;

1: "1" inclusion bit, Tag Tree 1 decode, layer # = 0;

2: "0001" Tag Tree 2 decode, # of zero bit-planes = 3;

3: "111101111" decode # of coding passes with Table 7.10; 6 + 15 = 21;

4: "110" has 2 indicators; $LBlock = 3 + 2 = 5$; decode length, $5 + \lfloor log_2 21 \rfloor = 9$;

5: "1 0011 0111" = $(01\ 37)_h$ = 311 (bytes).

The second packet header with sequence index number 1 contains information for three different subbands, HL2, LH2, and HH2, and can be decoded as follows:

```
FF 91 ==> SOP marker (start at byte 415)
00 04 ==> 4 bytes length for marker segment, excluding the marker
00 01 ==> packet sequence number = 1
```

	C7		D9		70		47	
(1)(1)(00	01)(11	1101	100)(1	0)(111	0000	0)(1)(00	01)(11
0 1	2	3		4		5	6 7	

```
       D9                    76                 C7                DB
   1101 100)(1     0)(111 0110    1)(1)(00 01)(11    1101 101)(1
       8            9              10        11    12        13         14

         66                  00
   0)(110 0110     0)000 0000
              15
```

HL2 with 1 × 1 code-block

Tag Tree 1 Inclusion	Tag Tree 2 Zero-Bit-Plane	# of Coding Pass	Length (bytes)
0	3	18	224

0: "1" means nonzero packet;

1: "1" inclusion bit, Tag Tree 1 decode, layer # = 0;

2: "0001" Tag Tree 2 decode, # of zero bit-planes = 3;

3: "111101100" decode # of coding passes with Table 7.10; 6 + 12 = 18;

4: "10" has 1 indicator; $LBlock = 3 + 1 = 4$; decode length, $4 + \lfloor log_2 18 \rfloor = 8$;

5: "1110 0000" = $(E0)_h$ = 224 (bytes);

LH2 with 1 × 1 code-block

Tag Tree 1 Inclusion	Tag Tree 2 Zero-Bit-Plane	# of Coding Pass	Length (bytes)
0	3	18	237

6: "1" inclusion bit, Tag Tree 1 decode, layer # = 0;

7: "0001" Tag Tree 2 decode, # of zero bit-planes = 3;

8: "111101100" decode # of coding passes with Table 7.10; 6 + 12 = 18;

9: "10" has 1 indicator; $LBlock = 3 + 1 = 4$; decode length, $4 + \lfloor log_2 18 \rfloor = 8$;

10: "1110 1101" = $(ED)_h$ = 237 (bytes);

HH2 with 1 × 1 code-block

Tag Tree 1 Inclusion	Tag Tree 2 Zero-Bit-Plane	# of Coding Pass	Length (bytes)
0	3	19	204

11: "1" inclusion bit, Tag Tree 1 decode, layer $\# = 0$;

12: "0001" Tag Tree 2 decode, $\#$ of zero bit-planes $= 3$;

13: "111101101" decode $\#$ of coding passes with Table 7.10; $6 + 13 = 19$;

14: "10" has 1 indicator; $LBlock = 3 + 1 = 4$; decode length, $4 + \lfloor log_2 19 \rfloor = 8$;

15: "1100 1100" $= (CC)_h = 204$ (bytes).

The third packet header with sequence index number 2 contains information for the last three subbands, HL1, LH1, and HH1, and can be decoded as follows:

```
FF 91 ==> SOP marker (start at byte 1098)
00 04 ==> 4 bytes length for marker segment, excluding the marker
00 02 ==> packet sequence number = 2
```

	E3			F6		F4		A9	
(1)(1)(1)(0	001)(1)		(1111	0110	1)(111	0)(100	1010	100)(1)	
0 1 2	3	4		5		6	7		8

	3E		7B		0E		3F		
(001)(1	1110	0111)(10)(11		0000	1)(1)(1)(0	001)(1)		(1111	
9	10	11		12	13 14	15	16		17

	6F		4D		93		E7	
0110	1)(111	0)(100	1101	100)(1)	(001)(1	1110	0111)	
	18		19	20	21		22	

	B2		67		F0		E9	
(10)(11	0010	0)(1)(1)(0	01)(1)(1		1111	0000)	(1110)	(1001
23	24	25 26	27 28		29		30	

	12		3E		7A		88	
0001	00)(1)(0	001)(1	1110	0111)(10)(10		1000	1)000	
31	32	33		34	35	36		

HL1 with 2 × 1 code-block

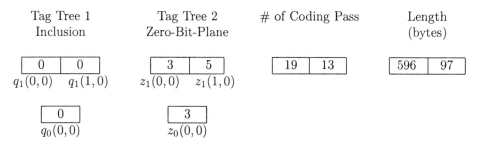

0: "1" means nonzero packet;

1: (Inclusion) Tag Tree 1 decode; upper-level node $q_0(0,0)$ need decode first; "1" $q_0(0,0) = 0$;

2: "1" $q_1(0,0) = 0$;

3: (Zero bit-plane) Tag Tree 2 decode; upper-level node $z_0(0,0)$ need decode first; "0001" $z_0(0,0) = 3$;

4: "1" $z_1(0,0) = 3$;

5: "111101101" decode # of coding passes with Table 7.10; $6 + 13 = 19$;

6: "1110" has 3 indicators; $LBlock = 3 + 3 = 6$; decode length, $6 + \lfloor log_2 19 \rfloor = 10$;

7: "10 0101 0100" $= (02\ 54)_h = 596$ (bytes);

8: "1" (Inclusion) $q_1(1,0) = 0$;

9: "001" $z_1(0,0) = z_0(0,0) + 1 + 1 = 5$;

10: "111100111" decode # of coding passes with Table 7.10; $6 + 7 = 13$;

11: "10" has 1 indicator; $LBlock = 3 + 1 = 4$; decode length, $4 + \lfloor log_2 13 \rfloor = 7$;

12: "110 0001" $= (61)_h = 97$ (bytes);

LH1 with 2 × 1 code-block

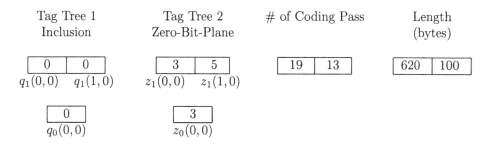

13: (Inclusion) Tag Tree 1 decode; upper-level node $q_0(0,0)$ need decode first; "1" $q_0(0,0) = 0$;

14: "1" $q_1(0,0) = 0$;

15: (Zero bit-plane) Tag Tree 2 decode; upper-level node $z_0(0,0)$ need decode first; "0001" $z_0(0,0) = 3$;

16: "1" $z_1(0,0) = 3$;

17: "111101101" decode # of coding passes with Table 7.10; $6 + 13 = 19$;

18: "1110" has 3 indicators; $LBlock = 3 + 3 = 6$; decode length, $6 + \lfloor log_2 19 \rfloor = 10$;

19: "10 0110 1100" $= (02\ 6C)_h = 620$ (bytes);

20: "1" (Inclusion) $q_1(1,0) = 0$;

21: "001" $z_1(0,0) = z_0(0,0) + 1 + 1 = 5$;

22: "111100111" decode # of coding passes with Table 7.10; $6 + 7 = 13$;

23: "10" has 1 indicator; $LBlock = 3 + 1 = 4$; decode length, $4 + \lfloor log_2 13 \rfloor = 7$;

24: "110 0100" $= (64)_h = 100$ (bytes);

HH1 with 2 × 1 code-block

Tag Tree 1 Inclusion		Tag Tree 2 Zero-Bit-Plane		# of Coding Pass		Length (bytes)	
0	0	2	5	22	13	580	81
$q_1(0,0)$	$q_1(1,0)$	$z_1(0,0)$	$z_1(1,0)$				
0		2					
$q_0(0,0)$		$z_0(0,0)$					

25: (Inclusion) Tag Tree 1 decode; upper-level node $q_0(0,0)$ need decode first; "1" $q_0(0,0) = 0$;

26: "1" $q_1(0,0) = 0$;

27: (Zero bit-plane) Tag Tree 2 decode; upper-level node $z_0(0,0)$ need decode first; "001" $z_0(0,0) = 2$;

28: "1" $z_1(0,0) = 2$;

29: "111110000" decode # of coding passes with Table 7.10; $6 + 16 = 22$;

30: "1110" has 3 indicators; LBlock $= 3 + 3 = 6$; decode length, $6 + \lfloor log_2 22 \rfloor = 10$;

31: "10 0100 0100" $= (02\ 44)_h = 580$ (bytes);

32: "1" (Inclusion) $q_1(1,0) = 0$;

33: "0001" $z_1(0,0) = z_0(0,0) + 1 + 1 + 1 = 5$;

34: "111100111" decode # of coding passes with Table 7.10; $6 + 7 = 13$;

35: "10" has 1 indicator; $LBlock = 3 + 1 = 4$; decode length, $4 + \lfloor log_2 13 \rfloor = 7$;

36: "101 0001" $= (51)_h = 81$ (bytes).

7.5 SUMMARY

In this chapter, we dealt with the fractional bit-plane coding (EBCOT) and the MQ-coder for implementation of the adaptive binary arithmetic coding scheme proposed in JPEG2000 standard. We described the terminology and their underlying concepts behind these algorithms. The EBCOT has three coding passes and four coding operations. We discussed in great detail the concepts behind these coding operations and how they are used in each coding pass in order to encode the bit-planes of the DWT coefficients. We took an example and showed how to generate the context and decision information by the EBCOT algorithm. This context and decision pair is then used by the MQ-coder to generate compressed codewords. We described the flowcharts for all the modules in both the EBCOT and the MQ-coder algorithms and their implementation issues. We discussed the Tier-2 encoding scheme using the Tag Tree coding mechanism. We discussed the basic definitions for the Tag Tree with an example and showed how the two-dimensional integer arrays can be mapped into a Tag Tree. This Tag Tree encoding is the basis for encoding the code-block and layer information in the compressed file header. We compressed a small component of size 80×60, generated the code-block information, and displayed the results as an example. We also showed the different progression orders achievable by the JPEG2000 standard in order to influence different areas of applications. In summary, we detailed entropy encoding (Tier-1 and Tier-2 encoding) in this chapter.

REFERENCES

1. D. S. Taubman, "High-Performance Scalable Image Compression with EBCOT," *IEEE Transactions on Image Processing*, Vol. 9, No. 7, pp. 1158–1170, July 2000.

2. W. B. Pennebaker, J. L. Mitchell, G. G. Langdon, Jr., and R. B. Arps, "An Overview of the Basic Principles of the Q-Coder Adaptive Binary Arithmetic Coder," *IBM Journal of Research and Development*, Vol. 32, No. 6, pp. 717–726, November 1988.

3. D. Huffman, "A Method for the Construction of Minimum Redundancy Codes," *Proc. IRE*, Vol. 40, pp. 1098–1101, 1952.

4. ISO/IEC 10918 (JPEG), "Information Technology—Digital Compression and Coding of Continuous-Tone Still Images."

5. ISO/IEC 15444-1, "Information Technology—JPEG2000 Image Coding System, Part 1: Core Coding System," 2000.

6. ISO/IEC 14492-1, "Lossy/Lossless Coding of Bi-level Images," 2000.

7. ISO/IEC JTC1/SC29/WG1 (ITU-T SG8) N2165, "JPEG2000 Verification Model 9.1 (Technical Description)," June 2001.

8

Code-Stream Organization and File Format

8.1 INTRODUCTION

Like any other image and video coding standards, JPEG2000 also defines syntax and rules to organize the compressed bitstream so that the compressed bitstream can be uniquely decoded by any system compliant to the standard. The file format of the compressed file needs to strictly follow the guidelines provided by the standard in order to be compliant with the standard. The JPEG2000 Part 1 standard defines an optional file format, called JP2, that any system compliant with the standard may choose to support.

In this chapter, we describe the basic code-stream organization (syntax and rules) and file format for the JPEG2000 Part 1 standard only. The syntax provides all the information that an application needs for decompression of the JPEG2000 code-stream. The file format for JPEG2000 Part 1 can be considered as a wrapper that applications may choose to adapt to contain JPEG2000 compressed code-stream.

8.2 SYNTAX AND CODE-STREAM RULES

Marker segments are used to indicate the characteristics of the image (such as image size, number of components in the image, the chosen tile size, etc.) and mark the code-stream. The markers and marker segments describe various features that are present in the compressed file and define the parameters used to compress the image (such as size of the code-block, precinct, quantization step-size, wavelet kernels used for transformation, number of resolution, type of multicomponent transformation, ROI parameters, and others). A marker segment includes a marker and associated marker parameters. On the other hand, headers of the compressed file are a collection of markers and marker segments. There are two types of headers in the JPEG2000 code-stream.

1. **The main header**: The main header is inserted at the beginning of code-stream and is used to delimit the code-stream as well as provide general information about the compressed file.

2. **The tile-part header**: The tile-part header is inserted at the beginning of the compressed bitstream of each tile-part and is used to delimit a particular tile-part and provides general information about a tile.

Every marker in the code-stream is two bytes long. The first byte is always 0xFF, and the second byte can have any value between 0x01 and 0xFE. In the JPEG2000 Part 1 standard, six types of marker segments have been defined.

- *Delimiting* marker segments: The delimiting marker segments are used to delimit the headers and the data.

- *Fixed information* marker segments: The fixed information marker segments contain information about the image. The only fixed information maker defined in JPEG2000 Part 1 is the image and tile size (SIZ) marker, which is required in the main header.

- *Functional* marker segments: The functional marker segments are used to describe the coding functions used; for example, the coding style default(COD) marker segment is used to describe the coding style information that is used as default for compressing all components of an image or a tile.

- *Bitstream* marker segments: The bitstream marker segments are used for error resilience. These markers are found in the bitstream, not as part of the main or a tile-part header.

- *Pointer* marker segments: The pointer marker segments point to specific offsets in the bitstream. These markers are optional, and they provide either a length information or a pointer into the bitstream.

- *Informational* marker segments: The informational marker segments provide additional information about the image; for example, comments can be put into the main or tile-part headers with a comment and extension (CME) marker segment.

The first two bytes after the marker should be an unsigned big-endian integer value, such as **Lmar** shown in Figure 8.1, which denotes the total length of the marker segment excluding the two bytes of the marker itself. The length of marker parameters could range from 1, 2, 4 bytes to variable length. Figure 8.1 shows a sample description of a marker segment.

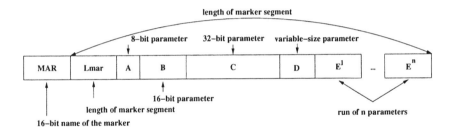

Fig. 8.1 Sample marker segment description.

8.2.1 Basic Rules

The following seven rules are provided in Annex A of the JPEG2000 Part 1 standard [2]. Any JPEG2000 compliance codec system needs to follow these rules.

1. All the markers and the marker segments and hence the headers are multiples of 8 bits (one byte). Further, if the number of bits in the bitstream data between the headers is not an integer multiple of 8, then the bitstream is padded so that it is a multiple of 8 bits. In other words, zero-padding (padded with 0 bits) will apply when the last (before the next header) compressed byte contains less than 8 bits.

2. All the markers and the marker segments within a tile-part header are applicable (or valid) only to the tile to which they belong. Different tiles may use the same markers with different parameters as specified in their own tile-part header.

3. All the markers and the marker segments in the main header are applicable to the whole image unless they are overridden by a marker segment in the tile-part header.

4. The "delimiting" marker segments and the "fixed information" marker segments must appear at the specific points in the code-stream. For example, the start of code-stream (SOC) marker must appear as the first marker in the main header.

5. The marker segments shall correctly describe the image as represented by the code-stream. If any alteration is applied to the code-stream, the marker segments shall be updated.

6. All parameter values in the marker segments are big-endian (i.e., the most significant byte first).

7. All markers between 0xFF30 and 0xFF3F have no marker parameters. They are reserved by the standard without marker parameter definition in order to enable backward compatibility and future extensions.

8.2.2   Markers and Marker Segments Definitions

Figure 8.1 shows an example of the marker segment description. The first two bytes are represented by a three-letter abbreviation of the marker segments, and the next two bytes (**Lmar**) specify the total length of the marker segment excluding the two bytes of the marker itself. Table 8.1 shows the marker names and code values of marker segments. The detail information and syntax for all the markers and marker segments can be found in Annex A of the JPEG2000 Part 1.

Table 8.1   Marker Segments: Marker Name and Value

	Name	Code Value
Delimiting Marker Segments		
Start of Code-stream	SOC	0xFF4F
Start of tile-part	SOT	0xFF90
Start of data	SOD	0xFF93
End of code-stream	EOC	0xFFD9
Fixed Info Marker Segments		
Image and tile size	SIZ	0xFF51
Functional Marker Segments		
Coding style default	COD	0xFF52
Coding style component	COC	0xFF53
Region of interest	RGN	0xFF5E
Quantization default	QCD	0xFF5C
Quantization component	QCC	0xFF5D
Progression order default	POD	0xFF5F
Pointer Marker Segments		
Tile-part lengths, main header	TLM	0xFF55
Packet length, main header	PLM	0xFF57
Packet length, tile-part header	PLT	0xFF58
Packed packet header, main header	PPM	0xFF60
Packed packet header, tile-part header	PPT	0xFF61
In Bitstream Marker Segments		
Start of packet	SOP	0xFF91
End of packet header	EPH	0xFF92
Informational Marker Segment		
Comment and extension	CME	0xFF64

8.2.3   Headers Definition

The **main header** as indicated in Figure 8.2 consists of segments known as main header marker segments. Some of the markers are essentially presented and some may or may not be presented. For example, the SOC and SIZ must be specified as the first and second marker segments in the main header. However, a PLT (packet-length) marker is not allowed to appear in the main

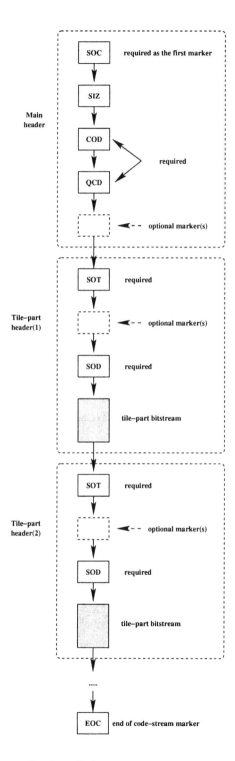

Fig. 8.2 Code-stream organization.

header and it is an optional marker in tile-part header. Table 8.2 provides an overview of these marker segments.

Table 8.2   Main Header Marker Segments

Name	Description	Required/Optional
SOC	Start of code-stream	Required as the first marker
SIZ	Image and tile size	Required as the second marker segment
COD	Coding style default	Required
COC	Coding style component	Optional and no more than one COC per component
QCD	Quantization default	Required
QCC	Quantization component	Optional and no more than one QCC per component
RGN	Region of interest	Optional
POD	Progression order change	Required in the main or tile-part header if any progression order changes
PPM	Packed packet headers	Optional, either PPM or PPT or code-stream packet headers are required
TLM	Tile-part lengths	Optional
PLM	Packet length	Optional
CME	Comments and extension	Optional

The **tile-part header** as indicated in Figure 8.2 consists of segments known as tile-part header marker segments. Some of the markers are essentially presented and some may or may not be presented in the tile-part header. Table 8.3 provides an overview of these marker segments.

8.3   FILE FORMAT FOR JPEG2000 PART 1: JP2 FORMAT

As shown in Figure 8.2, from SOC (start-of-code-stream) to EOC (end-of-code-stream), the code-stream of JPEG2000 is entirely self-contained. All the image components can be decompressed based on the syntax and code-stream rules discussed in the previous section. However, Annex I of the JPEG2000 standard Part 1 [2] defines an *optional* file format, **JP2** format, that can be used to contain JPEG2000 compressed image data. For the purpose of file identification, the file extension ".jp2" or ".JP2" should be used for traditional file systems. As on Macintosh file systems, the type code "jp2 " should be used for JP2 files.

The fundamental building block of the JP2 file format is called a **box**, which is used to encapsulate the JPEG2000 code-stream or other pieces of information, such as image properties, intellectual property rights, vendor-specific information, and so forth. Figure 8.3 shows the definition of a box. A box may contain four fields. The first field, **LBox**, specifies the length of the box, which includes all the fields of the box and the value is stored as a

Table 8.3 Tile-Part Header Marker Segments

Name	Description	Required/Optional
SOT	Start of tile	Required as the first marker segment of the tile-part header
COD	Coding style default	Optional and no more than one COD per tile
COC	Coding style component	Optional and no more than one COC per component
QCD	Quantization default	Optional and no more than one QCD per tile
QCC	Quantization component	Optional and no more than one QCD per component
RGN	Region of interest	Optional and no more than one QCD per component
POD	Progression order change	Required if any progression order changes from main POD
PPT	Packed packet headers	Optional, either PPM or PPT or code-stream packet headers required
PLT	Packet length, tile-part header	Optional
CME	Comments and extension	Optional
SOD	Start of data	Required, marks the beginning of the current tile-part data

32-bit big-endian unsigned integer. If a value 0 is specified in the **LBox** field, this box is the last box in the file. If a value 1 is specified in the **LBox** field, the actual length of the box is specified in the third optional field, **XLBox**, as a 64-bit big-endian unsigned integer. The second field, **TBox**, specifies the type of data stored in the last field, **DBox**. The size of the **DBox** field varies depending on the box type.

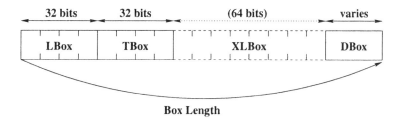

Box Length

Fig. 8.3 JP2 box definition.

8.3.1 File Format Organization

A JP2 file is organized as a *contiguous sequence of boxes*. Some boxes are required, and some of those boxes are optional as determined by the compressed file creator. Figure 8.4 shows a conceptual structure of a JP2 file with required boxes only. The *JP2 Signature* box should be the first box in the file and should be immediately followed by the *Profile* box. The *JP2 Header* box is a superbox that may contain other boxes, such as the *Image Header* box and *Color Specification* box. The *Contiguous Code-stream* box should not appear before the *JP2 Header* box. Other optional boxes may be found in a JP2 file without a particular order. However, all data should be in the box format; no other data should be found in a JP2 file.

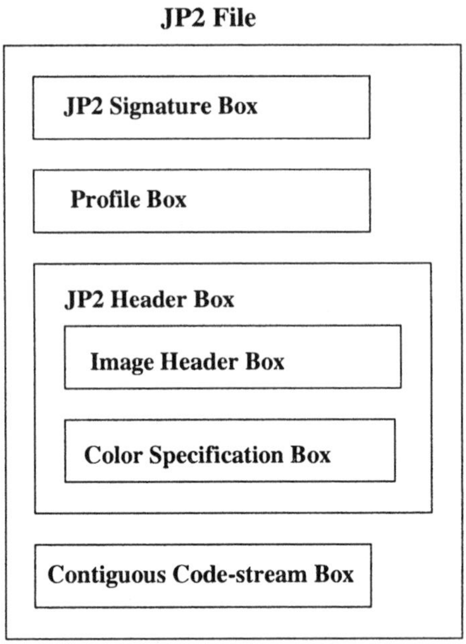

JP2 File

Fig. 8.4 A JP2 file structure with required boxes only.

8.3.2 JP2 Required Boxes

In this section, we provide detailed descriptions of only the JP2 required boxes. The detailed descriptions of optional boxes can be found in Annex I of the JPEG2000 standard Part 1 [2] document. Table 8.4 shows the name and type of required JP2 boxes. Figure 8.5 shows the binary structure of the required boxes. The first 64 bits of each box contain two fields (**LBox** and **TBox**) based on the length and type of the box. The details are described as follows.

Table 8.4 JP2 Required Boxes

Name	Type (TBox field in the box)
JP2 Signature box	'jP\032\032' (6A 50 1A 1A)$_h$
Profile box	'prfl' (70 72 66 6C)$_h$
JP2 Header box	'jp2h' (6A 70 32 68)$_h$
Image Header box	'ihdr' (69 68 64 72)$_h$
Color Specification box	'colr' (63 6F 6C 72)$_h$
Contiguous Code-stream box	'jp2c' (6A 70 32 63)$_h$

Note:

- JP2 Header box is a superbox.

- \nnn represents the value of a single byte character, where the three digits (nnn) specify the octal value of the byte.

JP2 Signature box: JP2 Signature box is the box that uniquely identifies the file as a JP2 file, and it should be the first box in the file. This box should have a fixed-length of a 12-byte string, which should have the value: **(00 00 00 0C 6A 50 1A 1A 0D 0A 87 0A)$_h$**.

Profile box: The Profile box should immediately follow the JP2 Signature box. The type of this box, which is the **TBox** field, should be 'prfl' = (70 72 66 6C)$_h$, and the **DBox** field should contain the brand (**BR**) and N compatibility list (**CL**^{i}, where $0 \leq i \leq N - 1$) information. Both the **BR** and **CL**^{i} fields are encoded as a four byte string of ASCII characters. For a JP2 file, the **BR** must equal 'jp2\040' = (6A 70 32 20)$_h$ and must have at least one **CL**^{i} with the value 'jp2\040'. The number of **CL**^{i} fields, N, is determined by the length of this box.

JP2 Header box: The JP2 Header box is a superbox that contains several boxes. There should be an Image Header box and at least one Color Specification box within the JP2 Header box. The type of the box is 'jp2h' = (6A 70 32 68)$_h$, and should appear after the JP2 Signature box but before the Contiguous Code-stream box.

Image Header box: The Image Header box contains fixed-length (24 bytes) generic information about the image, such as height, width, and number of components. The type of the box should be 'ihdr' = (69 68 64 72)$_h$, and the DBox field is broken into eight subfields as described in Table 8.5.

Color Specification box: The Color Specification box specifies the color space to the entirely decompressed image components. The type of the box should be 'colr' = (63 6F 6C 72)$_h$, and the DBox field contains up to five fields as described in Table 8.6.

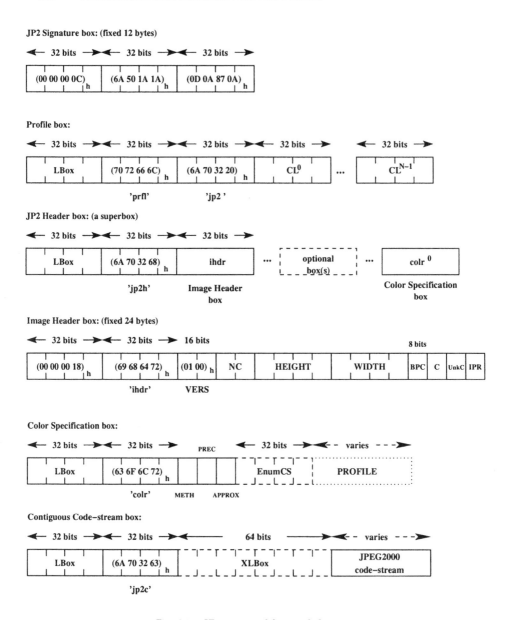

Fig. 8.5 JP2 required boxes definition.

Contiguous Code-stream box: This box contains a valid and complete JPEG2000 code-stream, and the type of the box is 'j2pc' = $(6A\ 70\ 32\ 63)_h$.

EXAMPLE   223

Table 8.5 Format of the Contents of the Image Header Box

Field name	Description	Size (bytes)	Value
VERS	Major/minor version number	2	$(01\ 00)_h$
NC	Number of components	2	$1 - (2^{16} - 1)$
HEIGHT	Image height	4	$1 - (2^{32} - 1)$
WIDTH	Image width	4	$1 - (2^{32} - 1)$
BPC	Bits per component	1	-127 - 127
C	Compression type	1	7
UnkC	Color space unknown	1	0 - known 1 - unknown
IPR	Intellectual property	1	0 or 1

Table 8.6 Format of the Contents of the Color Specification Box

Field Name	Description	Size (bytes)	Value
METH	Specification method	1	1 - Enumerated 2 - Restricted ICC profile
PREC	Precedence	1	0
APPROX	Color space approximation	1	0
EnumCs	Enumerated color space	4 (METH=1) 0 (METH=2)	$0 - (2^{32} - 1)$ (16/17 for sRGB/grayscale [4]) nonexistent
PROFILE	ICC profile [3]	varies	varies

8.4 EXAMPLE

In this section, we provide an example of JPEG2000 compressed code-stream with JP2 format. The image used for this example is a 24-bit RGB (three-component) image with width and height equal to $40 \times 30 = (28)_h \times (1E)_h$. As we can see, all six required boxes are present in the JP2 file and two optional boxes (Resolution box and Capture Resolution box) are also included just for reference. The JP2 box always starts with a 4-byte box length followed by a 4-byte box type. For example, the Resolution box has 26 bytes as indicated by the first 4 bytes of the box in this example, followed by a 4-byte box type, 'res ' = $(72\ 65\ 73\ 20)_h$. This box also is a superbox, which contains a Capture Resolution box with 18 bytes. The total length of this Resolution box is equal to $4 + 4 + 18 = 26$ bytes. The zero box length of the Contiguous Code-stream box indicates that this box is the last box in the file. The $(FF\ 4F)_h$ marks the start of code-stream (SOC marker), and the $(FF\ D9)_h$ marks the end of the code-stream (EOC marker). There is only one tile-part of a tile in this compressed code-stream, as shown in the last byte of the SOT marker segment. The image size, $40 \times 30 = (28)_h \times (1E)_h$, can be found in either Image Header box or SIZ marker segment.

```
00 00 00 0C   => JP2 Signature box (12 bytes)
6A 50 1A 1A 0D 0A 87 0A

00 00 00 14   => Profile box (20 bytes)
70 72 66 6C 6A 70 32 20
00 00 00 00 6A 70 32 20

00 00 00 47   => JP2 Header box (73 bytes)
6A 70 32 68

00 00 00 18 ==>> Image Header box (24 bytes)
69 68 64 72 01 00 00 03
00 00 00 1E 00 00 00 28
07 07 00 00

00 00 00 0F ==>> Color Specification box (15 bytes)
63 6F 6C 72 01 00 00 00 00 00 10
```

******************** Optional boxes ***********************

```
00 00 00 1A ==>> Resolution box (26 bytes)
72 65 73 20

00 00 00 12 ===>>> Capture Resolution box (18 bytes)
72 65 73 63 00 48 00 FE 00 48 00 FE 04 04
```

****

```
00 00 00 00   ==> Contiguous Code-stream box (last box)
6A 70 32 63

FF 4F (SOC) ---> Start of Code-stream

FF 51 (SIZ)
00 2F 00 00 00 00 00 28 00 00 00 1E 00 00 00 00
00 00 00 00 00 00 00 28 00 00 00 1E 00 00 00 00
00 00 00 00 00 03 07 01 01 07 01 01 07 01 01

FF 5C (QCD)
00 0D 40 40 48 48 50 48 48 50 48 48 50

FF 52 (COD)
00 0C 00 00 00 01 01 03 04 04 00 01
```

```
FF 64 (CME)
00 0C 00 01 41 56 4C 54 5F 31 31 34

FF 90 (SOT)
00 0A 00 00 00 00 09 49 00 01

FF 93 (SOD) ---> Start of tile-part

.....................................

FF D9 (EOC) ---> End of Code-stream
```

8.5 SUMMARY

In this chapter, we presented a brief summary of the JPEG2000 code-stream organization and the JP2 file format. The basic descriptions of markers, marker segments, and header and code-stream rules were introduced in this chapter. Also the concept of using *box* for the JP2 file format were reviewed in brief. We demonstrated a simple example to illuminate the code-stream organization syntax and the structure of a JP2 file.

REFERENCES

1. ISO/IEC 10918 (JPEG), "Information Technology—Digital Compression and Coding of Continuous-Tone Still images."

2. ISO/IEC 15444-1, "Information technology—JPEG2000 Image Coding System, Part 1: Core Coding System," 2000.

3. International Color Consortium, "ICC Profile Format Specification, ICC.1: 1998-09."

4. International Electrotechnical Commission. "Color Management in Multimedia System, Part 2: Color Management; Part 2-1: Default RGB Color Space—sRGB, IEC 61966-2-1," October 1999.

9

VLSI Architectures for JPEG2000

9.1 INTRODUCTION

JPEG2000 [1, 2] is a very versatile image compression standard with multipurpose capabilities and features achievable by a single unified system based on the salient features of the discrete wavelet transform and the scalable entropy encoding (bit-plane-wise) adopted in the standard. It not only offers superior compression performance, the scalable nature of the underlying algorithms of the JPEG2000 standard makes it perfectly suitable to achieve resolution scalability and picture fidelity scalability features essential in today's diverse imaging and multimedia applications. All these features in JPEG2000 standard can be achieved through a single syntax definition of the code-stream organization of the compressed file. Although some of these properties can be attained by the JPEG standard, they cannot be attained by a single unified algorithm and a single syntax definition of the code-stream organization of the compressed file. We discussed the core algorithms for the JPEG2000 standard in Chapters 6–8. We also presented different features of the JPEG2000 standard and their influence in the vast area of applications in this age of Internet and multimedia communication in Chapter 6.

All the rich features of JPEG2000 are achieved at the expense of tremendous computational and memory cost for implementation of the underlying algorithms in JPEG2000, which makes it difficult for its potential application in many real-time imaging and multimedia applications. Computational analysis [3] shows that the computational requirement for JPEG2000 compression algorithm is more than 30 times as great compared to the current baseline JPEG encoder, and the computational requirement of the decoder is almost 10 times that of the baseline JPEG decoder when it is implemented in a highly optimized manner in a general-purpose computing platform. As a result, there is a tremendous need to develop high-performance architectures and special-purpose custom VLSI chips exploiting the underlying data parallelism to speed up the DWT and entropy encoding phase of JPEG2000 to make it suitable for real-time applications.

To our knowledge, only a handful of papers have been published in the literature with full description of an overall JPEG2000 architecture suitable for VLSI implementation. In this chapter, we present an architecture for overall implementation of the JPEG2000 encoder and decoder proposed by Andra, Chakrabarti, and Acharya [4, 5] in greater detail. We also present a summary of other works that have been published in the literature in relation to different components of JPEG2000, mainly EBCOT and MQ-coder.

9.2 A JPEG2000 ARCHITECTURE FOR VLSI IMPLEMENTATION

A global architecture for implementation of JPEG2000 encoder proposed by Andra, Chakrabarti, and Acharya [4, 5] is shown in Figure 9.1. Key components of the architecture are as follows.

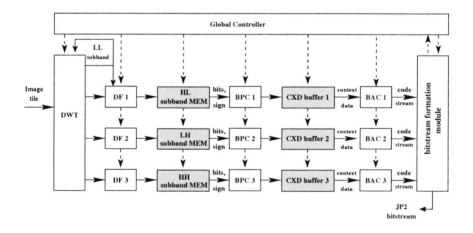

Fig. 9.1 A top-level architecture for the JPEG2000 encoder.

- **DWT computation module:** We devoted a complete chapter (Chapter 5) on VLSI algorithms and architectures for computation of discrete wavelet transform (DWT). We discussed the methodologies of convolution-based architectures and lifting-based architectures in Chapter 5. In the context of the JPEG2000 standard, the lifting-based architecture is more suitable compared to the convolution-based architecture because of the inherent features of lifting-based implementation of DWT, such as reduced number of computations both for $(9, 7)$ and $(5, 3)$ filter banks, in-place computation leading to reduced memory requirements, scope of parallel processing, etc., as described in Chapter 4.

The DWT computation module in Figure 9.1 computes the multilevel wavelet decomposition of the input image tile. In each level of decomposition, the DWT module produces four subbands (LL, HL, LH, and HH). The subband LL is input back to the DWT modules for the next level of decomposition. The other three subbands are input to the subsequent phases of the architecture for entropy encoding. In Chapter 5, we have described the concept behind the architecture of the DWT module [5, 6, 7, 8] that has been adopted in this overall architecture for the JPEG2000 encoder.

- **Data format module (DF):** The *data format modules* first quantize each input sample in each subband by the quatization parameter supplied by a *global controller* module. For lossless compression, the quantization parameter is 1. Each quantized sample (integer) is represented in a 16-bit word. After quanitation, each DF module converts the two's complement representation of each quantized sample to sign-magnitude representation required by the EBCOT algorithm executed by the BPC modules. The DF module then decomposes the subband into a number of code-blocks and stores them in a special local memory (SM). The data format module also determines the most significant bit-plane of each code-block. The most significant bit-plane is the first bit-plane that contains at least one 1 bit.

  There are three DF modules in the architecture. DF1 processes the samples from the HL subband, and DF2 and DF3 process the samples from the LH and HH subbands respectively and store the processed data into the special local subband memory (SM).

- **Subband memory module (SM):** A special *subband memory module* (SM) [5] has been used in this architecture such that the memory structure can handle word-in-bit-out format combined with the stripe structure in order to efficiently handle the input data by the BPC coder. The stripe structure for the bit-plane scan pattern has been described in Figure 7.1 in Chapter 7. Structure of the subband memory SM is depicted in Figure 9.2. There are 32×8 rows and each row is made of 64 bits. Each $b_{R,C}^{p}$ represents the bit value in row R and column C in the pth bit-plane of the code-block. In this structure, each column (stripe) of the scan pattern is grouped together and each row consists of 16 such columns. Hence 32 columns (each four-row stripe) are stored in two consecutive rows in SM. In this fashion, a 32×32 size code-block is represented by 128 rows each with 64 bits in the subband memory module. The concept can be extended to any size of code-block. A code-block of size $M \times N$ can be represented by $\frac{M}{4} \times N$ rows each with 64 bits.

$b_{0,0}^0$	$b_{1,0}^0$	$b_{2,0}^0$	$b_{3,0}^0$	$b_{0,0}^1$	$b_{1,0}^1$	$b_{2,0}^1$	$b_{3,0}^1$	.....	$b_{3,0}^{15}$
$\vdots$	$\vdots$	$\vdots$	$\vdots$	$\vdots$	$\vdots$	$\vdots$	$\vdots$	.....	$\vdots$
$b_{0,31}^0$	$b_{1,31}^0$	$b_{2,31}^0$	$b_{3,31}^0$	$b_{0,31}^1$	$b_{1,31}^1$	$b_{2,31}^1$	$b_{3,31}^1$	.....	$b_{3,31}^{15}$
$b_{4,0}^0$	$b_{5,0}^0$	$b_{6,0}^0$	$b_{7,0}^0$	$b_{4,0}^1$	$b_{5,0}^1$	$b_{6,0}^1$	$b_{7,0}^1$	.....	$b_{7,0}^{15}$
$\vdots$	$\vdots$	$\vdots$	$\vdots$	$\vdots$	$\vdots$	$\vdots$	$\vdots$	.....	$\vdots$
$b_{4,31}^0$	$b_{5,31}^0$	$b_{6,31}^0$	$b_{7,31}^0$	$b_{4,31}^1$	$b_{5,31}^1$	$b_{6,31}^1$	$b_{7,31}^1$	.....	$b_{7,31}^{15}$
$\vdots$	$\vdots$	$\vdots$	$\vdots$	$\vdots$	$\vdots$	$\vdots$	$\vdots$	.....	$\vdots$
$b_{28,0}^0$	$b_{29,0}^0$	$b_{30,0}^0$	$b_{31,0}^0$	$b_{28,0}^1$	$b_{29,0}^1$	$b_{30,0}^1$	$b_{31,0}^1$	.....	$b_{31,0}^{15}$
$\vdots$	$\vdots$	$\vdots$	$\vdots$	$\vdots$	$\vdots$	$\vdots$	$\vdots$	.....	$\vdots$
$b_{28,31}^0$	$b_{29,31}^0$	$b_{30,31}^0$	$b_{31,31}^0$	$b_{28,31}^1$	$b_{29,31}^1$	$b_{30,31}^1$	$b_{31,31}^1$	.....	$b_{31,31}^{15}$

Fig. 9.2 Structure of the subband memory for a 32×32 code-block; $b_{R,C}^p$ represents the bit at location (R, C) in the pth bit-plane of the code-block.

- **Bit-plane coder (BPC) module:** Each BPC module essentially executes the EBCOT algorithm. The EBCOT algorithm has been described in Chapter 7. The input to the BPC module is read from the SM module, which consists of both the sign bit and the bit-planes of the code-block. Output of the BPC module is a sequence of 5-bit context and 1-bit data pair (CD, D) temporarily stored in an internal buffer (CXD) before they are encoded by the QM-coder (BAC) in the subsequent pipeline stage of the architecture. In this JPEG2000 encoder architecture, three BPC modules are engaged to encode the code-blocks from the three subbands HL, LH, and HH as shown in Figure 9.1. However, multiple BPC modules can be engaged to process multiple code-blocks from each subband to exploit the data parallelism because the encodings of the code-blocks are independent from each other and hence speed up the architecture at the cost of additional hardware resources. We describe the logic behind each BPC module in greater detail in Section 9.3.

- **Context and Data (CXD) module:** The CXD buffer is a FIFO with a read port and a write port so that the BPC module can write the 6-bit data (5 bits for context and 1 bit for data) in the FIFO and BAC can read the 6-bit data from the FIFO in parallel. The size of the FIFO should be large enough in order to manage the speed difference between the BPC and BAC in the pipeline. The control circuit (global controller) manages the pointers of the FIFO for both the read and write operations.

- **Binary arithmetic coding (BAC) module:** Each BAC module executes the MQ-encoding scheme to encode the data bit of the context-data pair read from the CXD FIFO. The MQ-encoding algorithm and its implementation has been described in Chapter 7. An architecture for the MQ-coder is presented later in Section 9.4.

- **Global controller:** The global controller generates all the necessary control signals to enable all the modules in the architecture including loading the image tiles, reading and writing the subband memory, controlling the pointers to access the CXD FIFO, generating the control signals for the BPC and BAC encoders, and loading the Q-table for the BAC module. It is also used to handle the rate-control and generation of the final code-stream and the header of the compressed file. The Tag Tree coding and organization of the compressed code can be done by either a local microcontroller available in the chip or the host processor controlling the chip.

9.3   VLSI ARCHITECTURES FOR EBCOT

The block diagram of the VLSI architecture for the EBCOT encoder developed by Andra, Chakrabarti, and Acharya [4, 5, 9] is shown in Figure 9.3. Following are the key building blocks of this architecture.

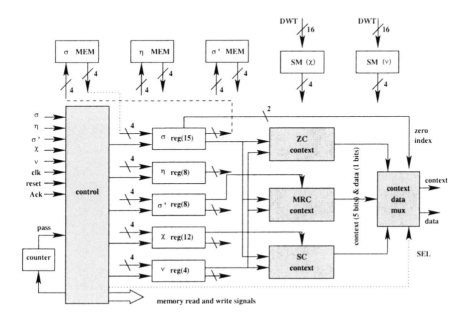

Fig. 9.3   VLSI architecture for the EBCOT encoder.

1. Three separate blocks of combinational logic circuits generate the context and data pairs (cx, d) for the ZC, MRC, and SC operations. Details of their logic of operations are further discussed in Section 9.3.1.

2. Five different special-purpose shift registers (σ-reg, η-reg, σ'-reg, v-reg, and χ-reg) process the state variables σ, η, σ', v, and χ as described in the EBCOT algorithm. The sizes of shift registers to hold σ, η, σ', v, and χ state variables are 15, 8, 8, 4, and 12 bits respectively, as shown in Figure 9.3. The working principles of these registers are further details in Section 9.3.2.

3. The local memory modules σ MEM, η MEM, and σ' MEM, each of size 32×4 bits, are used to load and store the three state variables σ, η, and σ' respectively. These three memories are updated in every pass by the corresponding σ, η, σ' registers. The magnitude (v) and sign (χ) bits are read from the subband memory (SM) bit-plane by bit-plane. All the memories have a single read and write port as shown in Figure 9.3.

4. The *context and data multiplexer* selects the right context (cx) and the corresponding data bit (d) generated by the ZC, MRC, and SC logic circuits and also the RLC logic, which is hard-coded. The possible context values from the RLC logic output are either 17 or 18 as explained in Chapter 7. The data bit (d) is chosen from the v, sign data χ, hard coded RLC data bits (0,1), or the zero-index ZI(MSB, LSB) bits (00–11, because the run-length could be 0, 1, 2, or 3). The multiplexer (mux) is controlled by a 3-bit control signal ($cntrl_{cx}$). Based on the particular coding pass (CUP, SPP, MRP) executed, the controller generates the control signals $cntrl_{cx}$. The contexts and data for different $cntrl_{cx}$ are shown in Figure 9.4.

$cntrl_{cx}$	Context	Data
000	-	-
001	ZC	v
010	SC	sign bit
011	MC	v
100	17	0
101	17	1
110	18	ZI[MSB]
111	18	ZI[LSB]

Fig. 9.4 Output of the *Context* and *Data* mux for different $cntrl_{cx}$.

5. The *controller* is basically a state-machine that generates control signals to control the *shift registers* (σ-reg, η-reg, σ'-reg, v-reg, and χ-reg) and

the *context and data multiplexer* (mux). The controller generates the read and write signals for the local memory modules σ-MEM, η-MEM, σ'-MEM. The controller also generates the control signal to control the *counter* that keeps track of the number of stripes processed and also the particular coding pass being executed. Further details of the function of the *controller* is presented in Section 9.3.3.

9.3.1 Combinational Logic Blocks

Tables 7.1 – 7.6 in Chapter 7 provide the basis of generation of 5-bit *context* (CX) for each of the coding operations. These contexts can be generated by combinational logic circuits for each of the coding operations as originally explained in [9, 10]. We presented a simplified form of the logic functions suitable to develop these combinational logic circuits below.

- **Zero coding (ZC) context block:** The ZC context block generates the relevant contexts (as presented in Tables 7.1 – 7.3) based on the status of the significance states of the eight neighbors (σ_{00}, σ_{01}, σ_{02}, σ_{10}, σ_{12}, σ_{20}, σ_{21}, and σ_{22}) of the current bit position X as shown in Figure 9.5.

σ_{00}	σ_{01}	σ_{02}
σ_{10}	**X**	σ_{12}
σ_{20}	σ_{21}	σ_{22}

Fig. 9.5 Neighborhood for *zero coding* context generation.

We present here the logic functions for generation of the 5-bit context $cx[4:0]$ by zero coding the LL and LH subbands. The same methodology is applied to generate the contexts for the HL and HH subbands as well. The logic functions for the bit $cx(i)$, for $i = 0$ to 4, of context $cx[4:0]$ are as follows. The output *data* bit from the ZC context block is the magnitude bit at position **X**,

$$cx(4) = 0$$
$$cx(3) = \sigma_{10} \wedge \sigma_{12}$$
$$cx(2) = P_h + \overline{H} \wedge \sigma_{01} \wedge \sigma_{21}$$
$$cx(1) = P_h \wedge (V + \overline{V} \wedge D) + \overline{H} \wedge (P_v + \overline{V} \wedge P_d)$$
$$cx(0) = P_h \wedge (V + \overline{V} \wedge \overline{D}) + P_v \wedge \overline{H}$$

where $+$ is the logical OR operation, $\wedge$ is the logical AND operation, and $\bar{x}$ represents the NOT of a logic variable x and

$$H = \sigma_{10} + \sigma_{12}$$
$$V = \sigma_{01} + \sigma_{21}$$
$$D = \sigma_{00} + \sigma_{02} + \sigma_{20} + \sigma_{22}$$
$$P_h = \sigma_{10} \wedge \bar{\sigma}_{12} + \bar{\sigma}_{10} \wedge \sigma_{12}$$
$$P_v = \sigma_{01} \wedge \bar{\sigma}_{21} + \bar{\sigma}_{01} \wedge \sigma_{21}$$
$$P_d = \sigma_{00} \wedge \sigma_{02} + \sigma_{20} \wedge \sigma_{22} + (\sigma_{00} + \sigma_{02}) \wedge (\sigma_{20} + \sigma_{22}).$$

- **Sign coding (SC) context block:** As explained in Section 7.3.1 in Chapter 7, *context* and *data* are determined by a horizontal reference value H (also called contribution of the horizontal neighbors) and a vertical reference value V (contribution of the vertical neighbors) by the sign coding algorithm. The context table for the sign coding is shown in Table 7.4. Let us assume that contributions of 0, $+1$ and -1 by the horizontal and vertical neighbors are expressed as hc_0, hc_{+1}, hc_{-1} and vc_0, vc_{+1}, vc_{-1} respectively. The contributions can be computed based on the status of the significance states of the horizontal neighbors (σ_{10}, σ_{12}) and vertical neighbors (σ_{01}, σ_{21}) and the corresponding sign states (χ_{10}, χ_{12}, χ_{01}, χ_{21}) from the χ memory block, using the following logic equations.

$$vc_{+1} = \sigma_{01} \wedge \sigma_{21} \wedge \bar{\chi}_{01} \wedge \bar{\chi}_{21} + \bar{\sigma}_{01} \wedge \sigma_{21} \wedge \bar{\chi}_{21} + \sigma_{01} \wedge \bar{\sigma}_{21} \wedge \bar{\chi}_{01}$$
$$vc_{-1} = \sigma_{01} \wedge \sigma_{21} \wedge \chi_{01} \wedge \chi_{21} + \bar{\sigma}_{01} \wedge \sigma_{21} \wedge \chi_{21} + \sigma_{01} \wedge \bar{\sigma}_{21} \wedge \chi_{01}$$
$$vc_0 = \overline{vc}_{+1} \wedge \overline{vc}_{-1}$$

and

$$hc_{+1} = \sigma_{10} \wedge \sigma_{12} \wedge \bar{\chi}_{10} \wedge \bar{\chi}_{12} + \bar{\sigma}_{10} \wedge \sigma_{12} \wedge \bar{\chi}_{12} + \sigma_{10} \wedge \bar{\sigma}_{12} \wedge \bar{\chi}_{10}$$
$$hc_{-1} = \sigma_{10} \wedge \sigma_{12} \wedge \chi_{10} \wedge \chi_{12} + \bar{\sigma}_{10} \wedge \sigma_{12} \wedge \chi_{12} + \sigma_{10} \wedge \bar{\sigma}_{12} \wedge \chi_{10}$$
$$hc_0 = \overline{hc}_{+1} \wedge \overline{hc}_{-1}.$$

Accordingly the logic functions for the context bits $cx(i)$, for $i = 0$ to 4, based on the above values are as follows.

$$cx(4) = 0$$
$$cx(3) = 1$$
$$cx(2) = vc_0 \wedge (hc_{+1} + hc_{-1}) + vc_{-1} \wedge hc_{-1} + vc_{+1} \wedge hc_{+1}$$
$$cx(1) = hc_{+1} \wedge vc_{-1} + hc_{-1} \wedge vc_{+1} + hc_0 \wedge (vc_{+1} + vc_{-1})$$
$$cx(0) = hc_{+1} \wedge (vc_0 + vc_{-1}) + hc_{-1} \wedge (vc_{-1} + vc_{+1}) + hc_0 \wedge vc_0.$$

- **Magnitude refinement coding (MRC) context block:** The context table for magnitude refinement coding is shown in Table 7.5. The inputs to the MRC context block are $\sigma'_{m,n}$ (value 1 indicates that it is not the first magnitude refinement for the current element) and the significance status of the eight neighbors (σ_{00}, σ_{01}, σ_{02}, σ_{10}, σ_{12}, σ_{20}, σ_{21}, σ_{22}) of the bit being encoded. Accordingly the logic functions for the context bits $cx(i)$, for $i = 0$ to 4, are as follows.

$$nhood0 = \sigma_{00} + \sigma_{01} + \sigma_{02} + \sigma_{10} + \sigma_{12} + \sigma_{20} + \sigma_{21} + \sigma_{22}$$

$$cx(4) = \sigma'_{m,n}$$
$$cx(3) = \overline{\sigma'_{m,n}}$$
$$cx(2) = \overline{\sigma'_{m,n}}$$
$$cx(1) = \overline{\sigma'_{m,n}}$$
$$cx(0) = \overline{\sigma'_{m,n}} \wedge nhood0.$$

- **Run-length coding (RLC) contexts:** There are two possible contexts in RLC. It is executed at the beginning of each stripe only when the RLC condition is satisfied (i.e., significance status of all the neighbors of all the four bits in the stripe are all 0's). The detailed coding mechanism was discussed in Chapter 7. In [5, 10], the RLC context generation methodology is hard-coded.

9.3.2 Functionality of the Registers

There are five different special-purpose shift registers (σ-reg, η-reg, σ'-reg, υ-reg, and χ-reg) of varying sizes to process the state variables σ, η, σ', υ, and χ as described in the EBCOT algorithm (see Figure 9.3). All these registers are capable of 1-bit left shift. For initialization and run-length coding, register σ is also capable of 5-bit left shift and the χ register is also capable of 4-bit left shift. The σ, η, and σ' registers have an "update" position where a 1 is written to set the corresponding state variable when applicable. Data from the relevant memory are written into 4 least significant bit positions in the registers. But data can be read from different positions of the registers and written into the memory. The registers are read and written at the end of coding of each stripe.

In Figure 9.6, we show the coding order of a 4×3 code-block as an example. Let us assume that the bit in position 5 is being currently coded to explain the functionality of the registers below.

1	**5**	9
2	6	10
3	7	11
4	8	12

Fig. 9.6 Coding order for a 4×3 code-block.

- σ **Register:** Register σ contains 3 stripes each time from the σ-MEM memory. The stripes from Figure 9.6 in vertical causal mode have been mapped in the σ register in a particular fashion as shown in Figure 9.7(a). The 0's preceding 1, 5, and 9 indicate that they represent bits outside the boundary (the last row in the previous scan) and their values are assumed to be all 0's. When bit position 5 is encoded, these three 0's along with 1, 2, 6, 10, and 9 form the 8 neighbors as shown in Figure 9.7(a).

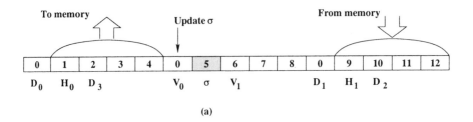

(a)

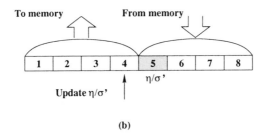

(b)

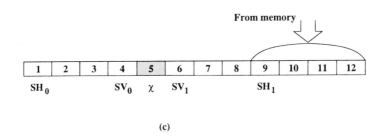

(c)

Fig. 9.7 (a) σ register, (b) η (also σ') register, (c) χ register.

During initialization, the register is reset and the first stripe is loaded from σ-MEM and shifted by 5 bits and then the same is repeated with the second and third stripes. This results in proper data alignment. For termination, no data are read while coding the last stripe. The "update" bit is set during the shift to change the σ of a particular bit. There are two zero detectors connected to the output of the σ register. The first zero detector detects whether σ of the 8 neighbors are all 0's in order to determine whether a bit is coded in SPP (indicated by the "nhood0" signal in Figure 9.3). The second zero detector detects whether σ of all the elements in all 3 stripes are all 0's in order to indicate that the RLC condition is satisfied (the RLC_C signal in Figure 9.3). When the RLC condition is satisfied in CUP and the stripe consists of all 0's, then no further coding is required and the data are shifted left by 5 bits.

- σ' and η **Registers:** Registers σ' and η are identical and shown in Figure 9.7(b). The data from the η-MEM (or σ'-MEM) memory are written to the 4 least significant bit positions 8, 7, 6, 5, as shown in Figure 9.7(b) and the updated data are read from the 4 most significant bit positions to write back to η-MEM (or σ'-MEM) memory. The "update" position is the bit position 4 shown in Figure 9.7(b).

- χ **Register:** The χ register has 12 bits as shown in Figure 9.7(c). It is loaded with 4 bits at a time for each stripe from the subband memory SM (χ) as shown in Figure 9.3 and shifted by 4 bits left in order to load the next stripe and continue to fill up 12 bit positions for three stripes. The data arrangement and the boundary conditions for the χ register are similar to the σ register. But when a neighbor is insignificant, the sign of the neighbor does not play a role in forming the context. This property helps to have 12 bits, unlike the special arrangement required in the σ register. The function of χ register during initialization, termination, and RLC coding is the same as for the σ register except the data are shifted by 4 bits instead of the 5-bit shift needed in the σ register.

- υ **Register:** This is a simple 4-bit register without any special functionalities. A zero detector is attached to the output to generate the "*All0s*" signal, which helps to determine what path the RLC primitive takes in the CUP. Also a 4-bit to 2-bit encoder is present to generate the ZI (zero-index) of the position of the first 1 bit in the stripe (with first position encoded as 00 and fourth position encoded as 11) for the RLC.

9.3.3 Control Mechanism for the EBCOT Architecture

The control signals in the EBCOT architecture are generated by a state machine comprising of 24 states [9, 10]. The state machine is divided into five phases: *initialization* phase, ZC and SC control phase, MRC control phase, RLC control phase, and *termination* phase, as discussed below.

- **Initialization Phase:** The *initialization phase* is enabled at the beginning of encoding each bit-plane. State transitions of the initialization phase are depicted in Figure 9.8. During this phase it sets the pointers to load the DWT coefficients of the code-blocks to the subband memory SM (υ and χ) at state 0 if the first bit-plane is encoded. All the registers and memory address pointers are reset at state 1. The first stripe is loaded into the σ and χ registers in state 2 from the σ-MEM and subband memory SM (χ). However, the σ memory is not accessed in the first bit-plane because none of the bit positions are significant yet. The σ register is shifted left by 5 bits and the χ register is shifted left by 4 bits in state 3 (indicated by Ishift in Figure 9.8) in order to align the data as described in the functionalities of these registers in the previous section. Based on the coding pass indicated by the counter, the state machine goes either to state 4 for significance propagation pass (SPP), state 12 for magnitude refinement pass (MRP), or state 16 for cleanup pass (CUP).

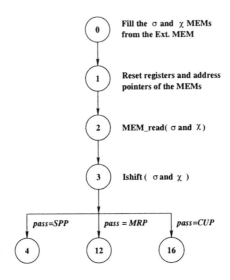

Fig. 9.8 Initial phase for the EBCOT encoder.

- **ZC and SC control phase:** State transitions of the *ZC and SC control phase* are shown in Figure 9.9. The σ, χ, and υ registers are loaded from the σ-MEM, χ-MEM, and subband memory SM (υ) in state 4 as shown in the state transition diagram in Figure 9.9. If either the coding pass is SPP and $\sigma = 0$ and $nhood0 \neq 0$ (i.e., at least one σ of the eight neighbors is 1), or the coding pass is CUP and $\sigma = 0$ and $\eta = 0$, or the RLC condition is satisfied and at least one bit in the stripe is 1 (i.e., $RLC\_cb = 1$), then it generates the control signal $cntrl_{cx} = 001$ in state 6 in order to output the corresponding ZC *context* and *data* (υ) as listed in the control signal table in Figure 9.4; otherwise it goes to state 5 without any coding. If the SPP condition is satisfied and the bit becomes significant (i.e., $\upsilon = 1$), then the control signal $contrl_{cx} = 010$ is generated in state 7 in order to output the SC *context* and the sign bit of the element in the current bit position as indicated in the table in Figure 9.4 and σ and η are set in state 9. If $\upsilon = 0$, then only η is set in state 8. In either of these states (5, 8, 9), the registers are shifted left by 1 bit and the *counter* is incremented. The counter keeps track of the coding position in the stripe (*end-of-row* signal). If the counter indicates *end-of-row*, it goes to state 10 to begin the termination phase; otherwise the coding continues in either state 6 or state 5 depending on the status of the coding pass and the state variables as shown in Figure 9.9.

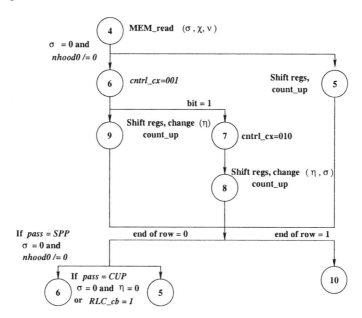

Fig. 9.9 ZC and SC phase.

- **MRC control phase:** The state transition diagram for the MRC control phase is shown in Figure 9.10. This phase is executed during the magnitude refinement pass (MRP). In state 12 of this phase, the σ, η, σ', and v registers are loaded from the σ MEM, η MEM, σ' MEM, and v SM. If $\sigma = 1$ and $\eta = 0$ (MRP condition), then the control signal $cntrl_c x$ = 011 in state 14 in order to output the corresponding MC *context* and output *data* bit (v) as listed in table in Figure 9.4 and the σ' is set in subsequent state 15; otherwise it goes to state 5 without generating any output or encoding the data. In either state (5 or 15), the registers are shifted and the counter is incremented. If the counter indicates *end-of-row*, it goes to state 10 to begin the termination phase; otherwise the coding continues in either state 14 or state 5 depending on the status of the coding pass and the state variables as shown in Figure 9.10.

- **RLC control phase:** State transition of the RLC control phase is shown in Figure 9.11. This phase is executed during the cleanup pass

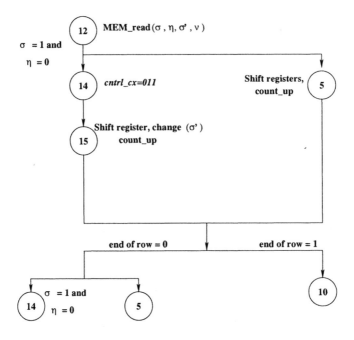

Fig. 9.10   MRC phase.

(CUP) and only when the first bit of the stripe is encoded. In state 16, the σ, η, χ, and v registers are loaded from σ MEM, η MEM, SM χ, and v respectively. If $\sigma = 1$ or $\eta = 1$ for the first bit in the stripe, it goes to state 5 without encoding the bit. If $\sigma = 0$ and $\eta = 0$ for the first bit in the stripe, then the RLC condition is checked. If the RLC condition is not satisfied then it goes to state 6 to execute the ZC phase. If the RLC condition is satisfied and all the bits in the stripe are 0's (indicated by $All0s = 1$), then it goes to state 17 and generates the control signal $cntrl_{cx} = 100$ in order to output $context = 17$ and $data = 0$ as suggested in the control signal table in Figure 9.4. It then shifts the σ register by 5 bits and the χ register by 4 bits as indicated by the $Ishift$ operation in Figure 9.11 and goes to state 11 in the termination phase. On the other hand if there is a 1 in the stripe (i.e., $All0s = 0$), then it goes to state 18 and generates the control signal $cntrl_{cx} = 101$ in order to output $context$ $= 17$ and $data = 1$ and then goes to state 19. In state 19, it generates the control signal $cntrl_{cx} = 110$ in order to output $context = 18$ and the first bit of the 2-bit zero-index (MSB[ZI]) and then goes to state 20. In state 20, it generates the control signal $cntrl_{cx} = 111$ in order to output $context = 18$ and the other bit of the zero-index (LSB[ZI]) and sets the RLC_cb signal to 1. $RLC\_cb = 1$ indicates that ZC and SC are applied on the rest of the bits in the stripe. Based on the value of the 2-bit zero-index (ZI), the registers are shifted and the counter is incremented as shown in Figure 9.11, and then it goes to state 7 for execution of the SC phase.

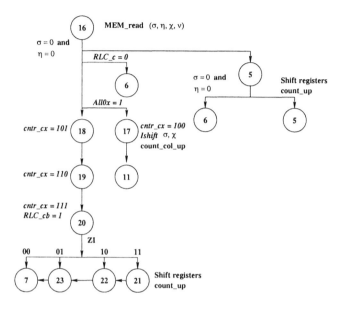

Fig. 9.11 RLC phase.

- **Termination phase:** The state transition diagram for the *termination phase* is depicted in Figure 9.12. When the counter indicates the *end-of-row* signal at the end of each stripe, the termination phase is computed. The σ register is shifted left by 1 bit in state 10. In state 11, the RLC_cb signal is set to 0. In state 11, the data in the registers are written back the appropriate memory depending on the coding pass. If coding pass is SPP, the contents from register σ and register η are written back to σ MEM and η MEM. On the other hand, content of the register σ' is written back to σ' MEM if the coding pass is a MRP, whereas content of the register σ is written back to σ MEM if the coding pass is CUP. The state machine goes to state *stop* (we may consider it state 13) after completion of encoding the last bit-plane of the code-block. If it is the end of a block but not the last bit-plane, the state machine goes to state 0 if the current pass is CUP and goes to state 1 otherwise (MRP or SPP) in order to start the next coding pass in the current bit-plane. If end of the block is not reached, the state machine goes to either state 4 if current coding pass is SPP or state 12 if current coding pass is MRP or state 16 if current coding pass is CUP as shown in Figure 9.12.

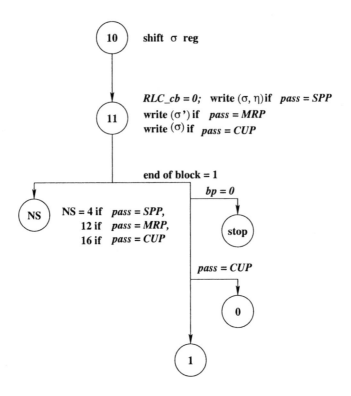

Fig. 9.12   Termination phase of the EBCOT encoder.

9.4   VLSI ARCHITECTURE FOR BINARY ARITHMETIC CODING: MQ-CODER

The block diagram of the VLSI architecture proposed by Andra, Chakrabarti, and Acharya [4, 5] is shown in Figure 9.13. The MQ-coder algorithm described in Section 7.3.3 in Chapter 7 has been directly mapped into this architecture. The key building blocks of this architecture are as follows.

- **Update logic:** The update logic has two components:(1) an informa-tion table (*info table*), and (2) a combinational logic circuit.

  - The *info table* essentially consists of 19 entries for all the possible contexts (0 – 18) generated by the EBCOT encoder during the bit-plane coding. Each entry consists of the MPS (1 bit) and an index (6 bits) to the Q-table representing the probability estimation of the MPS symbol. The info table is initialized with the 19 initial index values corresponding to the 19 different contexts shown in Table 7.6 in Chapter 7. The input to the info table is a 5-bit context (CX) and the output is the *Q-index* to address the *Q-table*

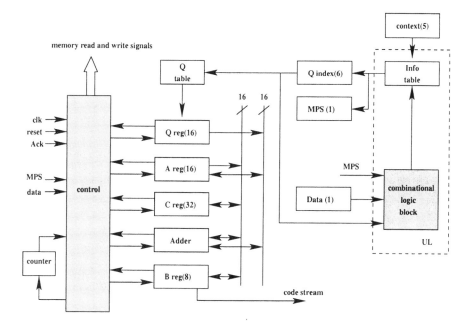

Fig. 9.13   MQ-encoder architecture.

in order to read the precomputed probability estimation (q_e) from the Q-table.

- The *combinational logic circuit* in the update logic module is engaged to update the *Info table* by generating the new Q-index based on the present Q-index, sense of MPS, and the input symbol (1 bit *data* output by EBCOT). If a renormalization step is executed during either the MPS or LPS coding, the info table is updated with the new Q-index and the MPS sense based on the principle described in Chapter 7.

- **Registers:**

  - *Register A*: Value of the interval at point of coding is actually contained in register A. This is a 16-bit shift register capable of shifting left by 1 bit. The most significant bit $A[15]$ of register A is used by the controller to determine whether the renormalization step needs to be performed. When the adder performs the subtract operations during LPS or MPC coding, it stores the results $A - q_e$ back to register A (see "CodeLPS()" and "CodeMPS()" in the MQ-coder algorithm in Chapter 7).

  - *Register C*: This is a 32-bit shift register representing the code at any point of coding. The register is capable of shifting left by

1 bit. When the adder performs the addition operation, it stores the result $C + q_e$ back to the C register (see "CodeLPS()" and "CodeMPS()" in the MQ-coder algorithm in Chapter 7). The 28th bit of the C register ($C[27]$) is used by the controller to determine whether a carry needs to be added to the B register as shown in the "ByteOut()" routine in the MQ-coder section in Chapter 7.

- *Register B*: This is a special-purpose 8-bit register. The compressed bitstream is actually output from the B register as shown in the 'ByteOut()' routine in the MQ-coder algorithm. There is a detector built with this register to determine whether all the bits of the register are 1's. If all the bits of the B register are 1, then the bit-stuffing operation is initiated by the controller.

- *Register Q*: This is just a 16-bit register to hold the probability estimation q_e obtained by accessing the Q-table based on the Q-index supplied by the update logic circuitry from the *info table*.

- **Adder:** The adder computes the basic arithmetic steps of the MQ-coder algorithm. It is capable of addition $(C + q_e)$, subtraction $(A - q_e)$, and comparison $(A - q_e < q_e)$ required in the MQ-coder algorithm. Since size of the registers C, A, and Q are 32 bits, 16 bits, and 16 bits respectively, the adder needs to be capable of computing 32-bit integer arithmetic operations.

- **Control circuit:** The control circuit generates control signals for all the registers and the tables. It is nothing but a state machine to generate the control signals during execution of the MQ-coder algorithm. The working principle of the state machine is similar to the controller in the EBCOT architecture. We avoid detailed discussion of the state machine here. The counter inputs the control circuit to control the B register to output the compressed bitstream. The counter is initialized by 12. As soon as the counter becomes 0 during the encoding process, the content of register B is output as the compressed bitstream and a new byte of data is loaded to B from register C.

- **Q-table:** The Q-table consists of 47 entries of Q_e values as shown in Table 7.7. The Q-table is addressed by the 6-bit Q-index. Depending on the Q-index, the corresponding Q_e entry (probability estimation value q_e) is read from the table and loaded into the 16-bit register Q, which is used by the adder to add it with C or subtract from A as shown in the "CodeLPS()" or "CodeMPS()" routines.

9.5   DECODER ARCHITECTURE FOR JPEG2000

The tope-level architecture for the JPEG2000 decoder is shown in Figure 9.14. The architecture is similar to the encoder architecture shown in Figure 9.1 with data flow in the reverse direction.

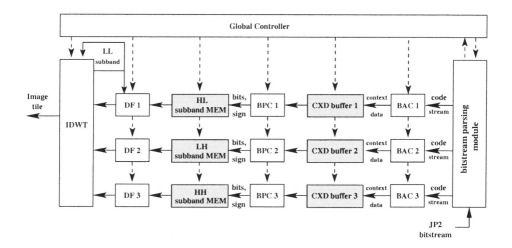

Fig. 9.14   A top-level architecture for the JPEG2000 decoder.

The *bitstream parsing module* parses the compressed file to generate the code-stream. The code-stream is decoded by the three MQ-decoders (BAC1, BAC2, BAC3) in order to generate the context and data pairs corresponding to each subband. The MQ-decoder architecture is very similar to the encoder architecture with few minor changes. The code byte in the MQ-decoder is loaded into the B register and the decoder decodes it using the MQ-decoding algorithm. The basics of the modules of the decoder are functionally similar to the encoder. After the *context* and *data* are generated by the MQ-decoder, they are stored in the CXD buffers (CXD buffer1, CXD buffer2, and CXD buffer3). The EBCOT decoders decodes the *context* and *data* to generate the bit-planes of the code-blocks. The EBCOT decoder algorithm is essentially the same as the encoder algorithm with small and obvious changes in v and χ memories and registers. For example, in the EBCOT decoder the data from v (value) and χ (sign) are written into the subband memory instead of reading from it. We leave the details of the EBCOT architecture as an exercise for the reader. The *data formatter* circuits (DF1, DF2 and DF3) convert these sign-magnitude values of the code-blocks into two's complement representation in order to be used by the inverse discrete wavelet transform (IDWT) architecture. The IDWT architecture generates the image tiles.

9.6   SUMMARY OF OTHER ARCHITECTURES FOR JPEG2000

There are only a few other papers published in the literature discussing the VLSI architectures for the critical components in the JPEG2000 encoder and decoder, as of writing this book. The JPEG2000 algorithm is very intensive both in computation and in memory requirements. It is evident from the discussions in previous sections that the entropy encoding part of the JPEG2000 algorithm consumes a significant portion (more than 50%) of the total clock cycles required to compress an image. The bit-plane coding (EBCOT) consumes the highest computation time because of bit-wise processing in every bit-plane of the code-blocks. In EBCOT processing, an N-bit element in a code-block is converted into N individual samples of 1 bit to be encoded. The memory organization of these bit-planes and access of the bits becomes very tricky in software implementation in a general-purpose computer or a digital signal processor (DSP) type media architecture. Special-purpose memory and register architectures have been proposed by Andra, Acharya and Chakrabarti [9, 5] in order to efficiently access the bit-planes of the code-blocks and encode each bit in each bit-plane. We have discussed this architecture in greater detail in previous sections in this chapter.

Because of the bit-wise processing inherent in the EBCOT algorithm and the MQ-coder, the entropy encoding part of the JPEG2000 standard is very difficult to be optimized on a general-purpose computing platform or media processor. As a result, special-purpose custom VLSI architecture is particularly suitable for optimization of the entropy encoder for JPEG2000 implementation. Most of the architectures in the literature have focused on designing the EBCOT architecture to reduce the number of clock cycles and on-chip memory requirements [11, 12, 13, 14]. We summarize the features of these architectures below.

9.6.1   Pass-Parallel Architecture for EBCOT

Chiang, Lin, and Hsieh [11] proposed a novel architecture for implementation of EBCOT in which the three coding passes of bit-plane coding process are merged into a single pass in order to improve overall systems performance. In this architecture, the authors proposed an efficient *pass-parallel context modeling* scheme in order to reduce the number of memory-access and clock-cycle requirements to implement EBCOT in hardware. The pass-parallel context modeling scheme processes the three coding passes of the same bit-plane in parallel by modifying the original bit-plane coding algorithm in a clever way by introducing two significance state variables σ_0 and σ_1 rather than single significance state variable σ in the original EBCOT algorithm.

In this algorithm, the coding operation in cleanup pass (CUP) is delayed by one stripe from the other two coding passes: significance propagation pass (SPP) and magnitude refinement pass (MRP). In the pass-parallel coding process, one of the two significance state variables $\sigma_0[m,n]$ and $\sigma_1[m,n]$ at location $[m,n]$ is toggled to 1 while this sample becomes significant in SPP and CUP respectively. Both the significant state variables are set to 1 immediately after the first magnitude refinement coding (MRC) is applied for this sample. Also the task of the magnitude refinement state variable σ' is replaced by XOR (Exclusive OR) operation of the σ_0 and σ_1

$$\sigma'[m,n] = \sigma_0[m,n] \oplus \sigma_1[m,n] \tag{9.1}$$

where $\oplus$ is the XOR operation. As a result, the on-chip memory requirement doesn't increase because of introduction of two significance state variables. The correct significant states of the samples within the context window are computed as follows.

- For samples belonging to SPP, the significance state of a visited sample at location $[m, n]$ is equal to $\sigma_0[m,n]$ and the significance state of the sample that has not been visited is

$$\sigma_{not} = \sigma_0[m,n] \vee \sigma_1[m,n] \tag{9.2}$$

where $\vee$ is the binary OR operation.

- For samples belonging to the magnitude refinement pass (MRP), the significance state of the visited sample at location $[m, n]$ is equal to $\sigma_0[m,n]$. The significance state of the sample at location $[m, n]$ that has not been visited is determined by

$$\sigma_{not} = \sigma_0[m,n] \vee \sigma_1[m,n] \vee v^p[m,n] \tag{9.3}$$

where $v^p[m,n]$ is the magnitude of the data bit at location $[m, n]$ in p^{th} bit-plane of the code-block to be encoded. This is possible because a sample at location $[m, n]$ becomes significant if and only if its magnitude bit $v^p[m,n]$ is 1 for the first time.

- For samples belonging to the cleanup pass (CUP), the significance states of all neighbors are determined by Eq. 9.2.

Because of the pass-parallel context modeling, one MQ-coder module can be used in the JPEG2000 encoder architecture instead of three by switching the right context and data bits into the MQ-coder module [11]. Based on this pass-parallel coding of the bit-planes and single-pass switching arithmetic encoder, overall systems performance of a JPEG2000 architecture in terms of computation time can be improved by more than 25% [11].

9.6.2 Memory-Saving Architecture for EBCOT

Hsiao, Lin, Lee, and Jen [12] proposed an efficient high-speed memory savings architecture for implementation of the embedded bit-plane coding to improve the overall systems performance of a JPEG2000 encoder. In this architecture, mainly three speedup strategies have been applied in order to accelerate the context formation module in the EBCOT engine. They are pixel skipping, magnitude refinement parallelization, and group-of-columns skipping. Based on these speedup strategies, the on-chip memory for implementation of EBCOT can be reduced by approximately 20% [12].

The *renormalization* step in the MQ-coder has been enhanced in the codestring register to improve the clock rate of the MQ-coder implementation in [12]. Adopting these speedup strategies for both bit-plane coding and the MQ-coder, overall systems performance of the JPEG2000 encoder can be enhanced by reducing the clock cycles and memory requirements.

9.6.3 Computationally Efficient EBCOT Architecture by Skipping

Lian, Chen, Chen, and Chen [14] recently proposed a very efficient hardware architecture for implementation of the EBCOT algorithm. Because of the characteristics of the fractional bit-plane coding by the EBCOT algorithm, distribution of the number of bits coded in three coding passes in EBCOT vary greatly from bit-plane to bit-plane. In the most significant bit-plane of the coding blocks all the samples are insignificant and only the *cleanup pass*(CUP) is executed. In the lower significant bit-planes, more and more bits are process by the the *magnitude refinement pass* (MRP), whereas the number of bits processed by CUP keeps on decreasing. The number of bits encoded by the *significant propagation pass* (SPP) increases at the beginning in first few bit-planes and then it decreases in lower significant bit-planes because the number of samples became significant in the previous bit-planes keeps on growing and the samples are encoded by the MRP in the following bit-planes. This skewed nature of distribution of the number of samples encoded in each coding pass has been exploited to develop an efficient architecture. As a result, experimentally it has been shown that sometimes it even reduces the number of clock cycles by almost 60% compared to the straightforward implementation of the EBCOT architecture.

In this architecture, the clocking requirements are reduced by applying two speedup techniques called *simple-skipping* (SS) and *group-of-columns skipping* (GOCS) to generate the context information. The basic principle of both the methods is to skip the samples not belonging to a particular coding pass in order to avoid any computation. In each coding pass, it identifies the *need-to-be-coded* (NBC) samples so that the bits can be simply skipped. In the SS method only n cycles are spent to encode the NBC bits if there are only n NBC samples in a stripe. Since each stripe contains 4 samples, $4 - n$ clock cycles can be saved by skipping $4 - n$ bits which are not NBC. If a stripe does not contain any NBC, only one clock cycle is spent to check the condition only. The GOCS method is to skip a group of columns all together, if there are no NBC samples in the group of stripes (columns). The GOCS method can be applied in both MRP and CUP. The number of NBC samples in each group are marked in the SPP. There is a special memory in the architecture called the GOC memory to indicate the status of the samples in the group of stripes. The best number of columns in a group has been found to be 8 based on experimentation to study the performance of the GOCS method. If a group of stripes contains no NBC samples, the GOC memory is marked by a bit 0, otherwise it is marked by 1. While coding in MRP and CUP, the contents of the GOCS memory are checked. If the value is 0 for the currently coding GOC, all the stripes of the group can be skipped all together. As a result, only one clock cycle is required to check this condition and results in saving 31 clock cycles because a group of 8 stripes contain 32 samples.

An extreme case of skipping is called pass skipping. If the samples become significant in an earlier bit-plane, it is possible that all samples are encoded in SPP and MRP resulting in skipping the whole bit-plane for CUP. It is also possible that all samples in the lower bit-planes belong to MRP and none of them to SPP and CUP and hence skipping both the passes for the whole bit-plane all together. Although the occurrences of these cases are very small, it significantly speeds up the bit-coding when they happen.

9.7 SUMMARY

In this chapter, we presented in a VLSI architecture for the JPEG2000 encoder [4, 5]. We also presented the underlying details of the EBCOT architecture including its key building blocks and control mechanism. We presented the MQ-coder architecture for binary arithmetic coding. We also briefly presented the JPEG2000 decoder architecture, which is architecturally similar to the encoder architecture with the data flow just in reverse direction with minor changes in the control mechanism and registers. There are not many architectures for the JPEG2000 standard algorithms available in the literature. Since entropy coding of JPEG2000 is the most computationally intensive, few researchers have focused on optimizing the EBCOT architecture in order to reduce clock cycle and memory requirements. We have reviewed the architectures in this chapter. Some preliminary commercial products for JPEG2000 architecture have been reported in the marketplace [15, 16, 17, 18]. However, detailed information of these architectures have not been published. Detailed review of the VLSI architectures for lifting-based discrete wavelet transform suitable for JPEG2000 was presented in Chapter 5.

REFERENCES

1. ISO/IEC 15444-1, "Information Technology—JPEG2000 Image Coding System Part 1: Core Coding System," 2000.

2. David S. Taubman, "High performance scalable image compression with EBCOT," *IEEE Transaction on Image Processing*, Vol. 9, No. 7, pp. 1158–1170, July 2000.

3. D. Santa-Cruz and T. Ebrahimi, "An Analytical Study of JPEG2000 Functionalities," *Proceedings of International Conference on Image Processing*, September 10–13, Vancouver, Canada, 2000.

4. K. Andra, T. Acharya, and C. Chakraborti, "A High Performance JPEG2000 Architecture," *Proc. of the IEEE Intl. Symposium on Circuits and Systems (ISCAS 2002)*, pp. 765–768, Scottsdale, Arizona, May 2002.

5. K. Andra, C. Chakraborti, and T. Acharya, "A High Performance JPEG2000 Architecture," *IEEE Transactions of Circuits and Systems for Video Technology*, Vol. 13, No. 3, pp. 209–218, March 2003.

6. K. Andra, C. Chakrabarti, and T. Acharya, "A VLSI Architecture for Lifting Based Wavelet Transform," *Proceedings of the IEEE Workshop on Signal Processing Systems*, Lafayette, Louisiana, October 2000.

7. K. Andra, C. Chakraborti, and T. Acharya, "An Efficient Implementation of a Set of Lifting-based Wavelet Filters," *Proc. of the IEEE Intl. Conference on Acoustics, Speech and Signal Processing (ICASSP 2001)*, Salt Lake City, Utah, May 2001.

8. K. Andra, C. Chakraborti, and T. Acharya, "A VLSI Architecture for Lifting-Based Forward and Inverse Wavelet Transform," *IEEE Transactions on Signal Processing*, Vol. 50, No. 4, pp. 966–977, April 2002.

9. K. Andra, T. Acharya, and C. Chakraborti, "Efficient VLSI Implementation of Bit-plane Coder of JPEG2000," in *Proc. of the SPIE Intl. Symposium on Optical Science and Technology, Applications of Digital Image Processing XXIV*, Vol. 4472, pp. 246–257, San Diego, July 2001.

10. K. Andra, "Wavelet and Entropy Coding Accelerators for JPEG2000," Ph.D. Dissertation, Arizona State University, December 2001.

11. J. S. Chiang, Y. S. Lin, and C. Y. Hsieh, "Efficient Pass-Parallel for EBCOT in JPEG2000," *Proc. of the IEEE Intl. Symposium on Circuits and Systems (ISCAS 2002)*, pp. 773–776, Scottsdale, Arizona, May 2002.

12. Y. T. Hsiao, H. D. Lin, and C. W. Jen, "High-Speed Memory Saving Architecture for the Embedded Block Coding in JPEG2000," *Proc. of the IEEE Intl. Symposium on Circuits and Systems (ISCAS 2002)*, pp. 133–136, Scottsdale, Arizona, May 2002.

13. H. H. Chen, C. J. Lian, T. H. Chag, and L. G. Chen, "Analysis of EBCOT Decoding Algorithm and its VLSI Implementation for JPEG 2000," *Proc.*

of the IEEE Intl. Symposium on Circuits and Systems (ISCAS 2002), pp. 329–332, Scottsdale, Arizona, May 2002.

14. C. J. Lian, K. F. Chen, H. H. Chen, and L. G. Chen, "Analysis and Architecture Design of Block-coding Engine for EBCOT in JPEG 2000," *IEEE Transactions of Circuits and Systems for Video Technology*, Vol. 13, No. 3, pp. 219–230, March 2003.

15. Analog Devices Inc. (2003), ADV202: JPEG2000 Video CODEC, preliminary data sheet (REV.PrT). *www.analog.com*

16. inSilicon Corporation (2001), JPEG2000 Encoder. *www.insilicon.com.*

17. DWPworx Inc. (2002) DSW2000S (Rev.0.7): JPEG2000 and MPEG Encoder Decoder. *www.dspworx.com/downloads/dsw2000s_pb.pdf*

18. Amphion(2003). CS6590: JPEG2000 Codec. *www.amphion.com/cs6590.html*

10

Beyond Part 1 of JPEG2000 Standard

10.1 INTRODUCTION

In this book, we mainly focused on the algorithms and VLSI implementation of the key modules in the JPEG2000 Part 1 standard. Part 1 is the *core coding system* of the JPEG2000 standard [1], which was published in 2000 as an international standard. We have dealt with the underlying algorithms, syntax of the compressed bitstream, and file format pertinent to Part 1 of the JPEG2000 standard in great detail in Chapters 6–8.

There are five more parts (Parts 2–6) that were completed or nearly completed by the standards committee as of writing this book [2, 3, 4, 5, 6]. We introduce these parts in this chapter in the following sections. Part 7 was proposed but has been abandoned lately. There are five more parts (Parts 8–12) currently under development as of writing this book [7, 9]. In this chapter, we give a quick introduction to these parts as well.

10.2 PART 2: EXTENSIONS

Numerous elements described in Part 1 have been further extended in Part 2 of the JPEG2000 standard [2]. These extensions have been described in Annex A to Annex M of the JPEG2000 Part 2 standard document [2]. In order to accommodate all the changes (extensions) from the Part 1 standard, new relevant marker segments have been introduced in JPEG2000 Part 2 Annex A with extensions of existing marker segments in Part 1. These new extended markers still follow the same syntactic rules as the syntax in JPEG2000 Part 1 [1] for code-stream organization explained in Chapter 8. Some of the key features adopted in the JPEG2000 Part 2 standard are discussed in the following sections.

10.2.1 Variable DC Offset

Annex B of Part 2 describes an extension that allows variable DC offset (for DC level shifting) prior to multicomponent transformations during encoding and after the inverse multicomponent transformations during decoding. In conjunction with a new marker segment **DCO** (DC offset) as described in Annex A of Part 2, users can select an arbitrary offset (integer or floating-point) for DC level shifting at the encoding time and pass the offset information via the **DCO** marker.

10.2.2 Variable Scalar Quantization Offsets

This extension allows users to select smaller or larger dead-zones for scalar quantization of their choice of applications. The visual appearance of low-level textures may be improved with different dead-zone scalar quantization step sizes. Accordingly, the variable quantization step-size can be represented as $2(1 - \xi)\triangle$, where $\xi \in [-1, +1)$ is a real number and can vary subband to subband, component to component, and tile to tile. Clearly, the value of ξ in Part 1 is 0. The extended versions of **QCD** and/or **QCC** marker segments are used to carry this information of ξ in the code-stream so that the decoder can parse the selected quantization step size from these marker segments in order to decode the compressed file uniquely. The presence of these extended marker segments (i.e., $\xi > 0$) is indicated by the first bit of the capability $Rsiz$ parameter ($Rsiz_1 = 1$) in the **SIZ** marker segment.

10.2.3 Trellis-Coded Quantization

The special case of the Trellis Coding algorithm [10], *trellis-coded quantization* (TCQ) [11], is provided as an alternative to the dead-zone scalar quantization in JPEG2000 Part 2. The TCQ algorithm is actually a spatial-varying scalar quantization technique [11]. One of four scalar quantization factors is chosen for each wavelet coefficient. No additional marker segment is used to implement the TCQ for quantization in Part 2. If the TCQ is chosen, it is signaled by the second bit of the capability $Rsiz$ parameter ($Rsiz_2 = 1$) in the **SIZ** marker segment.

Detailed discussion of the principles behind the Trellis-coded quantization algorithm is out of scope for this book. For Trellis Coding algorithm and the particular version of TCQ used in JPEG2000 Part 2, the reader is referred to [10, 11] and Annex D of the Part 2 standard [2].

10.2.4 Visual Masking

The visual masking extension provides improvement of image quality over areas like texture regions with low-intensity range in an image, and robustness against variations of image complexity for a given fixed bit rate. As shown in Figure 10.1, a "point-wise extended nonlinearity" module is inserted between the forward wavelet transformation and quantization modules at the encoder, and a "masking compensation" module is added after the dequantization, prior to the inverse wavelet transformation.

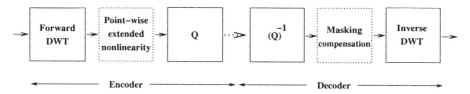

Fig. 10.1 Visual masking extension.

The quality improvement of visual masking (point-wise extended nonlinearity) is achieved in two steps. The first step, *self-contrast masking*, applies a point-wise power function to the original wavelet coefficients x_i with a normalized unit DC gain. That is,

$$y_i = sign(x_i)|x_i|^\alpha$$

where $\alpha \in [0, 1]$ is a real number. A typical value of α is 0.7 as suggested in Part 2, Annex E. The second step, *neighborhood masking*, normalizes y_i by a neighborhood weighting factor w_i, which is a function of the magnitudes of the neighboring pixels, that is,

$$z_i = \frac{y_i}{w_i} = \frac{sign(x_i)|x_i|^\alpha}{w_i}.$$

As described in Part 2, Annex E, the following weighting function for extended nonlinearity is adopted in the standard,

$$w_i = 1 + (a \sum_{k \in neighborhood} |\hat{x}_k|^\beta)/|\phi_i|$$

where $|\phi_i|$ denotes the size of the neighborhood, a is a constant with value of $(10000/2^{bit\_depth-1})^\beta$, bit_depth is the bit depth of the image component, $\hat{x}_k$ is the quantized neighboring coefficients, and β also assumes a value between 0 and 1. The size of the neighborhood and the parameter β are used to control the degree of neighborhood masking. A new marker segment **VMS** (*Visual MaSking*) is used to embed these control parameters for all tile-components in the code-stream. The presence of the **VMS** marker segment is signaled in the compressed file via the third bit of the capability *Rsiz* parameter ($Rsiz_3 = 1$) of the **SIZ** marker segment.

The inverse extended nonlinearity, masking compensation, is done based on the following equation,

$$\tilde{x}_i = sign(z_i)[|z_i|(1 + (a \sum_{k \in neighborhood} |\hat{x}_k|^\beta)/|\phi_i|)]^{1/\alpha}$$

where z_i is the dequantized wavelet coefficients.

10.2.5 Arbitrary Wavelet Decomposition

Instead of symmetrical *dyadic* wavelet subband decomposition, that is, filtering and downsampling by a factor of two in both horizontal and vertical directions as described in Part 1 of the standard, an extension is defined in Annex F of JPEG2000 Part 2 standard that allows arbitrary (more general, not necessarily dyadic) wavelet subband decomposition. Various wavelet subbands can be obtained through combination of vertical and/or horizontal filtering and decimation. As described in Part 1, the orientation of each subband is denoted by a two-letter code, where the first letter indicates horizontal filtering and the second letter indicates vertical filtering. There are three possible letters, *H*, *L*, and *X*, that can be used to denote a subband in this extended mode of arbitrary decomposition. The letter *H* (or *L*) implies that high-pass (or low-pass) filtering followed by a downsampling of factor two was applied. The letter *X* indicates no vertical or horizontal filtering and decimation was applied. Figure 10.2 shows an example of extended 3-level wavelet decompositions. For example, the 2XH subband was obtained at the second level of decomposition by a high-pass filtering in the vertical direction (column-wise) with downsampling, and no horizontal filtering and decimation was applied.

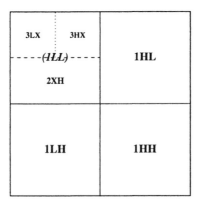

Fig. 10.2   Extended 3-level wavelet subband decompositions.

The key purpose for this extension is to provide the capability of fine tuning the compression performance by providing control over the decorrelation process. Two new marker segments, **DFS** (*down-sampling factor styles*) and **ADS** (*arbitrary decomposition styles*), along with two extended marker segments (**COD** and **COC**) are introduced in the Part 2 standard for the need of arbitrary decomposition. The application of this extension is signaled in the compressed file via the fifth bit of the capability *Rsiz* parameter ($Rsiz_5 = 1$) in the **SIZ** marker segment.

10.2.6   Arbitrary Wavelet Transformation

As discussed in Chapter 6, Part 1 of JPEG2000 specified only two filters for discrete wavelet transform: the (9, 7) filter pair for irreversible transform and the (5, 3) filter pair for reversible transform. Extensions in Part 2 of the standard also allow employment of the user-defined arbitrary wavelet filters. In order to specify all the parameters for arbitrary wavelet filter kernels, a new marker segment, **ATK** (*arbitrary transformation kernels*), is introduced to carry information such as

- Filter category based on boundary extension policy (as explained in Section 6.6.1.3); that is, whole-sample symmetric (WSS), half-sample symmetric (HSS), or arbitrary filters

- Transformation type, reversible or irreversible

- Number of lifting steps, numerical type of lifting step coefficients (integer or real), and other lifting-related information

The detailed descriptions for the arbitrary wavelet transformation can be found in Annex A and G of the JPEG2000 Part 2 standard document [2]. The application of this extension is signaled in the compressed file via the sixth bit of the capability *Rsiz* parameter ($Rsiz_6 = 1$) in the **SIZ** marker segment.

10.2.7   Single Sample Overlap Discrete Wavelet Transformation

As shown in Figure 6.2 in Chapter 6, the discrete wavelet transformation is applied to each tile-component independently. This tile-component-based processing provides convenience in terms of memory efficiency for both software and hardware implementation. If resources are available, we can even process tiles in parallel. However, if the size of the tile-component is too small, the resulting reconstructed image can have noticeable blocking artifacts at the tile boundaries. To avoid strong artifacts at the tile boundaries, JPEG2000 Part 2 provides extensions that allow *single sample overlap* (SSO) block-based discrete wavelet transform. In order to further improve the decompressed image quality, a tile can be partitioned into **cells** for wavelet transformation. So there are two types of SSO blocks, tile-based and cell-based. Figure 10.3 shows an example of overlapping tiles. The dashed lines show the tile grid, and the SSO block contains one extra row at the bottom and one extra column at the right of the current tile. The extended marker segments, **SIZ**, **COD**, and **COC**, are used to embed these SSO overlapping parameters into the code-stream.

The application of overlapped block-based DWT is signaled in the compressed file via the fourth bit of the capability $Rsiz$ parameter ($Rsiz_4 = 1$) in the **SIZ** marker segment.

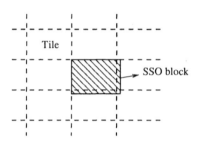

Fig. 10.3   Overlapping tiles.

10.2.8   Multiple Component Transforms

As discussed in Section 6.5.3, there are only two multi-component transforms, reversible color transform (RCT) and irreversible color transform (ICT), defined in JPEG2000 Part 1. These transforms can be applied on only the first three components of an image. The key purpose of these transforms is to exploit the intercomponent correlation in a standard color (RGB) image. By applying the RCT or ICT, the RGB image is transformed into a different color space and the components are decorrelated to reduce the intercomponent redundancies that might be present in the image. In JPEG2000 Part 2, the idea of multicomponent transform has been extended for images that have more components, such as multiple component medical images. In Part 2 extension, the components can be grouped together arbitrarily as **component collections** and a new marker segment, *multiple component collection* (**MCC**), is defined to describe the collection of input components, the collection of output intermediate components, and other associated information. Figure 10.4 shows an example of a seven-component image with three component collections.

There are three types of decorrelation transform presented in this extension: *linear block transforms*, *dependency transforms*, and *wavelet-based transforms*. For each component collection, one may apply any of the three decorrelation transforms. In some cases, more than one transform may be applied sequentially on the same component collection. The most powerful feature of this multiple-component point transform extension is that it is a unified framework with the ability to accommodate different decorrelation techniques.

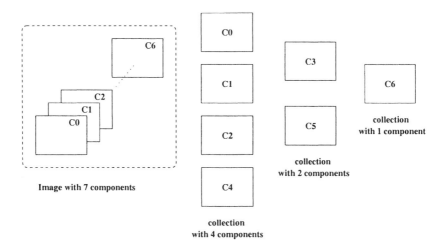

Fig. 10.4 A seven-component image with three "component collections."

Three more new marker segments are defined to accommodate these extensions in JPEG2000 Part 2. The *component bit depth* (**CBD**) marker segment is used to defined the bit depth of reconstructed image components. The *multiple component transformation* (**MCT**) marker segment is used to define the multiple component transformation matrices. The *multiple component intermediate collection* (**MIC**) marker segment is used to describe the input intermediate component collections, the output reconstructed image component collections, and the matrices for a multiple component dependency transform. When wavelet-based decorrelation is used, the **ATK** and **ADS** marker segments (as mentioned in Sections 10.2.6 and 10.2.5) are used to specify the wavelet transform kernel and arbitrary decomposition used in constructing the component collection. Presence of one of these extensions of multicomponent decorrelation transformation in the compressed file is signaled by the seventh bit of the capability *Rsiz* parameter ($Rsiz_7 = 1$) in the **SIZ** marker segment.

10.2.9   Nonlinear Transformations

In an image capturing system, such as a video system, **gamma** correction is usually applied at the camera. Gamma correction is a non-linear point transformation, which is usually used for precompensating the nonlinearity of a display device (such as CRT—cathode-ray tube, or LCD—liquid crystal display). It also increases the compression efficiency because the human eye is known to have a logarithmic response to light very similar to the characteristics of gamma correction. A gamma function contains two functional segments: a linear function, which is used to minimize the effect of sensor noise in the dark (near black) regions of the image, and a power function with exponent of *gamma* for pixels with large magnitude in the image. Figure 10.5 shows a forward gamma nonlinear function defined by ITU-R Rec. 709 (for HDTV)[13] that might be used by a JPEG2000 encoder. The actual function is given as follows:

$$R'_{709} = \begin{cases} 4.5R & R \leq 0.018 \\ 1.099R^{1/2.2} - 0.099 & 0.018 < R, \end{cases}$$

where R is the input value (normalized between 0.0 and 1.0) and R' is the gamma-corrected value, and gamma is equal to $1/2.2 \cong 0.45$. For most practical implementations, a lookup table (LUT) is used to approximate the actual nonlinear function.

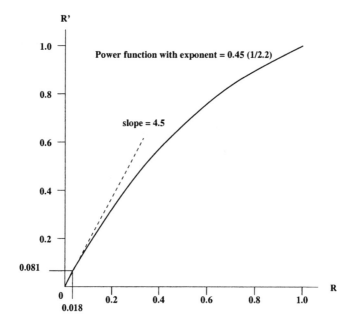

Fig. 10.5   Rec. 709 gamma correction function.

For more information about gamma correction and digital video, the reader is referred to the book by Charle A. Poynton [12].

This extension provides the ability of embedding the information about any nonlinear transformation applied at the encoding time into the code-stream. So a decoder can use it to map the reconstructed values back to their proper range after entropy decode processes and (if any) inverse multiple-component transformations. A new marker segment, *nonlinearity point transformation* (**NLT**), is used to describe the gamma function or a lookup table (LUT) for the function representing the nonlinearity.

10.2.10 Region of Interest Extension

We discussed ROI coding in great detail in Section 6.6.3. The MAXSHIFT algorithm for ROI coding [14] used in JPEG2000 Part 1 is simple to implement. In MAXSHIFT algorithm, no mask (a bit map describing the location of region of interest) information needs to be embedded in the code-stream. This is accomplished by choosing a scaling value in such a way that the smallest nonzero ROI coefficient is larger than the largest background coefficient. However, only one scaling value can be specified in the original RGN marker segment even though there are multiple regions of interest. The technical details of both the algorithms have been presented in Section 6.6.3.

The ROI extension as described in JPEG2000 Part 2 Annex K uses the general scaling-based method [15], which allows multiple regions of interest with different scaling values. The extension also specified how to generate the mask in the wavelet domain. The extended region of interest marker segment RGN is used to specify the locations, shifts (scaling values), and type of ROI in the code-stream. Specifically, the location and size information of multiple rectangular and/or elliptical regions of interest can be specified in the extended RGN marker segment.

10.2.11 File Format Extension and Metadata Definitions

An extended optional file format, called JPX, is included in JPEG2000 Part 2 that applications can choose to contain the JPEG2000 bitstream. The JPX is an extension of the JP2 file format defined in Part 1 of JPEG2000. We discussed the structure of JP2 file format in great detail in Section 8.3. The Part 2 extension adds more capabilities to JP2. For example, JPX adds a specification of a binary container for both image and metadata. It can indicate image properties such as the tone-scale or color space of the image inside the file format. JPX also provides mechanisms for combining multiple code-streams (JP2 style images as an example) into a single file, and allows to include metadata elements in files. Metadata is additional information that is associated with the image, such as how the image was created/captured, patient information for a medical image (as an example), etc. The complete specification for this extension and metadata definitions are provided in JPEG2000 Part 2 Annex L and Annex M [2].

10.3 PART 3: MOTION JPEG2000

Part 3 of JPEG2000 standard (called Motion JPEG2000) [3] specifies a file format called MJ2 or MJP2 and also the instructions for how to use images encoded with JPEG2000 Part 1 core coding codec for motion sequences. There is no new coding methodology defined in Part 3 of the JPEG2000 standard. All images in a Motion JPEG2000 file are compressed frame by frame using

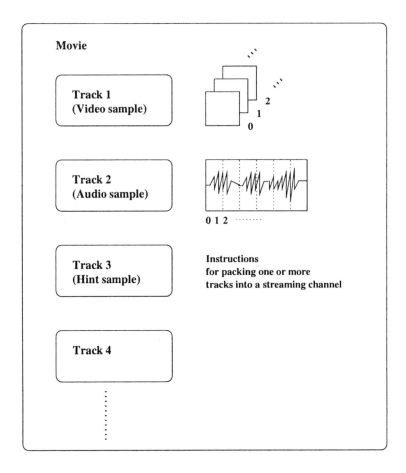

Fig. 10.6 A Motion JPEG2000 *movie* with multiple *tracks*.

JPEG2000 Part 1 codec without any interframe coding. The MJ2 format is designed to contain not just one or more JPEG2000 image sequences but also other information such as audio annotations and streaming requirements. The overall presentation of Motion JPEG2000 is called a **movie**. As shown in Figure 10.6, a *movie* is a collection of **tracks**. Each track is a timed sequence of media data, called **samples**. Samples are numbered in sequence based on timed unit. There are many different kind of tracks, but the three most important tracks are *video* track, *audio* track, and *hint* track. They are used for two different purposes. The video and audio tracks are used to contain media data. The purpose of a hint track is to carry instructions for packing one or more tracks for a streaming protocol.

Similar to the JP2 file format discussed in Section 8.3, the fundamental building block of the MJ2 file format is called a **box**. All the data are contained in structure boxes, and no data are outside the box structure. Basi-

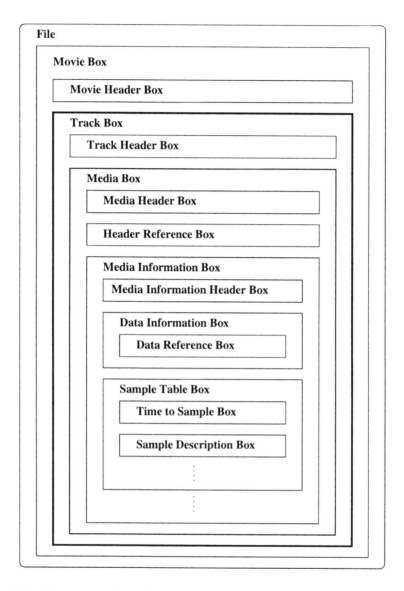

Fig. 10.7 File structure (boxes) of a Motion JPEG2000 *movie* with one *track.*

cally, Part 3 of the JPEG2000 standard is nothing but definitions of boxes and guidelines for how to use them. There are 30 boxes defined in this file format. Figure 10.7 shows an example of the box structure for a MJ2 file with one track. Part 3 also provides guidelines for how to use the JPEG2000 codec with frequency weighting in order to improve the subjective quality of reconstructed image sequence. Motion JPEG2000 has a very wide range of applications such as digital still cameras with video capture capability, remote surveillance, etc., where a *high-quality frame-based* approach is desired.

10.4 PART 4: CONFORMANCE TESTING

JPEG2000 Part 4 [4] defines the conformance testing for JPEG2000 Part 1 [1]. The standard specifies three procedures: decoder compliance testing procedure, encoder compliance testing procedure, and JP2 file format reader compliance testing procedure. The whole testing procedures are based on two **profiles** and three **compliance classes** (**Cclass**). The two profiles (*profile* 0 and *profile* 1) defined in "JPEG2000 Part 1, Amendment 1 Code Stream Restrictions", are used for compliance testing. Testing an arbitrary code-stream (which requires unlimited resources) is out of the scope of conformance testing. A profile provides limitations on compression parameters such as tile size, LL subband resolution, subsampling factor, marker locations, and others. So a decoder can define its capabilities for the bitstream within a profile. The three compliance classes (Cclass 0, Cclass 1, and Cclass 2) define different levels of image-quality guarantees for a decoder. The compliance level for an *implementation under test* (IUT) should be reported based on **profile x Cclass y**. The decoder and encoder compliance test procedures are as follows.

- **Decoder compliance test procedure:** The decoder compliance test procedure can be summarized as follows: First, decode all the test code-streams using the decoder under test (the test code-streams are supplied by the standard). Second, compare decoded images with the reference image; if all the errors are within the defined tolerance (based on the error metrics provided in the standard), then the decoder under test is reported as *profile x Cclass y* compliant.

- **Encoder compliance test procedure:** The encoder compliance test procedure can be summarized as follows: First, encode all the selected test images with different compression parameters using the encoder under test. Second, if the reference decoder can fully decode all the encoded code-stream, then the encoder under test passes the compliance test.

A compliant JP2 file format reader must be able to decode the code-stream within the JP2 file. In addition, if the decoded components are not all at the same resolution, the reader should be able to upsample them into the same resolution and convert to full resolution sRGB [17] color space from the source color space. A set of test JP2 files and reference images are provided in the Part 4 standard. The test procedure just simply decodes the test file and compares with the corresponding reference images. If the differences of all the test files are within the defined tolerances, the JP2 file format reader is compliant with the standard.

The Part 4 compliance test files include bare code-stream, JP2 files, reference decoded images, and description files for the test data. The reference decoder is defined in JPEG2000 Part 5: Reference Software [5], which we will review in the next section. However, it should be noted, it is explicitly stated in Part 4 of the JPEG2000 standard document that compliance testing does not include acceptance testing, performance testing, or robustness testing.

10.5 PART 5: REFERENCE SOFTWARE

As stated in JPEG2000 Part 5 [5], this standard is informative only. It consists of software source packages and short descriptions about the reference software. There are two software packages included in the standard, JasPer and JJ2000. JasPer is a C programming language [18, 19] based implementation of the JPEG2000 Part 1 codec; more information can be found at **http://www.ece.uvic.ca/~mdadams/jasper/**. JJ2000 is a *Java*^{TM} implementation of JPEG2000 Part 1 codec. More information about JJ2000 can be found at the JJ2000 project home web page at **http://jj2000.epfl.ch/**. The details of the software architecture and usage are beyond the scope of this book. The official JPEG2000 software and test data are available at web page **http://www.jpeg.org/software/** for further information and downloads.

10.6 PART 6: COMPOUND IMAGE FILE FORMAT

Part 6 of JPEG2000 [6] defines a file format JPM based on the same file format architecture used in JPEG2000 Parts 1 and 2. The JPM file format reuses many boxes that were defined in Part 1 for JP2 file format and Part 2 for JPX file format. The key purpose of JPM file format is to store compound images that may contain multiple continuous and bi-level images. The ITU-T T.44|ISO 16485 [20] multilayer *mixed raster content* (MRC) model is used to represent a compound image in Part 6 of JPEG2000 standard. Compound images are very useful for document image processing. A document can be represented by a compound image with one or more pages, and each page may contain multiple objects. It should be noted that under the JPM file format, an object may be compressed using a compression method other than JPEG2000. For example, a bi-level image object such as a scanned fax image can be compressed using JBIG2 [21].

10.7 OTHER PARTS (7–12)

Part 7 of JPEG2000 was proposed and has been abandoned. So we avoid discussing Part 7 in this book. There are four more parts currently under development in the JPEG2000 standards committee as of writing this book. Part 12 is already published [8]. The purpose of these parts are as follows.

- **Part 8—secure JPEG2000 (JPSEC):** Part 8 deals with security-related issues for JPEG2000 applications such as encryption, watermarking, source authentication.

- **Part 9—interactivity tools, APIs, and protocols (JPIP):** Part 9 is being developed as an interactive network protocol, and it specifies tools for efficient exchange of JPEG2000 images and related metadata.

- **Part 10—3-D and floating point data (JP3D):** Part 10 is being developed with the concern of three-dimensional data. It will be very useful for applications such as 3-D medical image reconstruction and other areas requiring 3-D imagery and floating point operations.

- **Part 11—wireless (JPWL):** Part 11 is being developed for wireless multimedia applications. The main concerns for JPWL are error protection, detection, and correction for JPEG2000 in an error-prone wireless environment.

- **Part 12—ISO base media file format:** Part 12 has a text in common with ISO/IEC 14496-12 for MPEG-4, and is already published (2004-02-01).

10.8   SUMMARY

As of writing this book, there are 11 parts in JPEG2000 standard (Part 7 has been abandoned). Part 1 of the JPEG2000 standard was dealt with in great detail in Chapters 6 to 8. In this chapter, we introduced the reader to Parts 2 to 12 of the JPEG2000 standard. The Part 2 extension offers some additional capabilities and features over Part 1 of the JPEG2000 standard. We discussed these capabilities and resulting marker segments to accommodate these extensions in this chapter. Part 3 of the JPEG2000 is called the Motion JPEG2000 standard. Part 3 specifies a file format (MJ2) that contains image sequence encoded with JPEG2000 core coding algorithm for motion video. Part 4 of JPEG2000 standard specifies compliance testing procedures for encoding/decoding using Part 1 of JPEG2000. In Part 5, two software source packages (using Java and C programming languages) are available for the purpose of testing and validation for JPEG2000 systems implemented by the developers. Part 6 of the JPEG2000 standard specifies compound image file format (JPM) for storing compound images. Part 8 of the standard deals with security aspects for JPEG2000 applications such as encryption, watermarking, etc. Part 9 defines an interactive network protocol, and specifies tools for efficient exchange of JPEG2000 images and related metadata. Part

10 is being defined to deal with the three dimensional image data. Part 11 deals with the issues related to error protection, detection, and correction for JPEG2000 for its usage in an error-prone wireless environment. Part 12 deals with ISO base media file format, which has a text in common with MPEG-4 standard for video compression.

REFERENCES

1. ISO/IEC 15444-1, "Information Technology—JPEG2000 Image Coding System, Part 1: Core Coding System," 2000.

2. ISO/IEC 15444-2, Final Committee Draft, "Information Technology—JPEG2000 Image Coding System, Part 2: Extensions," 2000.

3. ISO/IEC 15444-3, "Information Technology—JPEG2000 Image Coding System, Part 3: Motion JPEG2000," 2002.

4. ISO/IEC 15444-4, "Information Technology—JPEG2000 Image Coding System, Part 4: Conformance Testing," 2002.

5. ISO/IEC 15444-5, "Information Technology—JPEG2000 Image Coding System, Part 5: Reference Software," 2003.

6. ISO/IEC 15444-6, Final Committee Draft, "Information Technology—JPEG2000 Image Coding System, Part 6: Compound Image File Format," 2001.

7. ISO/IEC 15444-9, Final Committee Draft, "Information Technology—JPEG2000 Image Coding System, Part 9: Interactivity tools, APIs, and Protocols," 2003.

8. ISO/IEC 15444-12, "Information Technology—JPEG2000 Image Coding System, Part 12: ISO Base Media File Format," 2004.

9. http://www.jpeg.org/jpeg2000/index.html.

10. C. Schlegel, *Trellis Coding.* 1st ed., IEEE Press, Piscataway, 1997.

11. M. W. Marcellin and T. R. Fisher, "Trellis Coded Quantization of Memoryless and Gauss-Markov Source," *IEEE Transactions on Communication*, Vol. 38, pp. 82–93, January 1990.

12. C. A. Poynton, *A Technical Introduction to Digital Video.* Wiley, New York, 1996.

13. Recommendation ITU-R BT. 709, "Basic Parameter Values for the HDTV Standard for the Studio and for International Programme Exchange." Geneva: ITU, 1990.

14. D. Nister and C. Christopoulos, "Lossless Region of Interest with Embedded Wavelet Image Coding," *Signal Processing*, Vol. 78, No 1, pp. 1–17, 1999.

15. E. Atsumi and N. Farvardin, "Loss/Lossless Region-of-Interest Image Coding Based on Set Partitioning in Hierarchical Tree," *IEEE Int'l Conf. Image Processing*, pp. 87–91, Chicago, October 1998.

16. ISO/IEC 14496-1, "Information technology—Coding of Audio-Visual Objects, Part 1: Systems," 2001.

17. M. Stokes, M. Anderson, S. Chandrasekar, and R. Motta, "A Standard Default Color Space for the Internet—sRGB," Version 1.10, November 1996. http://www.w3.org/Graphics/Color/sRGB.html.

18. ISO/IEC 9899, "Programming Languages—C," 1999.

19. ISO/IEC 9945-1, "Information Technology—Portable Operating System Interface (POSIX), Part 1: System Application Program Interface (API) (C language)," 1996.

20. ITU-T T.44|ISO/IEC 16485, "Information Technology—Mixed Raster Content (MRC)," 2000.

21. ITU-T T.88|ISO/IEC 14492, "Information Technology—Coded Representation of Picture and Audio Information—Lossy/Lossless Coding of Bi-level Images," 2001.

Index

arbitrary wavelet decomposition, 256
  arithmetic coding, 9, 30

box, 218, 262
bypass mode, 177

cell, 257
code
  fixed-length, 8
  uniquely decipherable, 9
  variable-length, 8
code-block, 164, 165
CODEC, 9
coding, 5
  Arithmetic coding, 9
  Elias coding, 9
  entropy coding, 11
  Huffman coding, 4, 9
  Shannon-Fano coding, 9
coding operation
  Magnitude refinement coding,
    170
  Run-length coding, 171
  Sign coding, 169

Zero coding, 168
coding pass
  bypass mode, 177
  CUP, 165, 172
  MRP, 164, 173
  SPP, 164, 173
communication, 1
component, 200
component collections, 258
compression, 19
  lossless compression, 10
  lossy compression, 10
  perceptual lossless, 10
compression advantage, 2, 3
compression performance, 12
  coding complexity, 15
  coding delay, 15
  compression ratio, 13
compression ratio, 13
compression standard, 17
  G3, 17
  G4, 17
  H.263, 18
  H.263L, 18

JBIG, 18
JPEG, 17, 55
JPEG2000, 17, 137
MPEG, 18
MPEG-2, 18
MPEG-4, 18
computer, 1
CWT, 81

data compression, 3, 4, 10
    image compression, 2, 3
DC level shifting, 146, 254
DCT, 12, 63
decoding, 5
decompression, 5, 12
discrete cosine transform, 12
discrete memoryless source, 5
discrete wavelet transform, 12
DTWT, 82
dual lifting, 97
DWT, 12, 82, 108, 148, 228
    (5, 3) filter, 99, 151
    (9, 7) filter, 101, 109, 149
    arbitrary filters, 257
    in-place computation, 91, 102
    recursive, 124

EBCOT architecture, 231
    BAC module, 231
    BPC module, 230
    control, 237
    CXD module, 230
    data formation module, 229
    global controller module, 231
    memory-saving, 247
    pass-parallel, 246
    Q-table, 231
    registers, 235
    state machine, 237
    subband memory module, 229
entropy, 5
entropy coding, 11, 148
error resiliency, 141
Euclidean algorithm, 93

fixed-length code, 8

fractional bit-plane coding, 165

gamma correction, 259
greatest common divisor GCD, 93,
    98

HSS, 152, 257
Huffman coding, 4, 24, 163
Huffman tree, 25

ICC profile, 141
image, 1
image compression, 2, 3
information, 5, 7
    redundant information, 2
    source, 5
information content, 6
information theory, 5–7
Internet, 1, 138
IWT, 91

JasPer, 265
JJ2000, 265
JP2, 213, 218
    Color Specification box, 220,
      221
    Contiguous Code-stream box,
      220, 221
    Header box, 220, 221
    Image Header box, 220, 221
    Profile box, 220, 221
    Signature box, 220
JPEG, 55
    baseline JPEG, 60
    hierarchical mode, 76
    lossless, 56
    progressive DCT-based, 75
JPEG2000, 137
    conformance testing, 264
    EBCOT, 157, 164, 177
    main header, 214, 216
    markers, 216
    Part 1, 145
    Part 2, 253
    PCRD, 156

rate control, 156
Tier-1 coding, 157, 164
Tier-2 coding, 158, 195
tile-part header, 214, 218
JPM, 144, 265
JPX, 261

Laurent polynomial, 92
layer, 197
lazy wavelet transform, 96
Lempel, 19
lifting algorithm, 99
lifting factorization, 98
lossless compression, 10
lossy compression, 10
LZ77, 19, 44
LZ78, 19, 46
LZW, 19, 49

marker segments, 216
markers, 216
Mathematical Theory of Communication, 5
metadata, 261
MJ2, 144, 261
model, 6
modeling, 5
mother wavelet, 79
Motion JPEG2000, 261
hint track, 262
movie, 262
sample, 262
track, 262
MP3, 19
MPEG-21, 18
MPEG-7, 18
MQ-coder, 44, 158, 185
MQ-coder architecture, 242
control circuit, 244
Q-table, 242
registers, 243
update logic, 242
MRC, 265
MRC model, 144
MSE, 156

multicomponent transform, 146, 258
ICT, 147
RCT, 146
multimedia, 1, 3, 17
multiresolution analysis, 83
multiresolution decomposition, 80

noiseless source coding theorem, 6, 7
nonlinear transform, 259

packet, 197
packet header, 201
polyphase, 94
polyphase matrix, 95
polyphase representation, 94
precinct, 197
preferred neighborhood, 167
progression order, 200
pyramid algorithm, 80, 85

Q-coder, 39
QM-coder, 39
conditional exchange, 42
interval inversion, 41
LPS, 40
MPS, 40
renormalization, 41
quad tree, 196
quality, 2, 3
MOS, 14
objective quality metrics, 14
PSNR, 14, 139
SNR, 14
subjective quality metrics, 14
quantization, 12, 148, 152
dead-zone, 152
trellis-coded quantization, 254
variable scalar quantization, 254

redundancy, 2, 5, 11
region of interest, 153
MAXSHIFT, 155
ROI, 140, 153, 261

resolution, 197
run-length coding, 24, 163

scan pattern, 166
    vertical causal mode, 166
single sample overlap SSO, 257
source coding, 23
    arithmetic coding, 30
    binary arithmetic coding, 34
    Huffman coding, 24
    run-length coding, 24
    Ziv-Lempel coding, 44
sRGB, 264
storage, 2

Tag Tree, 196
Tag Tree coding, 158, 196
TCQ, 254
text, 1
text compression, 19
tiling, 145
Trellis Coding, 254
    trellis-coded quantization, 254

uniquely decodable, 7

variable-length codes, 8, 9, 203
video, 1
visual masking, 255
VLSI architecture, 107

2M architecture, 129
4M architecture, 130
DWT, 110
EBCOT (see EBCOT architecture), 227
enhance pipeline, 120
flipping, 121
folding, 120, 126
IDWT, 112
lifting-based DWT, 118
MQ-coder (see MQ-coder architecture), 242
pipeline, 119
recursive, 124
semi-systolic algorithm, 110

wavelet, 79
    dilations, 80
    dual lifting, 96, 99
    lifting, 91
    mother wavelet, 80
    primal lifting, 96, 99
    translations, 80
wavelet transform, 81
WSS, 152, 257

z-transform, 92
zig-zag ordering, 69
Ziv, 19
Ziv-Lempel coding, 44

About the Authors

Dr. Tinku Acharya is currently Senior Executive Vice President and Chief Science Officer of Avisere Inc., Tucson, Arizona. He is also Adjunct Professor in the Department of Electrical Engineering, Arizona State University, Tempe, Arizona since 1997. He received his B.Sc. (Honors) in Physics and his B.Tech and M.Tech in Computer Science from the University of Calcutta, India in 1984, 1987, and 1989, respectively. He received his Ph.D. in Computer Science from the University of Central Florida, Orlando, in 1994.

Dr. Acharya served in Intel Corporation from June 1996 to June 2002, where he led several R&D teams in numerous projects toward development of algorithms and architectures in image and video processing, multimedia computing, PC-based digital camera, high-performance reprographics architecture for color photocopiers, biometrics, multimedia architecture for 3G cellular mobile telephony, analysis of next-generation microprocessor architecture, etc. Before joining Intel Corporation, he was a consulting engineer at AT&T Bell Laboratories (1995–1996) in New Jersey, a research faculty member at the Institute of Systems Research, University of Maryland at College Park (1994–1995), and held visiting faculty positions at Indian Institute of Technology (IIT), Kharagpur (on several occasions during 1998–2003). He also served as Systems Analyst in National Informatics Center, Planning Commission, Government of India (1988–1990). He held many other positions in industry and research laboratories. He collaborated in research and development with Palo Alto Research Center (PARC) in Xerox Corporation, Eastman Kodak Corporation, and many other institutions and research laboratories worldwide.

Dr. Acharya is an inventor of 74 U.S. patents and 14 European patents in the areas of electronic imaging, data compression, multimedia computing, biometrics, and their VLSI architectures and algorithms, and more than 50 patents are currently pending in the U.S. Patent Office. He contributed to over 60 refereed technical papers published in international journals, conferences, and books. He is a co-author of the book *Data Mining: Multimedia, Soft Computing and Bioinformatics* published by John Wiley & Sons, Hoboken, New Jersey, 2003. He also co-edited the book *Information Technology: Principles and Applications*, published by Prentice-Hall India, New Delhi, 2004. His pioneering works won him international acclamation. He has been awarded the *Most Prolific Inventor* in Intel Corporation Worldwide in 1999 and *Most Prolific Inventor* in Intel Corporation Arizona site for five consecutive years (1997–2001). His contribution in generation of intellectual properties in the state of Arizona has been specially mentioned in the Business Journal of Phoenix, Arizona in its January 2002 issue.

Dr. Acharya is a Life Fellow of the Institution of Electronics and Telecommunication Engineers (FIETE), and Senior Member of IEEE. He served on the U.S. National Body of JPEG2000 standards committee (1998–2002) and represented Intel Corporation on this committee as its primary member. He served in program committees of several international conferences and many other professional bodies in academia and industry. His current research interests are in computer vision for enterprise applications, biometrics, multimedia computing, multimedia data mining, and VLSI architectures and algorithms.

Dr. Ping-Sing Tsai is currently Assistant Professor in the Department of Computer Science, The University of Texas—Pan American. He received his B.S. in information and computer engineering from Chung Yuan Christian University, Taiwan, R.O.C., in 1985. He received his Ph.D. in computer science from the University of Central Florida, Orlando, in 1995.

Dr. Tsai was a staff systems engineer/R&D scientist at Intel Corporation, Arizona from 1997 to 2002, where he worked with Dr. Acharya on numerous projects toward development of algorithms in multimedia-related applications. Dr. Tsai contributed to over 20 refereed technical papers published in international journals and conferences. He is also the co-inventor of 13 U.S. patents. His current research interests are in biomedical image analysis, computer vision, multimedia computing, and biometrics.